COMIC BOOK WOMEN

WORLD COMICS AND GRAPHIC NONFICTION SERIES
Frederick Luis Aldama and Christopher González, editors

The World Comics and Graphic Nonfiction series includes monographs and edited volumes that focus on the analysis and interpretation of comic books and graphic nonfiction from around the world. The books published in the series use analytical approaches from literature, art history, cultural studies, communication studies, media studies, and film studies, among other fields, to help define the comic book studies field at a time of great vitality and growth.

OTHER BOOKS IN THE SERIES

Mark Cotta Vaz, *Empire of the Superheroes: America's Comic Book Creators and the Making of a Billion-Dollar Industry*

Anna Peppard, ed., *Supersex: Sexuality, Fantasy, and the Superhero*

Allan W. Austin and Patrick L. Hamilton, *All New, All Different? A History of Race and the American Superhero*

Jorge Santos, *Graphic Memories of the Civil Rights Movement: Reframing History in Comics*

Benjamin Fraser, *The Art of Pere Joan: Space, Landscape, and Comics Form*

Jan Baetens, *The Film Photonovel: A Cultural History of Forgotten Adaptations*

Marc Singer, *Breaking the Frames: Populism and Prestige in Comics Studies*

Matt Yockey, ed., *Make Ours Marvel: Media Convergence and a Comics Universe*

Mark Heimermann and Brittany Tullis, eds., *Picturing Childhood: Youth in Transnational Comics*

David William Foster, El Eternauta, Daytripper, *and Beyond: Graphic Narrative in Argentina and Brazil*

Christopher Pizzino, *Arresting Development: Comics at the Boundaries of Literature*

Frederick Luis Aldama and Christopher González, eds., *Graphic Borders: Latino Comic Books Past, Present, and Future*

COMIC BOOK WOMEN

CHARACTERS, CREATORS, AND CULTURE IN THE GOLDEN AGE

Peyton Brunet and Blair Davis
Foreword by Trina Robbins

University of Texas Press
Austin

First edition, 2022
First paperback edition, 2023

Requests for permission to reproduce material from this work should be sent to:
Permissions
University of Texas Press
P.O. Box 7819
Austin, TX 78713-7819
utpress.utexas.edu/rp-form

♾ The paper used in this book meets the minimum requirements of ANSI/NISO Z39.48-1992 (R1997) (Permanence of Paper).

Library of Congress Cataloging-in-Publication Data

Names: Brunet, Peyton, author. | Davis, Blair, 1975– author. | Robbins, Trina, writer of foreword.
Title: Comic book women : characters, creators, and culture in the Golden Age / Peyton Brunet and Blair Davis.
Other titles: World comics and graphic nonfiction series.
Description: First edition. | Austin : University of Texas Press, 2022. | Series: World comics and graphic nonfiction series | Includes bibliographical references and index.
Identifiers: LCCN 2021027221
ISBN 978-1-4773-2412-7 (paperback)
ISBN 978-1-4773-2413-4 (PDF)
ISBN 978-1-4773-2414-1 (ePub)
Subjects: LCSH: Women cartoonists—United States—History—20th century. | Comic books, strips, etc.—United States—Women authors—History—20th century. | Comic strip characters—United States—History—20th century. | Women superheroes—United States—Comic books, strips, etc.—History—20th century. | Comic books, strips, etc.—Social aspects—United States. | Women in literature—History—20th century. | Heroines in literature—History—20th century.

Classification: LCC PN6725 .B78 2022 | DDC 741.5/973—dc23

LC record available at https://lccn.loc.gov/2021027221

doi:10.7560/324110

PEYTON

For my superheroine sisters, Paige and Perrin.

BLAIR

For my Mum. And yours, too.

CONTENTS

FOREWORD

Trina Robbins

I was lucky enough to have a schoolteacher mother who not only taught me to read at the age of four but who supplied me with books—and comics—to read, and I did, avidly. But the comics, while beautifully drawn and absolutely charming, were the kind mothers approved of: funny animals, Raggedy Ann and Andy, cute kids' comics like *Our Gang*. The candy store that sold comics was two blocks away, which meant I had grown big enough to cross two streets before I could choose and buy comics on my own.

When I did, for the first time, I was faced with a dizzying array of choices: superheroes, teen humor, mystery and adventure, cowboys! What to choose? The decision was automatic and easy. I chose any comic with a girl or woman on the cover, but not the pretty girls tied to a chair so the hero could rescue them. I went for the women who had their own comic, with their own name on the cover, women who could take care of themselves. And there were plenty: of course Wonder Woman, but also Sheena, Queen of the Jungle, with her flowing golden hair and her leopard skin dress, and Mary Marvel, a preteen girl who said the magic word "Shazam" to become a girl who could fly and punch out the bad guys. I played with the idea that maybe if I could find my magic word, my "Shazam," I too could gain superpowers.

And there were the teenagers: Patsy Walker, Millie the Model, Katy Keene, who you could even design clothes for if you were brave enough to mail them to Katy's creator, Bill Woggon. I was never brave enough, but I enjoyed the sometimes bizarre designs other kids sent in, and I quietly drew my own paper dolls and fashions at home.

Never mind if there was only a Patsy Walker comic once a month or a *Jumbo* comic starring Sheena every two months; I never ran out of girls' comics. If I finished Sheena, there was still *Fight Comics*, starring Tiger Girl, and if I finished Millie the Model, there was Hedy De Vine the movie star. If I was faced with waiting a month for the next Wonder Woman, there were the four superheroines from Timely (later Atlas, and later Marvel) comics: Sun Girl, Namora, Venus, the goddess herself come down to Earth, and Blonde Phantom, fighting crime in a slinky red evening gown.

I never read the superheroes; they were boring, and I couldn't relate to them. I only wanted to lose myself in page after brightly colored page of adventures of girls and women. They were somehow more human than the men. Many didn't have superpowers at all. Wonder Woman didn't fly in those days; she simply was able to run incredibly fast and leap incredibly high because of her Amazon training. The idea of her creator, William Moulton Marston, was to show that ordinary girls, with the right training, could be almost as powerful as the Amazon princess. Others had powers that were attainable if you found the right magic word, like Mary Marvel, or pressed the right nerve, like Scarlet O'Neil, who pressed a nerve on her left wrist to become invisible. Teen heroines like Patsy Walker and Katy Keene had no powers except their smarts and optimistic resilience.

About a year ago, I discovered the answer to a question: Do women and men react differently to comics? I was being interviewed by a filmmaker for a documentary on the late underground cartoonist Spain Rodriguez. When I told her I'd loved Sheena comics as a kid, she told me that Spain and cartoonist Victor Moscoso, both around the same age as me, had also loved Sheena. Both Spain and Moscoso, she said, told her they used to draw Sheena naked. Did I, she asked, also draw Sheena naked?

I was outraged. "How dare they?" I sputtered. "Of course I didn't draw Sheena naked! I wanted to *be* her!"

COMIC BOOK WOMEN

INTRODUCTION

Comics studies has chronicled the history of the medium in ways that are centered almost exclusively on men. Two of the most influential and widely cited histories of comics are *Men of Tomorrow* by Gerard Jones and *Of Comics and Men* by Jean Paul Gabilliet. Both are exceptional works, but women play a very small role in both. The male-dominated focus of comics historians is also seen in the titles of books such as David Kunzle's *Father of the Comic Strip*, Jan Bernard Stoltz's *The Men Who Made the Comics*, Bob Batchelor's *Stan Lee: The Man behind Marvel*, and Matthew J. Pustz's *Comic Book Culture: Fanboys and True Believers*, as well as the cover blurb for Joe Simon and Jim Simon's *The Comic Book Makers* ("The young men in the Golden Age of comics were as bizarre as the characters they created!").

Comics history regularly describes the medium as one built by men who told tales about male heroes. But what would a female-centric history of comics—one that placed women at the center of comics history instead of on the sidelines—look like? Our understanding of genres like the western, crime, horror, superhero, and sci-fi comics would shift dramatically, and the narratives surrounding how auteurs such as Stan Lee and Will Eisner built their careers would also be altered. The story of how comic books were born and how they evolved changes significantly when we place women up front rather than at the margins of this history.

In their introduction to a special issue of *Inks: The Journal of the Comics Studies Society* in 2019 on underground comics, Margaret Galvan and Leah Misemer urge "the application of feminist praxis to how we tell the history of comics in comic studies." They argue, "A practice of feminist historiography involves looking at things differently and questioning the accepted methods that reproduce the same narratives, which exclude by building a lineage through dominant forces, through straight, white, cis men rather than through another route."[1] In turn, a feminist history of comics should include the reclaiming of women's efforts as writers, artists, editors, and other roles within the industry in its early decades, as well as the re-centering of the female characters who were often much more pivotal to the evolution and success of various genres than given credit for.

Both on the page and in publishers' studios, women fought for legitimacy throughout the early history of comic books. Many strong heroines arose, certainly, such as Wonder Woman, the Black Cat, Phantom Lady, Miss Fury, and Señorita Rio, but there were far more damsels in distress, conniving temptresses, boy-crazed teenyboppers, haggard crones, nosy old biddies, bossy battle-axes, and other overworked clichés. In the humor series *Dizzy Dames*, for example, the tagline read "Screwballs in Skirts!" and the first issue's cover featured a young woman asking, "You mean this isn't where they pick Miss America?" to the shocked judges at a dog show. When any particular group of people sees itself portrayed in hurtful, hateful, thoughtless, boorish, ignorant, awkward, or indifferent terms, the consequences for how that group sees itself (along with how others see them from the outside) can be lasting. As fictional stories regularly depict one's culture, race, or gender in disparaging or inaccurate ways, it becomes difficult to counteract the steady drumbeat of those stereotypes. If these patterns are repeated often enough over time, negative attitudes and opinions can become solidified across generations.

The ways in which women have been represented in comics are one such instance of how media images can have lasting consequences. What most comics fans refer to as the Golden Age of comics, spanning much of the 1930s, '40s, and '50s, has been a forum for frequently problematic, often uncomfortable, at times complex, and occasionally inspiring depictions of women.[2] While the comics industry saw women such as Lily Renée, Toni Blum, and Marcia Snyder working across a range of different genres in this era, most female characters were created, written, and drawn by men—a pattern that has only recently begun to see any significant degree of change. For every appearance of a strong heroine or powerful villain like Miss Fury or Madam Satan, there were even more blatantly sexist moments, such as the time Batman threatened Catwoman with the phrase "Quiet or Papa spank!" during her first appearance in *Batman* #1 (1940).[3] Comic book publishing is still a predominantly male industry even today, despite the inroads made by female writers, artists, editors, and executives. The 1960s, '70s, and '80s saw pioneering comic book creators such as Marie Severin, Trina Robbins, Louise Simonson,

Cover of *Dizzy Dames* #1, 1952, American Comics Group.

and Ann Nocenti working for both DC and Marvel Comics on such top characters as Spider-Man, Wonder Woman, the Hulk, and Daredevil, but their work was regularly overshadowed by their male counterparts.

Now, decades later, there are more women working in comics than at any point in history, but the symptoms of past neglect still linger. It wasn't until 2018 that a female creator first won an Eisner Award (the comics industry's top honor since its 1988 debut) for Best Writer. Marjorie Liu won for *Monstress*, but she shared the award with Tom King for his work on *Mister Miracle* and various *Batman* titles—the first tie in that category's history. Consider this moment a bit further: a woman wins an Eisner for Best Writer (for a series about a powerful female hero) for the first time in the three decades of the award's history, but she has to share it with a male writer who writes about male characters. Liu's win is a key moment in the history of female comics creators, but it comes with a glaring footnote.

Few women earned public recognition for their work making comic books in the initial decades of the medium. For every woman like June

Batman #1, 1940, Detective Comics Inc.

Tarpé Mills whose name appeared within the pages of their creations (albeit under the pen name Tarpé Mills to disguise her gender), far more labored in uncredited roles as editors, letterers, and colorists. Some were even ghost-artists and ghost-writers for their male counterparts, while others took over as lead artists during World War II when numerous comics creators were drafted. Comics scholar and Image Comics editor Jennifer M. Smith notes,

> It's important to realize that there have always been women as characters in comics, as readers of comics, and as creators of comics. And I don't just mean of independent comics or romance comics. . . . Comics as a medium has always had tons of women in various areas. But even within the narrow domain of superhero comics, it's important not to erase the contribution of the women who have been there since the Golden Age: as artists, as writers, as editors. Women as editors have been really integral to comics production for decades. . . . It's important for us to acknowledge that history.[4]

The comics industry continues to be regarded as a male-dominated space where women—whether characters, creators, or readers—are at best routinely tokenized and at worst perpetually marginalized. In more recent years, the presence of female creators producing work for and about complex and compelling women, girls, and nonbinary people has certainly increased, but the public face of feminism in comics remains lacking. If the endless array of T-shirts, tote bags, and blockbuster films featuring spandex-clad superheroines are to be believed, the only powerful women in comics are those with superpowers. This "superfeminism" risks neglecting not only that characters from other genres can be equally empowering but also that there are women on the creative side who have crafted countless stories dating back more than eighty years about women who don't have superstrength or immortality. Unless we acknowledge that women have had a longer and richer history as comics characters and creators than most people realize, the current moment, in which cinematic superheroines such as Wonder Woman and Captain Marvel have captured the public's attention, risks being little more than a patronizing pat on the head seeking to reassure us, *See, girls can be strong too.*

The current state of women in comics stems in no small part from the early history of comic books, which is typically chronicled from the perspective of male creators such as Will Eisner, Jerry Siegel, Joe Shuster, Bob Kane, Stan Lee, Jack Kirby, Joe Simon, Jack Cole, and Joe Kubert. Comic books, we are told, were built primarily by these "men of tomorrow" as a male-driven endeavor that succeeded via such characters as Superman, Batman, the Human Torch, Captain America, Captain Marvel, Archie Andrews, Blackhawk, Plastic Man, and other male heroes. But this grand narrative of comics history has excluded the vital contributions made by creators such as Ruth Atkinson, Toni Blum, Barbara Hall, Fran Hopper, June Tarpé Mills, Lily Renée, and Ruth Roche to the industry's development; Maurice Horn's *The World Encyclopedia of Comics* does not contain entries for any of these women, for instance.[5]

Equally neglected are the pivotal roles played by such characters as Sally the Sleuth, Olga Mesmer, Fantomah, the Magician from Mars, Sandra of the Secret Service, the Black Cat, Moon Girl, Sheriff Sal, Gale Allen, Sally O'Neil, and Two-Gun Lil to the development of numerous genres. As feminist scholar bell hooks writes, "Feminist critiques of all-male canons of scholarship or literary work expose biases based on gender," a process that is "central to making a place for the recovery of women's work and contemporary place for the production of new work by and about women."[6] In turn, a feminist history of comics must reclaim the forgotten work done by women in the industry, along with examining both the cultural and industrial consequences of how women were represented across various genres. Our intention is not merely to point out instances of misogyny or to chart the oppression of women in every corner of the comics world; instead, we aim to reinsert female creators and characters into the canon of comics history. This re-situation of women in the history of comics requires a deeper look at how women wielded the (however little) power they possessed and how female characters worked as an outlet for creators to both uphold and overturn hegemonic norms of gender, class, race, and sexuality.

Women worked at most of the earliest comic book companies. One of the first was Centaur Publications, which began in 1938 (the same year that Superman debuted in *Action Comics* #1). Two of their first creators were Claire S. Moe and June Tarpé Mills, both of whom wrote and drew for Centaur between 1938 and 1940 on such series as *Amazing Man Comics*, *Amazing Mystery Funnies*, *Funny Pages*, *Funny Picture Stories*, and *Keen Detective Funnies*. Moe did the story and art for such features as "Circus and Sue," "Dean Masters," "Sonny Darling," and "Yellow Terror," while Mills was writer/artist on "Barry Finn," "Cat-Man," "Diane Deane," "The Ivy Menace," and "The Vampire"—the latter two being some of the earliest examples of horror comics—as well as a cover artist.

A revisionist history of comics might even start with the origins of the companies that eventually became Marvel and DC Comics, given how these two publishers have come to dominate the male-driven histories of the comics industry. DC's origins stem from the efforts of Major Malcom Wheeler-Nicholson, who formed National Allied Publications Inc. in 1934, after more than a decade of writing for pulp magazines.[7] On January 11, 1935, his first comic book, *New Fun*, hit newsstands. It was the first comic book to feature original stories rather than reprinted material, making it a milestone in the history of the medium. It is also notable for being the first comic book to feature a female character in its lead story. While the series' covers offered stories in panel form (featuring a rotating cast of male characters such as cowboy Jack Woods and space adventurer Don Drake), the lead story in all six issues of *New Fun* was "Sandra of the Secret Service," featuring the serialized adventures of globetrotting American secret agent Sandra McLane. The cover stories are not included in each issue's table of contents, which always list Sandra's stories on page 1. When the series was rebranded as *More Fun* with its seventh issue (and then *More Fun Comics* with #9), Sandra continued to lead off each issue for more than two years until her final appearance in 1938's *More Fun Comics* #34. The character also inspired competing versions in 1937, including "Hope Hazard, G-Woman" in 1937's *Detective Comics* #3 and "G-Woman" in *New Adventure Comics* #22. All three of these series were integral to the early development of DC Comics, which thrived on female heroes well before the debut of Superman in 1938.

A forgotten female figure also factors into the history of Timely Comics, which later became Marvel Comics. The company's first effort, 1939's *Marvel Comics* #1, offered readers two new heroes who would go on to become mainstays of Marvel Comics throughout later decades—the Human Torch and the Sub-Mariner. Both were created by Funnies Inc., which was co-owned by Lloyd Jacquet (who had been Wheeler-Nicholson's

"Sandra of the Secret Service," *New Fun* #1, 1935, National Allied Publications Inc.

lead editor on *New Fun*). Funnies Inc. was a "packaging shop," which created original material for sale to various comic book publishers (a process known as "packaging" within the industry). All of the stories and characters featured within the first issue of *Marvel Comics* originated at "the Jacquet Shop," including the Angel, the Masked Raider, and Ka-Zar, along with the Sub-Mariner and the Human Torch.[8]

But Funnies Inc. was not led by Lloyd Jacquet alone. His wife, Grace

Jacquet, was co-owner of the shop from its inception in 1939 to her death (and the company's demise) in 1961, and was often closely involved in its production efforts. In an article for the fanzine *Alter Ego*, Jack Elmy describes his conversation with writer Joe Gill, who did freelance work for Funnies Inc. in the 1940s. Gill recalls Grace Jacquet as a "wonderful woman" who, he says, "was an essential part of the shop's day-to-day operations."[9] Timely owner Martin Goodman stopped using the services of Funnies Inc. in 1942 (while simultaneously hiring "much of Jacquet's staff" in the process).[10] When Lloyd was deployed as a naval intelligence officer in World War II between 1942 and 1946, Grace became editor in chief of Funnies Inc. With Grace at the helm, the Jacquet Shop hired numerous female creators, especially during the war years, including such artists as Nina Albright, Dolores Carroll, Jill Elgin, Lucy Feller, Florence Magarian, June Tarpé Mills, Claire S. Moe, Ramona Patenaude, and Janice Valleau. Grace's specific role in the production of early Timely Comics material prior to Lloyd's absence remains mostly unknown, but her larger contributions in this era have been overlooked in existing histories of both Funnies Inc. and Timely/Marvel Comics.

Timely's creative ranks in the 1940s also included a writer who would soon go on to become a prominent novelist: Patricia Highsmith, whose first novel, *Strangers on a Train*, was published in 1950 before being adapted as a film by Alfred Hitchcock. Highsmith wrote comics such as *Nellie the Nurse* for Timely in the late 1940s while also completing her first novel in this era. Earlier in the decade, she had created the propagandistic hero (and unfortunately named) Jap-Buster Johnston for Timely, along with writing the adventures of characters such as the Black Terror for Better Publications and Spy Smasher for Fawcett Comics in addition to work for Dell Publications and Novelty Press. In *The Talented Miss Highsmith: The Secret Life and Serious Art of Patricia Highsmith*, biographer Joan Schenkar describes Highsmith's work in comics as an "apprenticeship" several times, noting how her early comics writing helped her to develop some of the key themes in her later novels even though she was embarrassed by her early work in the medium.[11] Drawing a direct parallel between Highsmith's comic book work and her characterization of Tom Ripley in her fourth novel, *The Talented Mr. Ripley* (1955), Schenkar explains,

> When Pat gave her "criminal hero" Tom Ripley a charmed and parentless life, a wealthy, socially posed Alter Ego (Dickie Greenleaf), and a guilt-free modus operandi (after he kills Dickie, Tom murders only when necessary), she was doing just what her fellow

> comic book artists were doing with their Superheroes: allowing her fictional character to finesse situations she herself could only approach in wish fulfillment. And when she reimagined her own psychological split in Ripley's character—embodying him with both her weakest traits (paralyzing self-consciousness and hero-worship) and her wildest dreams (murder and money)—she was turning the material of the "comic book" upside down and making it into something very much like a "tragic book."[12]

Though the language Schenkar uses here fails to appreciate the full value of comics and their place in American popular culture, she is clear in her assertion that American comics held influence over Highsmith long after she left the industry. Schenkar writes that while Highsmith's crime novels, such as *Strangers on a Train*, were influenced by authors like Dostoevsky, Poe, Proust, and James, the themes of her work "had also been marinating for seven long years in the colorful tropes of the American comic book."[13] While Highsmith was loath to discuss her early career in comics, her work for numerous publishers throughout the 1940s made her what Schenkar calls "the most frequently employed female scriptwriter during the Golden Age of American Comics."[14]

Much of the problem in reclaiming the history of non-male creators and characters lies in the historiography that has been used to write existing accounts of the comics industry's evolution. Interviews with male creators who worked in the Golden and Silver Ages of comics have given us valuable firsthand accounts of the day-to-day workings of various publishers as well as the business decisions and creative choices made in the conception of new titles and characters. But when recalling their non-male counterparts, many interviewees default to describing the physical appearance or emotional temperament of the women they worked with more than their talents or their work (if these latter aspects were mentioned at all). Recalling Lily Renée, artist Nick Cardy says, "She was a good-looking girl, but she stayed pretty much to herself." Of artist Fran Hopper, Cardy adds, "She was a nice girl, very quiet and unimposing, and cute"; of artist Jean Levander, he points out that she "was big-bosomed and when she used to stop and give you something at the table, she'd hand the drawing or something over the table and she'd sit there and she'd sway from side to side with her body."[15] When asked if he recalled Timely inker Valerie Barclay, artist Lou Cameron said, "She was very attractive, and she looked like Vampira. She had white, white makeup, and the first time I saw her, sizing her up from across the room, I said, 'Gee, I'd like to take that home. But if there are no reflections in the mirrors, she gets a wooden stake between the boobs!'" Cameron also added that Barclay reminded him of "Julie Newmar with normal proportions."[16]

Similarly, when asked if he remembered artist Ann Brewster, who worked for such publishers as EC Comics, Fawcett, Fiction House, and Timely throughout the 1940s and 1950s, the esteemed writer/artist Joe Simon immediately focused on her body, replying, "Sure. She was quiet and she was of normal size, normal build; a nice woman."[17] So too does Will Eisner bring in writer Toni Blum's appearance when recalling her career: "Toni was like a 'den mother,' very attractive, and she worked hard."[18] While men are remembered for their work, what comes to mind about the women who made comics throughout the Golden Age in interviews with their male peers is often not what they created but what they looked like. The way these women were often described by the men around them ("like Vampira," "big-bosomed") doesn't just diminish their autonomy; it reduces them to something cartoonish or one-dimensional, much like the female characters these men often created. Given how much comics fans and scholars rely on these interviews to retrace the medium's history, this pattern has been detrimental to a full understanding of the vital contributions that women have made to the comics industry.

Women created comics in a range of roles throughout the twentieth century. In addition to the writers and artists discussed in this book, women worked as inkers (Valerie Barclay, Ray Herman, Ruth Harris, Jean Levander), letterers (Judith Christ, Veda Lufkin, Daisy Swayze, Alberta Tews), colorists (Lillian Proctor, Marie Severin), and proofreaders (Adele Hasan, Polly Schwartz). There were also female editors at most publishers in the Golden Age who made key creative decisions and oversaw, gave input to, and ultimately approved the work done by the male creators who worked for them. Bonnie Hano was Stan Lee's assistant editor in the early 1950s.[19] Gwen Hansen worked as an editor at Quality Comics. Ray Herman was an editor at Continental Magazines and Holyoke Publishing before forming her own company, Orbit Publications, in 1946. Helen Meyer was president of Dell Publishing and editor in chief of their comics line (which, Meyer has said, accounted for almost one-third of all comics sold by 1954, thanks to the success of their Walt Disney comics and other licensed titles).[20] Virginia A. Provisiero was an editor at Fawcett from 1943 to 1953, working on top titles such as *Hopalong Cassidy*, *Nyoka the Jungle Girl*, *Spy Smasher*, and *Whiz Comics*. Evonne Rae was an editor for Dell Publishing and Story Comics, and also wrote for the latter. Ruth Roche served as editor in chief at Fiction House, while Jean Alipe and Jean M. Press were also editors there. Roberta "Bobbie" Ross was Grace Jacquet's main editor at Funnies Inc. throughout the mid-1940s and was in charge of hiring.[21] Katherine "Kay" Woods worked as an editor at Fawcett Comics, as did Edna Hagen. Dorothy Woolfolk was an editor at All-American Publications, EC Comics, Timely Comics, and DC Comics.

Ruth Roche's career has gone especially unheralded among most comics historians despite how central she was to the industry's early years. After Jerry Iger's partnership with Will Eisner dissolved, Roche joined Iger's studio in 1940 as a writer and editor, but she soon became Iger's business partner. Roche served as executive editor at the Roche & Iger Studio until it folded in 1961. With Eisner gone, Iger realized he needed a strong creative talent to help helm the studio: artist Bill Bossert recalls that "Iger was the money man. . . . He watched the bottom line, but that's not the wrong thing to do." When asked whether there was anything creative about Iger, Bossert replied, "No, nothing creative at all, but he supplied the money, and Eisner provided the impetus and the creative work."[22]

Once Eisner split with Iger, Roche provided the needed creative impetus to keep the company running. But while the Eisner-Iger partnership is well chronicled in comics history, little gets said about Roche & Iger. Roche was also a prolific writer, working for more than two decades on such male characters as Ka'a'nga, Kayo Kirby, and Rip Carson, and such heroines as Phantom Lady and Señorita Rio, along with the jungle queens Camilla and Sheena. She also cocreated the first Muslim superhero, Kismet the Man of Fate, in 1944 for Elliot Publishing Co.'s *Bomber Comics* #1. An Algerian hero who battled Axis forces ("Have a barrelful of liquid cement, you infidels!" he shouts while subduing a group of Nazis), Kismet's religious faith was made prominent for readers, such as when he prays, "Allah be with me!" while preparing for a mission.[23]

While many women thrived in these behind-the-scenes roles, female creators struggled early on to gain acceptance as artists in the male-dominated field of illustration—a pattern that predates comic books. When a professional group called the Society of Illustrators was formed in 1901, they allowed a handful of women (Elizabeth Shippen Green, Florence Scovel, Violet Oakley, Jessie Willcox Smith, and May Wilson) to join as associate members in the years that followed but did not grant full membership to women until the 1920s.[24] Some women of this era, like Jessie Willcox Smith, illustrated children's books—a vital precursor to comic books that still serve as an important parallel to comics in how they offer readers a combination of words and images. After finding success with her 1905 edition of *A Child's Garden of Verses* by Robert Louis Stevenson,

"Kismet, Man of Fate," *Bomber Comics* #1, 1944, Elliot Publishing Co. Inc. Written by Ruth Roche.

Smith went on to draw and/or paint more youth-oriented books of poetry before producing an illustrated version of *Heidi* in 1922.[25] Fanny Young Cory drew "at least eleven books, including works by L. Frank Baum and Lewis Carol," while Maginel Wright Enright Barney drew several books from her own childhood, including 1931's *Weather Signs and Rhymes*.[26]

The suffrage movement was one area in which women cartoonists were especially active in the early decades of the twentieth century. As Alice Sheppard chronicles in *Cartooning for Suffrage*, female artists such as Blanche Ames, Nina Evans, Ida Proper, and Lou Rogers used comics as a forum for political expression in such publications as *Judge*, *New York Call*, *The Suffragist*, and *Woman's Journal*. As Sheppard notes, political cartoons had long been a forum for male artists to raise questions about societal injustice and power structures, but issues of gender were rarely a factor. As more women used comics as a political forum to challenge long-held beliefs about female identity and the role of women in society during the suffrage movement, these artists, "united by vocation and by suffrage at a critical time in women's history, reveal a commonality of purpose, hope and vision demonstrated though their art," writes Sheppard.[27]

Newspaper comic strips were another forum where some women found success. Grace Drayton drew numerous strips between 1903 and her death in 1936, including *Naughty Toodles*, *The Adventures of Bobby Blake and Dolly Drake in Storyland*, *Dolly Dimples and Bobby Bounce*, and *The Pussycat Princess*. Edwina Dumm created the strip *Captain Stubbs and Tippie* in 1918, followed in 1934 by *Tippie*. In the 1920s, the flapper craze inspired Virginia Huget's strips *Babs in Society*, *Flora's Fling*, and *Molly the Manicure Girl*. Huget went on to create other strips, including *Double Dora* and the fantasy opus *Miss Aladdin*.[28] In *Drawn to Purpose: American Women Illustrators and Cartoonists*, Martha H. Kennedy explains,

> From about 1917 into the 1920s, a period that included women's organizational leadership and service in World War I, and women at last winning the vote, comics by both male and female cartoonists gradually came to reflect the changing roles of women as many of them sought fulfilling activity outside the home. Popular imagery reflecting these changes began somewhat earlier, with the appearance of the New Woman in the 1890s, but the theme expanded with depictions of women campaigning for suffrage, a cause supported by many (but not all) women cartoonists, and, in the 1920s, of flappers, such as those drawn by Nell Brinkley and Virginia Huget. Not until the late 1930s and 1940s, however, were women able to successfully introduce comics with heroines who focused on careers and adventures outside the home, as seen in the work of Jackie Ormes and Dale Messick.[29]

Both Ormes and Messick, however, "labored for years to win syndication and reasonable distribution for their strips."[30] Ormes, an African American cartoonist, found a lasting career working for several newspapers serving Black communities. Her long-running character Torchy Brown first reached readers on May 1, 1937, in the *Pittsburgh Courier*, while in 1945 she debuted the single-panel strips *Candy* in the *Chicago Defender* and *Patty-Jo 'n' Ginger* in the *Pittsburgh Courier*. Torchy Brown appeared in numerous strips, culminating in *Torchy in Heartbeats*, which was syndicated by Smith-Mann Syndicate from 1950 to 1954.[31]

While creators like Ormes and Messick often struggled in their dealings with newspaper syndicates, comic strips were still more welcoming to female talent in the early twentieth century than were the comic book publishing houses. Indeed, several of the strips created by women during the early twentieth century remain in production today. Martha Orr's

1934 strip *Apple Mary*, for example, evolved into the better-known *Mary Worth*, about a gray-haired matron whose sensible advice guided the supporting characters through various melodramatic scenarios. Orr sold the strip in 1938 to raise her young child, and her assistant, Dale Connor, took over as the artist on the new version, which is still distributed to hundreds of newspapers by King Features Syndicate.[32] Another famous comic strip that debuted in the mid-1930s was Marge Henderson Buell's *Little Lulu*. Buell drew Lulu in the *Saturday Evening Post* from 1935 to 1947, at which point she sold the rights to *Little Lulu* comic books and a daily syndicated comic strip that ran from 1950 through 1969.

There were also numerous comic strips by male creators that were centered on female protagonists in this era. In the 1920s, readers followed the ongoing adventures of *Babs in Society*, *Dashing Dot*, *Ella Cinders*, *Flapper Fanny*, *Gay and Her Gang*, *Little Annie Rooney*, *Little Orphan Annie*, *Marianne*, *Tillie the Toiler*, and *Winnie Winkle*. Some strips, such as *Ella Cinders* and *Tillie the Toiler*, were adapted into feature films by major studios. *Little Orphan Annie*'s success continued into the 1930s, with the strip spawning a popular radio program (sponsored by Ovaltine, a fact made famous in the 1983 film *A Christmas Story*) and two less remembered films. Another strip, Dale Messick's *Brenda Starr*, was adapted as the thirteen-chapter serial *Brenda Starr, Reporter* in 1945. While male superheroes such as Batman, Captain America, Captain Marvel, and Superman also got their own film serials in the 1940s, the same wasn't true for female comic book characters; not even Wonder Woman made it to the screen. The fact that so many comic strips featuring female characters were adapted into movies while their comic book counterparts weren't further demonstrates just how marginalizing the comic book industry could be for women in the 1930s, 1940s, and 1950s—characters and creators alike.

Our work chronicling the early history of women in comic books is divided into eight chapters, each examining a specific genre or a unique role inhabited by women in the mid-1930s through the 1950s: crime comics, horror titles, jungle comics, romance books, science fiction, superheroes, western comics, and books in which women were the title characters. The rise of superhero comics (chapter 1) in the late 1930s saw several costumed heroines throughout the 1940s. Some remain at the forefront of popular culture today, such as Wonder Woman. Others, such as Phantom Lady, remain familiar to well-read comics fans, but most others have faded from popular memory. The Black Cat and Lady Luck had their own series, while others—including Golden Girl, Lady Satan, Miss Victory, Red Tornado, and the Woman in Red—appeared regularly in anthology titles like *All-American Comics*, *Dynamic Comics*, *Marvel Mystery Comics*, and *Thrilling Comics*. In addition to tracing the contributions that these heroes made to comics' evolution, chapter 1 also examines the innovative roles played by creators such as Barbara Hall, June Tarpé Mills, Nina Albright, Joye Hummel, and Toni Blum (who pioneered the so-called Marvel method of writing comics two decades before Stan Lee claims he invented the process). It also chronicles the pervasive sexual harassment that women faced while working in comics.

Jungle comics (chapter 2) were also a popular genre in this era, including titles such as *Jumbo Comics* and *Jungle Comics*. Women adventurers were a mainstay of the genre, and most had their own series, including *Jann of the Jungle*, *Lorna the Jungle Girl*, *Rulah the Jungle Goddess*, *Nyoka the Jungle Girl*, and *White Princess of the Jungle*. Others, such as Camilla and Tiger Girl, appeared in anthologies like *Jungle Comics*, while *Sheena, Queen of the Jungle* proved popular in other media as well, spawning multiple television series and a feature film in 1984. Along with examining both the empowering and sexist roles for women in these books, chapter 2 traces the problematic ways in which racist and colonialist ideals are expressed in otherwise lighthearted titles. We also examine the vital contributions made by creators such as Ruth Atkinson, Ruth Roche, and Marcia Snyder in addition to exploring how jungle tales were crossed with other genres in the work of Lily Renée's *Señorita Rio* and June Tarpé Mills's *Miss Fury*.

Crime comics (chapter 3) became best sellers in the 1940s, with women playing leading, supporting, and all roles in between in titles such as *All-Famous Crime*, *Crime and Punishment*, *Crime Does Not Pay*, *Famous Crimes*, and *Gangsters and Gun Molls*. But before the genre's emphasis on famous criminals, crime comics saw female sleuths, detectives, and policewomen as regular fixtures from the mid-1930s through early 1940s. Sally the Sleuth, Sandra of the Secret Service, and Sally O'Neil were among comics' earliest crime busters, though their contributions to the genre's origins have gone overlooked. At the dawn of the 1950s, crime comics also became a vital forum for exploring female identity in connection with issues of power, morality, and sexuality in books like *Crime SuspenStories*, *Crimes by Women*, and *It Rhymes with Lust*, the latter often credited as a pioneer of the graphic novel format.

Horror comics (chapter 4) arose by the late 1940s and predictably featured women in a range of villainous roles, from green-tinged witches and sorceresses to buttoned-up domestic murderers and unsuspected killers. Titles such as *Adventures into Terror*, *Eerie Comics*, and *Weird Horrors* frequently depicted women as hapless victims, while others, such as *Witchcraft* and *Witches Tales*, often centered around female villains. Publisher EC Comics dominated the marketplace by the early 1950s with titles like *Haunt of Fear*, *Shock SuspenStories*, *Tales from the Crypt*, and *Vault of Horror*, until the efforts of psychiatrist Fredric Wertham and other critics, as well as the rise of the Comics Code Authority (CCA), effectively killed the genre. While women were routinely murdered in the pages of these horror comics, the genre was an early forum for creators like June Tarpé Mills and Lily Renée to experiment in between the late 1930s and mid-1940s. Their work on such characters as the Purple Zombie and the Werewolf Hunter remains little known today, but it stands in stark contrast with the genre's steady output of dead female bodies as it evolved by the decade's end.

Western comics (chapter 5) also offered women prominent roles, led by famed sharpshooter Annie Oakley in titles from both Dell and Atlas Comics. Screen star Dale Evans had two titles, *Dale Evans Comics* and *Queen of the West, Dale Evans*, while many other books combined the western and crime genres, such as *Western Crime Busters*, *Western True Crime*, and *Women Outlaws*. Many of these comics starred characters like Belle Brander, Bronco Moll Malloy, Cattle Kate, Trigger Tess, and Wilma West, who rode alongside their male counterparts from the genre's early days. Westerns have long been thought of as a forum for exploring issues of American history and masculine identity across numerous media, but western titles regularly placed women—and, notably, often indigenous women—at the center of their narratives throughout the Golden Age of comics.

Comics with women as title characters (chapter 6) encompassed several genres, though most mixed humor and romance in titles such as *Boots and Her Buddies*, *Candy*, *Dixie Dugan*, *Dotty*, *Ginger*, *Kathy*, *Katy Keene*, *Linda*, *Miss Beverly Hills of Hollywood*, *My Little Margie*, *Nellie the Nurse*, *Penny*, *Starlet O'Hara*, *Suzie Comics*, *Torchy*, and *Vicky Comics*. This chapter looks at the role that popular titles like *Millie the Model* and *Patsy Walker* played within the comics industry, and their financial importance to how Marvel shifted to superheroes in the early 1960s. It also traces the way these titles offered a diverse array of characters for both younger and older readers—from high school high jinks to career-driven escapades—as well as the numerous ways in which fans were able to actively engage with the titles (such as advice columns, fashion designs, and more).

Science fiction (chapter 7) was another genre in which female characters were prevalent, in the pages of such titles as *Amazing Man Comics*, *Planet Comics*, *Sun Girl*, and *Venus*. Science fiction's ability to embed social, cultural, and political messages within its narratives meant that sci-fi comics could be a forum for exploring (whether in subtle or overt ways) questions of gender and personal identity in ways that other genres were less willing or able to do. Though early heroes like Alice of the Winged People, Amazona the Mighty Woman, and the Magician from Mars, who were among the earliest sci-fi heroes in comics in the late 1930s and early 1940s, have largely been written out of the sci-fi canon, their existence as lead characters remains significant within a genre that had—and continues to have—a complicated relationship with issues of social and cultural progress.

Finally, the rise of romance comics (chapter 8) saw industry legends Jack Kirby and Joe Simon shift from superheroes to a new genre in 1947 with *Young Romance*, and its overwhelming success led to a flood of imitators. Some books were devoted exclusively to the ritual of dating, like *Hi-School Romance*, *School Day Romances*, and *Teen-Age Romances*. But many more focused on the trials and delights of married life, such as *Bride's Diary*, *Just Married*, *Romantic Marriage*, *Secrets of Love and Marriage*, *Teen-Age Brides*, *True Brides*, and *Young Brides*. While other genres came and went by the 1950s, such as crime and horror, romance comics endured well into the 1970s by appealing to female readers. While romance comics regularly reinforced hegemonic norms of masculinity and femininity in mid-century American society, some stories proved to be a vital forum for explorations of gender issues, race, sexuality, and even—to an extent—queer identity. The genre also saw numerous creators, such as Phyliss Reed, Isabel Mangum, and Ray Herman, frequently challenge traditional notions of femininity in their work, often creating characters with more autonomy than seen in other genres.

Unlike previous scholarly studies of women and comics, ours is the first to focus on a wide range of genres throughout the Golden Age of comics. Whenever possible, we examine female characters of color closely, whether they appear in leading roles or supporting ones (although relatively few such characters overall were seen in this era). Women of color, when we did see them in comics, were often reduced to stereotypes. As Rebecca Wanzo notes in *The Content of Our Caricature: African American Comic Art and Political Belonging*, this often took the form of racist caricatures, "reducing people to real and imagined excesses in order to represent something understood as essential about their character."[33] While few comics aimed at nonwhite readers lasted for long due to the systemic racism found within the ranks of many comics distributors and retailers,[34] the few issues that were published in the 1940s and '50s, including *All-Negro Comics* and *Negro Romance*, stand as valuable records of how comic books handled diverse racial identities. The same is true of Latina characters like Señorita Rio; indigenous characters like Nelvana of the Northern Lights, Moon Maiden, and Starlight; and Moon Girl, the sole Arabic heroine of the Golden Age.

In reclaiming the work of women and their contributions to these eight genres, we look at gender and comics through the lenses of media form, access, and cultural representation to uncover the larger discourses at work in how these creators navigated an industry fraught with sexism and harassment, and how non-male characters were portrayed across gender lines during comics' Golden Age. In early chapters we trace a revisionist history of women working as pioneers in many of comics' most popular genres, while in later chapters we trace the ways in which other genres served as a forum for complex negotiations of women's societal, sexual, cultural, and gendered identities. In recovering the work done by women in a range of creative roles in this era, we analyze their contributions to various genres' development while also examining the consequences of women's representation for both readers at the time and comics fans, creators, and scholars in subsequent years. By studying a large cross section of comics to discover the larger patterns surrounding how women created comics and were represented in them, we often intentionally turn away from the best-known and canonical titles and characters, such as Wonder Woman, Catwoman, Lois Lane, and Betty and Veronica. Much like how film genre studies shifted away from auteurism to explore patterns of meaning across non-canonical examples, studying a wider pool of comics and characters (from major and minor publishers alike) allows for more nuanced patterns and evidence to emerge about how comics represented women in this era.

Just as comics scholar Leonard Rifas reminds us that "scholars who study racial imagery in comix do not merely check for the presence of offensive stereotypes," the task of studying female comics characters must involve doing more than simply pointing out the presence of sexist and patriarchal images and discourses.[35] Similarly, Deborah Elizabeth Whaley notes in *Black Women in Sequence: Re-inking Comics, Graphic Novels, and Anime* that we need to push "beyond a discourse of inclusion, exclusion, representation and stereotype to ask critical questions" about the larger social and historical patterns that specific texts and characters lead us toward, including contexts of "politics, gender, race and sexualities."[36] By pushing past the simplistic representation of woman-as-victim, we consider what "female empowerment" in comics means when the vast majority of characters and creators are white, as well as call into question the social, cultural, and political frameworks through which these characters obtain "empowerment." Comics are a medium with rich potential for representing women's identities, experiences, and histories, and our aim is to look at the unique potential that comics held for depicting gender, cultural identity, and sexuality.

Our approach to determining which characters qualify as "female" or "woman" takes cues from Judith Butler's theory of gender performativity, which maintains that gender is not an inherent, biological aspect of an individual but a culturally and socially determined, unstable identity.[37] Because the identities of most Golden Age characters were shaped by men, our analysis emphasizes *how* each character's gender is represented through the narrative, aesthetic, and stylistic choices made by their creators at a time when gender was understood to be strictly binary. Butler writes,

> To be female is, according to that distinction, a facticity which has no meaning, but to be a woman is to have *become* a woman, to compel the body to conform to an historical idea of "woman," to induce the body to become a cultural sign, to materialize oneself in obedience to an historically delimited possibility, and to do this as a sustained and repeated corporeal project. The notion of a "project," however, suggests the originating force of a radical will, and because gender is a project which has cultural survival as its end, the term "strategy" suggests the situation of duress under which gender performance always and variously occurs.[38]

Gender, in other words, is both a performance and a means of conforming to or challenging historically accepted notions of "womanhood." Butler's understanding of gender as a "project which has cultural survival as its end" is especially salient when considering which female characters and creators thrived within the industry and which were ultimately shut out. Nevertheless, it is this definition—that gender is constituted through repeated bodily acts and signifiers—that informs our understanding of "male" and "female."

The titles and characters examined here are crucial to a deeper understanding of comics history given the ways in which comics intended for non-male readers began to disappear by the early 1960s. As the Silver Age took shape, there seemed to be less and less room for comics about women at most publishers. Titles starring female characters were often the first to go, with books like *Katy Keene* canceled in 1961, and *Kathy* and *My Little Margie* ending in 1964. Some romance comics hung on until the early 1970s at publishers such as Charlton, but they vanished as the Bronze Age of comics emerged. Even such genres as horror, science fiction, crime, and jungle comics, which regularly spotlighted female characters (if not always in flattering roles), steadily declined by the time superheroes took over at Marvel and DC in the early 1960s. This eventual absence of comics about women makes these books from the 1930s through the 1950s all the more valuable to explore.

It's also important to note that the comics, creators, and characters we examine throughout this book are of an era that fewer and fewer comics fans can recall with the vivid memory of lived experience. As comics scholarship continues to delve deeper into women's roles from the past few decades, it is vital to place such discussions in conversation with the work done by prior generations of comics creators. Recent years have seen mainstream and independent publishers alike release award-winning and fan-favorite comics by and/or about women, including *America*, *Batgirl*, *Bingo Love*, *Bitch Planet*, *Boundless*, *Captain Marvel*, *Birds of Prey*, *Black Widow*, *Goldie Vance*, *Kindred*, *Love and Rockets*, *Lumberjanes*, *Monstress*, *Ms. Marvel*, *My Favorite Thing Is Monsters*, *Spinning*, *This One Summer*, *The Unbeatable Squirrel Girl*, *The Unstoppable Wasp*, and *Patsy Walker, A.K.A. Hellcat*. Hillary Chute notes that "while a few decades ago comics by women about their lives had to be published underground, today they are taking over the conversation about literature and the self."[39]

Similarly, Ana Merino noted in 2001 how

> in the world of comics, the true integration of women has been a relatively recent phenomenon, thanks in part to the effort of pioneers such as Mary Fleener, Diane Noomin, Aline Kominsky, Roberta Gregory, Trina Robbins and Phoebe Gloeckner, who over the course of several decades have tried to include and create dialogue over the differences in the predominantly masculine universe of comics.[40]

While the past few decades have seen advancement in the roles played by women both as comics characters and creators, the early history of women and comics remains largely untold. The representations of women in the comics analyzed throughout this book offer vital insights into how female identity was constructed during the pioneering decades of the comic book industry, while the reinsertion of female creators into the grand narrative of the comic book industry's early years allows us to understand how women were a foundational force in the origins of many popular genres.

CHAPTER 1

SUPERHERO COMICS

As comic book sales soared in the late 1930s and into the 1940s, superheroines fought alongside male superheroes almost from the start. Women wore colorful costumes, capes, and cowls in the pages of such prominent titles as *All-American Comics*, *Captain America Comics*, *Feature Comics*, *Police Comics*, *Speed Comics*, and *Thrilling Comics*, although most modern comics fans only remember one female superhero from this era—Wonder Woman. Since her first adventures, Wonder Woman has been regarded by her fans as an inspiring icon of strength and justice, but she was just one of many heroines from the first years of comics' Golden Age.[1] "Wonder Woman tends to be the first female superhero people think of, whether or not they have ever read a comic," writes comics scholar Carolyn Cocca.[2] Yet throughout the late 1930s and early 1940s, dozens of costumed women crime fighters debuted from comics publishers such as All-American Publications, Better Publications, Holyoke Publishing, Harvey Comics, Quality Comics, and Timely Comics, including the Woman in Red, the Black Cat, the Red Tornado, Golden Girl, and Miss Victory, all of whom offered readers new possibilities for how heroes were embodied.

But non-male characters faced numerous hurdles in this era. Most of the creators working on their adventures were men, and nearly all (characters *and* creators) were white, limiting the range of voices and lived experiences that could be represented using costumed heroes as a vehicle for inspiring tales of social justice. While a few superheroines challenged and commented on sexism directly in their adventures, many more became subject to patriarchal norms, rhetoric, and imagery, offering readers conflicting representations of female empowerment.

Such concerns were compounded by the fact that many of the visual and narrative tropes surrounding how women were represented in comics were born well before the comic books themselves, with the format preceded by not only newspaper comic strips but also pulp magazines. Comic books, we must remember, emerged out of older publishing traditions: while newspaper strips were formative in how visual and narrative storytelling patterns developed in the comics medium, the pulps contributed to many of the thematic elements so common to the early years of comic books. Several publishers produced pulp magazines before turning to the burgeoning comic book market in the late 1930s: Martin Goodman published titles including *All Star Adventure Fiction*, *Marvel Science Stories*, and *Uncanny Tales* before launching Timely Comics with the release of *Marvel Comics* #1 in 1939, while Harry Donenfeld specialized in "girlie pulps" like *Spicy Detective* and *Spicy Mystery Stories* before heading up the publishing companies that would eventually become DC Comics.[3] Both men's magazines specialized in titillating genre stories, with covers featuring scantily clad women in perilous situations, often involving bondage—a tradition that would continue on comic book covers into the early 1940s. The superhero genre might have been an outgrowth of the new comic book format, but its sexist and patriarchal depictions of women were a continuation of prior literary traditions.[4]

Women in Peril: Comic Book Publishing and Sexual Harassment

Timely Comics was among the worst offenders for covers portraying women in peril. Series such as *Daring Mystery Comics*, *Mystic Comics*, and *Marvel Mystery Comics* featured women tied up, hanging from the ceiling, trapped inside diabolic machinery, and similar situations as various male heroes rush to their rescue. The cover to *Marvel Mystery Comics* #3 shows a masked villain restraining a woman whose dress has begun to slide away from her chest; this series, alongside many others from Timely (such as *Daring Mystery Comics*), regularly depicted women who were bound with ropes, chains, or steel straps, often while they were trapped inside glass cylinders. The cover artwork, usually drawn by Alex Schomburg, regularly places these endangered women in the center of the page to emphasize their distress. Goodman built what eventually became the multimedia empire known as Marvel Comics (with Timely becoming Atlas Comics in 1951 and then Marvel by 1961), but he did so off of the initial success of comic books that regularly promoted lurid, misogynist images depicting violence against women.

The perils faced by women in comics were found not just on the printed page. For those women who did find work in the comics business, a culture of sexual harassment was commonplace at most publishers. Examining the industry's origins, historian Michael Schumacher explains, "Aside from taking jobs as secretaries, women were extremely rare in the early days of comics. Studios, like baseball clubhouses, were men-only environments inhabited by adults working in a children's game. The bad behavior, language, practical jokes, off-color humor and drinking after hours, and in some cases fooling around were all practiced freely, without concern for disapproving female perspectives."[5] Publisher Harry Donenfeld, who ran both Detective Comics Inc. and National Allied Publications (home of Batman and Superman, respectively), often came in drunk to the office: "He'd grab secretaries' breasts and walk off laughing."[6] As the owner of one of the leading publishing houses in the business, Donenfeld's behavior helped set a top-down tone for the industry that condoned sexual assault and harassment.

Comics history rarely acknowledges the predatory behavior that defined the working culture of most publishers in this era, and that drove many women away from a career in comics. Such abuses occurred regularly among all levels of staff. Artist Gil Kane, whose career spanned six decades and included work on most major characters at Marvel and DC, recalls how he and fellow creators Charles Biro and Bob Wood used to "write and draw and chase skirts day and night," often fueled by heavy drinking. Historian Gerard Jones tells of how "they bragged incessantly about the women they'd talked into coming to their rooms to be painted nude, only to stay to drink and get screwed. Biro was almost adolescent in his predations, contriving to peek into the women's dressing room and groping the female elevator operators at the Pep offices [MLJ Publications]. Wood beat women when he was drunk."[7]

At Timely, male staffers regularly rushed to the window to ogle women: artist Mort Meskin would shout from his seat, "'Get up! Get up! Get up!' And then everyone would get up, and there was a girl walking around in a wet bathing suit. . . . This happened almost every day. Some of those guys were like little boys with arrested development," artist Jack Katz recalls.[8]

Fiction House artist Lily Renée remembers how she often received "lewd notes" from male artists in the margins of their artwork. The male staffers also ogled her constantly: "They would all stop and stare at me as

I was walking out, as if they were undressing me," she says.[9] She recalls how she felt "totally miserable because the men thought of nothing but sex, and they were always making innuendos, and they just stared at me which made me very uncomfortable."[10] In a 2011 interview, Renée still recalled the men at Fiction House "making suggestive comments and trying to 'teach' her English—the dirty words."[11]

Renée faced an all too common dilemma for female creators in this era: quit in the face of constant harassment or stay silent and accept the behavior as part of the industry's working conditions for women. "I never wanted to come back. . . . At the same time I wanted to do good work; I wanted very much to succeed for my own sake," says Renée, who remembers how she often cried herself to sleep while working at Fiction House.[12] Her treatment didn't improve much when she quit and moved over to St. John Publications in 1948. She describes the publisher, Archer St. John, as "a lovely man, but he drank too much, and he chased me around the desk once. I mean it was awful. It was like a cartoon."[13]

Similarly, letterer Patricia Sprang, who worked on *Batman* with her husband, Dick, as well as at Quality Comics, left National Allied Publications because of steady harassment. Editor George Kashdan recalls how Sprang "was just tired of coming in there, and all the guys trying to make out with her." She told editor Mort Weisinger on her last day, "Mort, I'm leaving. Hell, I've had it. I just want you to know I've had it."[14] Female creators regularly struggled to do their jobs without being sexually harassed, and their voices were largely silenced both in the Golden Age of comics and in the subsequent histories written about this era.

This predatory behavior continued into the 1950s; artist Ramona Fradon (*Aquaman*, *Metamorpho*) recalls that "there was all this repartee going back and forth, and I just didn't feel as though I wanted to be seen." Fradon regularly experienced sexual harassment on the job at DC Comics. "There was one smart-ass nephew up there who was really fresh. He was sort-of insulting to me," she says. Another employee often surprised her from behind with kisses on the back of her neck. Fradon found the working environment at DC to be largely inhospitable for women: "It seemed so anomalous to me. I kept thinking, 'What am I doing here?'"[15]

Toni Blum and the So-Called Marvel Method of Writing Comics

One of the first women who navigated this male realm was Toni Blum, who worked as the head writer for the Eisner & Iger Studio in the late 1930s (and for Roche & Iger in the early 1940s). Blum regularly collaborated with studio cohead Will Eisner on story ideas and would then "type out scripts for the pencillers to break down into comic panels," writes Schumacher.[16] "She was the staff writer," says Eisner, describing how prior to Blum's arrival "the staff would work on features created initially by me or written by someone under my direction." Blum was then hired on as the company's "one internal writer later on, when we got affluent," Eisner recalls.[17]

While not spoken of in the same breath as her male peers, such as Otto Binder, John Broome Gardner Fox, and Stan Lee, Blum was one of comics' most important writers because she pioneered what would later become known as the "Marvel method" of writing. When most comic book writers drafted a story in this era, it was written as a full script for the artist to work with, with plot details and dialogue completed before any artwork was started. Blum, however, often used a different method. Creating a story outline for an artist page by page, Blum then later came up with the dialogue for the letterer to finish only after the artwork was completed, an approach that nearly everyone attributes to Stan Lee's work at Marvel Comics. This writing style has proven popular with many creators; writer Chris Claremont praises the collaborative nature of this approach, noting that "when it's really working well you get kind of a group where everybody has something to contribute . . . spark[ing] the writer to really consider what he's doing on the next step."[18]

The prevailing legend has it that Stan Lee pioneered this Marvel method of writing comics in the early 1960s as his new line of superhero titles soared: a 1991 article about Lee by Alastair Mabbott, for instance, recounts Stan taking credit for a style Blum pioneered, telling of how

> sales snowballed and, with unprecedented reader response, the company started producing more and more books per month. So many were on the go that Lee could not script them all and would give only a brief summary to the artist, who would draw the story however he (invariably he, rather than she) saw fit. Lee would get the pages back and add dialogue to suit the penciled pages. So the disputed legend goes, anyway. Thus was born "The Marvel Method."[19]

The term has become a ubiquitous one: Mark Salisbury begins his book *Writers on Comics Scriptwriting* with the declaration that there are "two distinct styles of comic book writing, full script and (Marvel style) plot."[20] Lee regularly took credit for this approach, championing himself as having reinvented comics' mode of production to the betterment of his artists' talents: "'It was totally born out of necessity,' says Lee, 'but then we found out it's a great system, because artists could use their imagination to the fullest.'"[21] This "great system," however, was originated by Blum, not Lee.

Blum's husband, comics artist Bill Bossert, describes Blum's process: she "wrote an outline, and she'd make up the whole thing. She'd write the outline, and she'd help them break it down page-by-page. Then she would get the pages back [from the artist], and she would pencil in the actual dialogue on the page. Then the lettering man would letter the dialogue."[22] When asked about Blum's innovative writing method, Eisner recalled,

> Well, that was the way Stan Lee did it years later. It was an act of desperation on Stan's part, because he didn't have time to write the stories. It's possible we worked that way, because I remember her working at a typewriter all day long. Generally, I would discuss the story with the writer first, and after Toni typed up the story, she gave it to an artist. . . . I have no trouble believing Toni worked [that way]. Toni was always at her typewriter. But I doubt she worked that way all the time; it was just sporadically. She might have worked that way with certain people. Some people needed a full script, like Lou Fine, who was only interested in drawing.[23]

This "desperation" on Lee's part saw him alter his initial writing approach to match Blum's when he realized its efficiency. The standard way that stories were written throughout the Golden Age was to write a full script that included dialogue before any artwork was produced. The DC Comics writer/editor George Kashdan, who began at the company in 1947 when it was still National Comics Publications, describes how writers would start by submitting a brief story synopsis to their editor. "Back in those days, if an editor liked an idea, he chatted with the writer about it, and out of that came a good verbal storyline. That would be an assignment. I'd go home and write a script. Every editor at DC worked this way," says Kashdan.[24] While Blum and Eisner "chatted" about story lines in a similar fashion, Blum would often forego the actual scripting, working instead in the so-called Marvel method that Lee later claimed he invented.

There are different accounts of Lee's writing process at Timely. Artist Jack Katz recalls how it was "always full scripts" that he received from Timely's writers (Lee included): "I know some of the writing was his."[25] On the other hand, Vince Fago, a writer/artist at Timely Comics who took over as editor in chief while Lee served in World War II, recalls that although Lee didn't write full scripts, he would write all the dialogue in addition to a story outline before giving things over to his artists: "He wrote the story and the dialogue but he didn't break it down into panels." Since Lee "had to handle writers and artists and production" in his dual role as writer and editor in chief, "it didn't leave him with much time," says Fago.[26] Regardless of which of these methods he used more in the 1940s and 1950s, Lee further streamlined his writing process in the early 1960s, only adding dialogue after receiving the artwork back, similar to how Blum did it two decades prior.

Bossert recalls the high level of creative control Blum had over the finished product, especially when dealing with "guys who didn't have a clue" what they were doing: "She'd have to keep rewriting the whole thing because they made such a mess. She'd say, 'This is supposed to be on the fifth page and you have it on the second page. You're giving away the whole story in the beginning.' So she had to re-do the whole story as it went along."[27] Blum was well respected by the artists she worked with: Chuck Mazoujian describes her as a "talented woman, and a good writer. . . . Most of Toni's stories were pretty interesting, so I didn't have any urge to change them. I wasn't going to criticize a story as long as it was interesting and it worked. I was always happy with what she wrote. . . . Toni was good."[28]

Sometimes Eisner would simply pass on the initial designs for a new character and leave it to Blum to fully develop the new hero in her scripts.[29] Blum wrote the early adventures of many characters who still exist today as a team called the Freedom Fighters at DC Comics (which have since acquired the rights to certain Quality titles): Black Condor, Dollman, the Ray, and Uncle Sam. She cocreated many other characters, such as Prop Powers and the Kid Patrol in the pages of *National Comics*, and regularly wrote the adventures of heroes like Don Glory, Lion Boy, the Red Bee, and Betty Bates, Lady at Law for *Hit Comics*. She also created a superpowered teenager named Wonder Boy (who was reinvented by DC in the 1990s) and worked as a ghostwriter in 1942 for Eisner's *The Spirit* while he served in World War II.[30]

Eisner even wanted Blum to write *The Spirit* regularly while he was overseas, but the two creators argued over page rates. When Eisner wouldn't pay Blum enough, she refused. In an April 1942 letter to Eisner, she explains,

> You see, Bill, it isn't that I'm such a mercenary wench, but to me, my time is worth precious dollars. I had expected to devote at least four or five days to the Spirit, or more, to do research, to rehash, to work

up breakdowns, etc. etc. At thirty dollars it's hardly worth it as I can make that in two or three days on a nine page feature. It isn't that I want time to work on other comic features, I am desperately trying to do some "good work" and I'll sacrifice money to it.[31]

Instead, Jack Cole and Manly Wade Wellman wrote scripts in Eisner's absence. Jules Feiffer took over writing *The Spirit* in 1946, but not without help from ghostwriter (and Eisner's secretary) Marilyn Mercer. Feiffer recalls how Mercer "actually did some script work in the early years, but no one else did any writing after I began working on The Spirit."[32] Mercer, however, tells it differently: "As I remember it, I was a writer and Jules was an office boy. As Jules remembers it, he was an artist and I was the secretary. Will can't really remember it very clearly. It is his recollection that Jules developed into an excellent writer and I did a good job of keeping the books." Mercer later went on to write for such publishers as Fiction House and Harvey Comics.[33]

Like many women creators, Blum often worked under male pseudonyms. While it was common practice in the 1930s and 1940s for comics writers and artists to use pseudonyms in order to fool readers into thinking that publishers used a wider range of talent, there was another reason why women often used male pen names. Writer and artist June Tarpé Mills went by the name Tarpé Mills in her early work for such series as *Amazing Man Comics*, *Amazing Mystery Funnies*, *Prize Comics*, *Star Comics*, and *Target Comics*.[34] She continued using her more masculine-sounding middle name when she started her own newspaper strip, *Miss Fury*, and has described how the use of male pseudonyms was a necessity for female creators at the time: "It would have been a major let-down to the kids if they found out that the author of such virile and awesome characters was a gal."[35] Blum, in turn, used such pseudonyms as Tony Boone, Anthony Bloom, and Tony Blum in her work. The comics creator and historian Trina Robbins traces this pattern back to newspaper strips, noting that many female cartoonists, including Rose O'Neill, Grace Dayton, Ethel Hays, and Nell Brinkley, "had no trouble getting published under their own feminine names" but that "a male pseudonym seemed to be required for action strips."[36] While some women found success in the comics industry in this era, most publishers didn't want their readers to know that women were behind some of their most powerful heroes.[37]

Publishers and the creators who worked for them were, at this time, content to not only take credit for creative methods pioneered by women but also sit idly by while their male coworkers (or they, themselves) sexually harassed and abused their female coworkers. In light of this, we should rethink both whom we venerate as icons of the industry *and* what moral issues and ideologies guide their storytelling, especially with regard to a genre as concerned with notions of justice as the superhero comic. If the male writers who regaled Golden Age audiences with tales of justice believed it permissible to make unwanted advances on the women they worked with, can audiences in turn trust that their notions of justice are unproblematic? Comics studies has long debated what role American exceptionalism (or patriotism, or jingoism) and politics play in the superhero genre, and superheroines are a part of the conversation that must be examined in more depth.

The First Superheroines

At most publishers, female superheroes were an afterthought, entering the marketplace only after male heroes such as Superman, Namor, the Human Torch, and Blue Beetle had established the genre in the late 1930s. While most historians and fans point to Superman as the first superhero in comics, definitively proclaiming the first comic book superheroine becomes a more difficult task due to the many variances in (a) which genres they appeared in, (b) whether they debuted in newspaper strips or comic books, (c) whether they possessed fantastic abilities, (d) whether wearing a mask and/or distinctive outfit while fighting crime is enough to qualify as a superhero, (e) whether we should take a character's civilian debut into account or just their costumed debut, and (f) whether it is enough to simply use special training to fight for justice, no matter whether the backdrop is urban, rural, the jungle forest, or the frozen tundra, to be labeled a superhero.

The very definition of what constitutes a superhero is still being debated within comics studies (and among fans), with questions often centered around whether costumed crime fighters need to have superpowers to be categorized within the superhero genre. Batman, for one, lacks the fantastic powers of a character like Superman or the Human Torch, but he is still widely considered a superhero. In Batman's case, his status as a genius with seemingly limitless wealth allows him to access both the training and technology to elevate himself above the average person. So, does one need special powers to be a superhero, or can she just fight crime in a costume? This is a key question in trying to label the first female superhero. In *The Superhero Reader*, Charles Hatfield, Jeet Heer, and Kent Worcester ask what they call "a relatively simple question: What are the origins of the superhero genre?"[38] The answers are far less simple when examining how

"Amazona the Mighty Woman," *Planet Comics* #3, 1940, Fiction House. Written by Toni Blum.

women fit into the equation, however. There simply is no easy answer to who the first superheroine was, because any assertion depends on numerous contextual factors—a symptom of the general thorniness surrounding how women were represented in the early years of comic books.

Hatfield, Heer, and Worcester describe how Wonder Woman's 1941 debut marks her "as arguably the first female superhero (though preceded by June Tarpé Mills's costumed crime fighter Miss Fury earlier that year), and is significant for her long popularity and in particular for her appeal to girl and women readers as an emblem of female power."[39] But Wonder Woman was preceded by several other characters who could each potentially claim the mantle of the first superheroine, although none attained the same lasting popularity of DC's Amazonian hero. One contender is Amazona the Mighty Woman, cocreated by Toni Blum for Fiction House's *Planet Comics* #3 in 1940 (her one and only appearance), who lives in "the vast cold reaches of the far north" and is one of "the last survivors of a super race that perished during the period of the last ice age."[40] While she possesses superstrength, the overt science fiction nature of that series problematizes how we determine which genre Amazona should be categorized in. Appearing alongside such features as "The Planetary Adventures of Flint Baker on Pluto," "Buzz Crandall of the Space Patrol," and "Spurt Hammond, Planet Flyer," Amazona was clearly framed for readers of *Planet Comics* as a science fiction hero (see chapter 7 for more on the character).

Another candidate for the title of "first superheroine" is Russell Stam's Invisible Scarlet O'Neil, a character whose invisibility certainly qualifies as a superpower. She first appeared in her own newspaper strip in the *Chicago Daily Times* in 1940, which was reprinted in *Famous Funnies* starting the following year before O'Neil briefly gained her own title series from Harvey in 1950. But her stories were less violent than most superhero tales of the period, with one early story seeing her use her powers to secretly type up several letters for a secretary worried about getting fired.[41] With her comic strip origins, and adventures often centered around helping her community rather than stopping powerful villains, Invisible Scarlet O'Neil has been largely forgotten in most histories of the superhero genre.

Miss Fury, who fought crime in a black leopard-skin costume much like that worn today by Catwoman, was another early hero who debuted in newspapers before being reprinted in comic books. As a civilian, Miss Fury's everyday identity was that of a wealthy woman named Marla Drake, but as a heroine, Miss Fury fought foes ranging from evil scientists to Nazis. And unlike Invisible Scarlet O'Neil's, Miss Fury's stories were much more violent, as she regularly left her opponents the worse for wear. Originally created by June Tarpé Mills as *Black Fury* in 1941, the *Miss Fury* strip was reprinted by Timely as a comic book biannually from 1942 to 1946. The character proved so popular that she even graced the sides of World War II–era military aircraft.[42]

Advertisement for "Invisible Scarlet O'Neil."

But if Miss Fury's and Invisible Scarlet O'Neil's comic strip origins potentially disqualify them from being crowned the first superheroine, a strong contender is the masked hero the Woman in Red. Alter ego of police officer Peggy Allen, the Woman in Red first appeared in Better Publications' *Thrilling Comics* #2 in 1940. She was skilled in physical combat and handy with a gun, making her a forceful character whose red mask, hood, gloves, and dress gave the crimson-clad avenger a distinctive costume to disguise herself while fighting crime. Her cocreator, artist George

"The Woman in Red," *Thrilling Comics* #3, 1940, Better Publications.

Mandel, describing himself as "an early feminist," considered the idea of a female superhero a completely natural step for the genre:

> I was always fighting for women's rights. I didn't think of it as a fight, though. But I have two sisters who I love very much, and I resent how women are treated just by being around. So when it came to "The Woman in Red," I wasn't conscious of it as a feminist strike. It was just unique. It was interesting because we didn't have women battlers in the comics, and [writer/co-creator] Richard Hughes deserves the credit for it.[43]

While the Woman in Red was a strong costumed crime fighter, her lack of superpowers means that she hasn't enjoyed the same recognition as such better-known figures as Wonder Woman who followed. Another such character (who was actually an honorary member of the Justice Society of America alongside Wonder Woman) was Ma Hunkel, also known as Red Tornado, created by Sheldon Mayer. Hunkel first appeared in *All-American Comics* #3 in 1939, and assumed her costumed identity as the Red Tornado in issue 20 the next year, one month before Wonder Woman's debut in *All Star Comics* #8. When a gangster named Tubbs Torpini kidnaps two of her children, Hunkel is inspired by the exploits of Green Lantern to create her own costumed alter ego ("Well . . . whaddaya know. He puts on his costume an' goes to town, eh? Hmm . . ." she muses).[44] Hunkel's costume consisted of red long underwear and a silver sauce pot—complete with eyeholes—proving that anyone can fashion a heroic costume with just a few common household items.

She lacked any powers but was never afraid of a fight; her costumed entrance at the end of issue 20 sees her smash a bottle over Torpini's head, knocking him out cold. With her cape draped over her right shoulder as she poses with one foot on the crime boss's back, she taunts the henchmen who enter the room: "C'mon in boys. . . . I'm just in the mood to give you some trouble! Ya wanna wrassle?"[45] Her second appearance, in issue 21, picks up where we left off, as Red Tornado grabs one of the henchmen by his leg and swings him like a baseball bat into his fellow thugs, clobbering them all with one blow. "Pull in your heads, boys! You're going through a tunnel!" she yells before knocking their lights out.[46]

While the character is a parody of costumed superheroes like Green Lantern and the Atom who appeared in the very pages of *All-American Comics*, Mayer also uses Red Tornado as a vehicle for some subtle commentary on the gender roles surrounding costumed heroes in the early years of comics. With her costume concealing all visible traces of her gender (and her cooking-pot helmet presumably muffling her voice), Red Tornado is assumed to be a man by all who encounter her. Hunkel never corrects the use of male pronouns to describe her alter ego, playing along when her friends and family say things like "Th' kids insist they were rescued by a mystery man!" and "He was a great big feller!" Modestly, Hunkel replies, "He was, eh? What did he look like?" with a knowing smile. Similarly, as her children read about Red Tornado in the newspaper, Hunkel smirks as one says, "Wow, he's some guy, eh Scrib!" When her other son, Scribbly, wishes he could get "a real good look at th' guy," Hunkel slyly states, "Well ya never kin tell, Scrib . . . maybe you will . . . maybe you will!" At this point, the narrator ends the story by telling the reader, "And if Ma Hunkel says he will, he will! . . . After all—who should know better than the Red Tornado himself. . . . Er, herself!"[47]

Mayer regularly plays with gendered language in Red Tornado's early adventures ("Any talk you hear about that Red Tornado is pure nonsense! There ain't no such person!" the police chief says before Tornado crashes through his window). While we can read such deliberate gender fluidity as simply a way for a non-male character to be taken seriously in a patriarchal era by disguising the fact that she is a woman, Mayer's rhetoric still allows for a reclaiming of Red Tornado as a character who challenges traditional norms of gender identity. When Scribbly draws a picture of Red Tornado, Hunkel teases him by saying, "Aw go on—I don't believe it! You made up that pitcher, outta your head! No human being is dumb enough to go around dressed like that!"[48] With the regular deflection of gender labels and pronouns in favor of inclusive terms like "person" and "human being," Mayer allowed Red Tornado to be a hero who performed a gender identity that moved beyond a strictly dual binary, in keeping with how cultural theorists hail the move beyond binary gender identities for its "liberatory" potential.[49]

"Scribbly and the Red Tornado," *All-American Comics* #22, 1941, All-American Comics Inc.

Hunkel's debut as the Red Tornado in the November 1940 issue of *All-American Comics* arrived several months after the Woman in Red and Amazona debuted in the March issues of *Thrilling Comics* and *Planet Comics*, respectively. If we consider Ma Hunkel's civilian debut in 1939's *All-American Comics* #3 the first appearance of a superheroine, then the debate gets somewhat easier. But if only costumes, powers, and/or displays of great physical strength should be counted, then consider how all of these heroines were preceded by a woman with amazing superpowers who debuted in the February issue of *Jungle Comics* (#2) that same year—Fantomah. A young woman with flowing blonde hair and wearing a sheer gown, described as "the mysterious Fantomah" and "The Mystery Woman of the Jungle" in her first appearance, she thwarts a pair of ivory hunters seeking to steal tusks from a secret elephant graveyard by transforming into a skeletal figure (at first disembodied, then full-bodied and flying, but at all times retaining her long blonde hair).[50]

By issue 3, her creator, Fletcher Hanks, describes her in the opening narration as "Fantomah, the most marvelous woman ever known," playing up her fantastic abilities. Hanks's narration stresses that she "has such remarkable insight that she can see all that ever happens in jungleland. . . . By using her strange powers, she has discovered two white men planning to rob the jungle of its most sacred treasure" within an "ancient city of gold." Despite the jungle setting, Fantomah's "strange powers" clearly establish her as a superhuman force: we soon see her fly toward the city while encircled by an ethereal white mist described as a "protective aura."[51] In addition to her powers of flight, omniscience, transformation, and disembodiment, we soon learn of another superpower: when her warnings

"Fantomah," *Jungle Comics* #2, 1940, Fiction Comics.

to leave the city's sacred jewels alone are ignored by the two thieves, she again transforms into a floating skull with flowing hair before changing the two men into hairy green creatures resembling a Dr. Seuss creation.

Fletcher Hanks's penchant for the surreal has made him a cult figure in comics history.[52] He drew Fantomah through to the fifteenth issue of *Jungle Comics* in 1941, after which he left the comics business. Fantomah

"Fantomah," *Jungle Comics* #3, 1940, Fiction Comics.

continued on in the series, but not before other creators changed some of the stranger aspects of Hanks's character. When a new writer (credited as W. B. Hovious) took over in #16, Fantomah stopped transforming into her skull-like visage while still retaining some of her other powers. In *Jungle Comics* #27, Fantomah gains an origin story, in which it is explained that she is the "legendary daughter of the Pharaohs" with the ability to draw on the powers of ancient Egyptian gods including Ammon, Ra, and Osiris.[53] By her final appearance in 1944 in issue 51, Fantomah's powers were no longer referenced; she had been reduced to an Egyptian-themed jungle goddess who no longer resembled the heroic, golden-tressed, disembodied skull of early issues.

Fantomah's fantastic powers clearly made her a superheroine, but her status as the protector of unnamed jungle civilizations in a series called *Jungle Comics* undoubtedly situates her within the jungle genre, much like how Amazona's appearance in *Planet Comics* has aligned her with science fiction. This generic instability makes it difficult to declare any one woman the first superheroine outright because of the problems surrounding how the term "superhero" itself and the genre as a whole get defined. Hatfield, Heer, and Worcester describe how superhero comics have been a dominant force within comics for the near entirety of the comic book format's history:

> Superheroes have played a central role in the story of comic books almost from their inception. Moreover, despite the genre's relative dormancy from the late 1940s through the late 1950s, superheroes have stood the test of time. Indeed, the superhero has been a staple of the medium and, since the sixties, the one overwhelmingly dominant market genre. As a result, the sheer number of superhero comics that have been published over the years is staggering.[54]

The stakes, then, are high for how comics fans and scholars define what a superhero is and what defines the genre's boundaries. Similar to how the jungle protector in the Phantom's 1936 debut two years before Superman arrived in *Action Comics* offers a controversial challenge to the label of "first superhero,"[55] calling Fantomah the first superheroine risks similar critique: she starred in a book whose title was at the forefront of an entirely different genre, and her superpowers were downgraded along the way after Fletcher Hanks left the series, before the character's adventures were scrapped altogether.

As Richard Reynolds notes in *Superheroes: A Modern Mythology*, "The superhero genre is tightly defined and defended by its committed readership," making it more difficult for comics historians to point to a character who originated within a non-superhero genre title to claim the mantle as the first superheroine.[56] Indeed, the late 1930s/early 1940s saw several non-male characters make their debuts as potent protectors of the innocent (whether they possessed what we might call superpowers or not). Characters like Fantomah, the Woman in Red, Red Tornado,

Invisible Scarlet O'Neil, Phantom Lady, and the Silver Scorpion all debuted before Wonder Woman, and each had remarkable powers and/or were costumed crime fighters, yet none has enjoyed the popular distinction among fans of being the first superheroine in the way that Wonder Woman has.

In a widely cited definition of what constitutes a superhero, Peter Coogan explains that superpowers can be extended to include "highly developed physical and/or mental skills . . . which raise a person's performance above that of ordinary people."[57] He also sees superheroes as guided by a "prosocial mission" to protect their community from harm, with these two criteria allowing for characters, such as Batman, who lack outright superpowers to still be categorized as superheroes.[58] Consider, too, that the one female character before Wonder Woman whom Hatfield, Heer, and Worcester cite as having a credible claim to the title of first superheroine is Miss Fury—a woman of wealth with a mission, just like Batman. Given that Invisible Scarlet O'Neil, the Woman in Red, and Ma Hunkel/Red Tornado *also* possess, respectively, an inhuman power, above-average crime-fighting abilities, and unexpected strength, it seems curious that a wealthy woman in an enchanted leopard-skin suit should emerge as their main contender for Wonder Woman's crown (or cape). In light of this, the fact that Batman and Miss Fury are readily accepted as superheroes despite lacking traditional superpowers, the access to training, tools, and technology that their wealth buys them should be considered in conversation with Coogan's "highly developed physical and/or mental skill" criterion.

Through this lens, the qualifier that superheroism requires extraordinary physical and mental capabilities takes on new connotations. Ma Hunkel/Red Tornado and the Woman in Red, however, fight crime and protect their communities in a "prosocial" manner as members of the working class who fashion their costumes and tools out of what they have available rather than advanced materials or cutting-edge technology. Miss Fury's widespread recognition as a figure of power and justice during the Golden Age, and the fact that she has the same backstory of wealth and social status as Batman, highlights that the question of what constitutes superhero status is an issue of both gender *and* wealth disparity. Obscene wealth buys these characters not only political and social power, but superpower too.

If, however, we don't accept Miss Fury as a superheroine, then perhaps Fantomah and her superpowers more readily fit the mold (if we can accept that the first superheroine starred in jungle comics). But we also have to consider another highly trained jungle protector with a prosocial mission who predated Fantomah by several years—Sheena, Queen of the Jungle. Sheena debuted in 1937 in the series *Wags* by American creators Will Eisner and Mort Meskin (published in the United States but distributed in the United Kingdom). These stories were soon reprinted in Fiction House's *Jumbo Comics* #1 in 1938; although its September cover date places its release three months after that of *Action Comics* #1, Sheena's international origins unmistakably mark her as a forerunner of the Man of Steel. Having been trained by a medicine man named Koba since she was a young girl, Sheena's strength and skill (along with the visual appeal of her leopard-skin dress and flowing blonde hair) quickly made her one of comics' leading figures in any genre. In *Jumbo Comics* #2, Koba describes how he "made Sheena a Goddess" after her father died; he says, "She is cunning and knows the great jungle[;] . . . my people follow her and though she is a women, she is fearless in battle."[59] She appeared in every issue of *Jumbo Comics* between 1938 and 1953, and received her own series in 1942, which lasted ten years.

Whether we can extend Coogan's definition of the superhero to apply to her or not, Sheena became a template for future crime fighters. She may not have the uncanny powers of Fantomah or the Invisible Scarlet O'Neil, but she does have special training, weapons, and skills like Batman, the Sandman, Blue Beetle, and other costumed crime fighters who are typically deemed superheroes. In *Jumbo Comics* #10, she takes down a killer lion with just her brawn and her blade, all while her male companion, Bob Reynolds, stands by and watches. In *The World Encyclopedia of Comics*, Maurice Horn sees Bob's relationship with Sheena as akin to that of another famous comics couple, drawing further parallel with the superhero genre: "But Sheena was always the leader. Her companion was a hapless man named Bob who functioned in much the same way Lois Lane did in Superman: Bob would always be caught or captured by some African interloper and Sheena was pressed into service to defeat Bob's captors and rescue her assistant."[60]

Sheena proved to be a vital example of how there was indeed a market for the adventures of a powerful woman in a starring role. With few non-male characters in comic books overall around the time of Superman's debut in the late 1930s, Sheena's arrival was all the more memorable. With male soldiers fighting overseas, more women entered the workforce (a trend associated with the pre-feminist Rosie the Riveter campaign). The rise in superheroines can in turn be read as a reflection of the new economic and social roles played by women in wartime America, with patriotic heroes such as Miss America and Miss Victory often fighting Axis threats at home and abroad while embodying the new potentials of women as both enforcers *and* protectors.

Cover of *Sheena Queen of the Jungle* #1, 1942, Fiction House.

While these wartime comics *did* offer new ways for women to view their roles in society, they also perpetuated questionable ideas of American exceptionalism. Comics studies scholars have increasingly interrogated the ideologies of superhero comics and the kinds of justice depicted within them. Drawing connections between American propaganda literature and superhero comics from the World War II era, Chris Murray criticizes the assumption that Golden Age superheroes embodied essential American ideals:

> The question we have to ask is whose America were superheroes? By and large they weren't an America for women, or for African-Americans, or indeed any minority or disempowered group. Where were the homosexual heroes, the black Batmans or the Captain Conscientious Objectors? Far from representing America as it was, superhero comics represented a view of America that was constructed by and within the ideology of the dominant power structures and institutions. If superhero comics represent something about America it

> has to be understood not only what was represented, but also what was excluded, and why.[61]

In many ways, superhero comics were more about instilling jingoistic ideas through vague messages of democracy and freedom than about making persuasive arguments *against* America's historical enemies. While Golden Age superheroines fought against German, Japanese, and Italian enemies just as often as their male counterparts did, publishers often seemed to shy away from explicitly naming what it was these patriotic heroines were fighting against. The result of this is that these heroines participated in the same valorization of violence and xenophobia in the name of justice as their male peers. In other words, they taught readers, young and old, male and female, that women—so long as they were, for the most part, white and conventionally attractive—were as capable as any man of carrying out the project of American nationalism. To return to Coogan, the question of *who* is encompassed within the term "prosocial" must be asked. Sure, the American superheroes and superheroines of the Golden Age ostensibly fought for *all* American citizens, and some even claimed to fight for the citizens of the world. But often they were depicted rescuing (white) children from danger, protecting genteel (white) families, aiding the military in the war effort, or protecting private property. It is not enough to take at face value that these heroines somehow fought for more just causes than the superheroes who preceded them, that they escaped the propaganda found in almost all forms of popular culture at the time; if anything, they forged stronger links between American women and American nationalism. The strength that these protectors and enforcers represented should be commended, but their ideologies should be critiqued and questioned too.

One of the earliest of these enforcers was Quality Comics' Phantom Lady, who debuted in 1941's *Police Comics* #1 alongside Plastic Man. Using a blinding black ray to simulate invisibility, Phantom Lady lasted two years at Quality but was brought back by a different publisher in 1947. Fox Feature Syndicate gave Phantom Lady her own series that year, written by Ruth Roche (who often used the male pseudonym Rod Roche) and primarily drawn by African American artist Matt Baker. The fact that both a woman and a Black man were simultaneously part of the character's creative team in the 1940s is a milestone in comics history, but Phantom Lady remains better known for her skimpy costume than her creative pedigree. Baker converted her costume in 1947 from an outfit that concealed her waist and breasts to one that included a tiny skirt and showed off most of her chest. But Trina Robbins argues that while many male critics see Baker's women as "drawn to appeal to men . . . they also appealed strongly to a female audience. His dashing and glamorous women have a kind of forties movie star appeal."[62]

Phantom Lady's costuming choice became a recurrent pattern in this decade. The Canadian heroine Nelvana of the Northern Lights, for example, was based on an Inuit legend that creator Adrian Dingle described as "pretty gruesome," prompting him to "'ma[ke] her into an attractive doll' by slipping her into a miniskirt."[63] The daughter of Koliak, the Inuit god of the Northern Lights, Nelvana is one of the few female heroes representing indigenous cultures in the early history of comics, and she was created in an earnest attempt to celebrate Inuit mythology. At the same time, the writer/artist Dingle's costume designs regularly emphasize the female body—be it Nelvana's skirt, which flaps up to show off her legs, or the skimpy outfits worn by the villainous Queen of Statica and her female guards, which reveal most of their chest and midriff.[64] This objectification of women's bodies has regularly defined the female superhero ever since.

Even when a heroine's costume isn't revealing, she is often mocked within the story simply for being a woman. The Silver Scorpion's costume—a full-bodied yellow jumpsuit along with a mask and red cape—is one of the least skimpy outfits worn by any superheroine. But still, in her first adventure in 1941's *Daring Mystery Comics* #7 from Timely Comics, her efforts to fight crime are mocked rather than celebrated: "Imagine . . . a girl rounding up all these counterfeiters!" a police officer chuckles after she subdues the very criminals that the police showed up too late to catch. The officer's snide comment is compounded by a newspaper headline the following day that serves as a cruel punchline to the debut of Timely's first female superhero: "Girl Breaks Up Counterfeiting Ring."[65]

Despite how they were often undermined in their own adventures, superheroines like jujitsu expert the Silver Scorpion and the Woman in Red subverted many conventional notions of femininity of this era by using brute force in the name of justice. While the Silver Scorpion routinely tossed criminals through the air and kicked them in the face, the Black Cat challenged gender norms in other ways. The Black Cat first appeared in *Pocket Comics* #1 (1941) as Linda Turner, a Hollywood stuntwoman and actress who became a masked crime fighter to aid in the war effort and fight Axis agents in America.[66] She regularly teams up with reporter Rick Horne, who is frequently depicted as love-sick for the Black Cat, visually indicated by hearts drawn in his dialogue balloons. He is also shown as being inferior to the Black Cat in both temperament and physical ability, such as in *Pocket Comics* #3, when he complains about having to climb out onto a window ledge with her. "Hey, I'm not a human fly!" shouts

Rick. "Don't be a sissy!" she shoots back, indicative of how the character regularly challenged traditional representations of masculinity in a way that few comics characters of this era ever did.[67]

The Black Cat was cocreated by Barbara Hall, who often signed her work B. Hall to hide her gender.[68] Her comics career was brief—after five years she left the business in 1946, focusing on oil painting and marrying playwright Irving Fiske[69]—but Hall's artwork was formally inventive and she created several popular female characters. In 1942, she cocreated the crime-fighting newsreel camerawoman the Blonde Bomber, who appeared in *Green Hornet Comics* through 1947. Hall also cocreated Pat Parker, War Nurse, and a team of Girl Commandos in 1942's *Speed Comics* #23, which appeared in that series through 1946. The Girl Commandos combined the war and superhero genres, with Pat Parker donning a mask and colorful costume in her first adventure.[70] It was also progressive in its representations of race and body type: as Robbins notes, "Pat Parker and her Girl Commandos defied comic book tradition not only by including an overweight girl, Ellen, as an action heroine who was just as tough as her sisters, but by the realistic, nonracist depiction of Mei Ling, the Chinese member of the group."[71] Artist Jill Elgin also worked on the Girl Commandos between 1942 and 1945, in addition to drawing some Black Cat stories during this period.

Hall's artwork is notable in the way she drew her figures. While many artists draw superhero costumes so form-fitting that they essentially become extensions of the hero's body, Hall gave the Black Cat's costume visible depth and weight. In her *Pocket Comics* #1 debut, the character's mask and gloves are often drawn in a way that suggests they are made with a rigid, textured material like leather: they give the costume a distinct physicality that is often lacking for most spandex-clad superheroes, a problem that film and television producers struggle with when making live-action versions of such characters. Varying textures was something that Jack Kirby felt was important for artists to emphasize, once noting how it is a problem when you "can't tell the difference between wood and clothing."[72]

The enhanced depth that Hall created with her artwork stems from both her shading techniques and how her linework positions these costume elements to look like they are worn *on* the character's body rather than blending seamlessly (i.e., improbably) into the curves of the body in the way that other heroes' costumes do. Hall's approach has been used with more frequency in twenty-first-century comics as superhero film adaptations have led artists to rethink how heroes appear on the page—so that, for instance, the scales on Aquaman's shirt or the details on

"The Black Cat," *Pocket Comics* #1, 1941, Harvey Comics. Art by Barbara Hall.

Captain America's helmet give the impression of a greater depth beyond the two-dimensional flatness of the comics page.

The Black Cat soon moved from the pages of *Pocket Comics* to *Speed Comics* and then to her own title in 1946, *Black Cat Comics*. In 1951, the title was changed in issue 30 to *Black Cat Mystery* and the stories shifted to the horror genre. The Black Cat herself appeared on the cover and first page in a host role in #30 but not thereafter: a symptom of how the horror genre's popularity was pushing superheroes out of the marketplace. But after a decade's worth of comics by 1951, the Black Cat's series outlasted those of many well-known superheroes (with *Captain America Comics*, *Flash Comics*, and *Green Lantern* all canceled in 1949), making her one of the most enduring superheroes of the era, thanks in large part to the efforts of Hall and Elgin.

As new superheroines continued to make their debuts throughout the 1940s, opportunities for readers to identify with non-male characters increased. The year 1941 saw the debut of several new characters, including Betty Ross (who later became Golden Girl), Miss Victory, USA (also called the Spirit of Old Glory), and Wonder Woman, offering readers images of powerful, unconventional women (even if many male readers still did take pleasure in seeing drawings of pretty young heroines). "Most of these heroines were designed to appeal to men and women alike during the war years," sociologist Christina M. Knopf argues, "offering new civic ideals for the women, and shapely young pinups" for the men.[73]

As World War II progressed, many of the new characters who debuted in 1941 were patriotically themed, such as USA, the Spirit of Old Glory, who got her start in Quality's *Feature Comics* #42. When a young girl watching Betsy Ross sew the first American flag in 1776 places some of its threads in a locket, it allows her to be reborn in the twentieth century as a powerful hero who fights for America; she is alerted to nearby danger whenever the flag she carries droops. Her first task is to stop a schoolteacher who is training her students to become young Nazi agents: "I'm protecting these children from the danger of your teaching . . . with my flag and my torch of liberty!" she cries as she whisks the teacher away.[74] The same year saw two new heroines with American flag–themed costumes: Pat Patriot began in Lev Gleason Comics' *Daredevil Comics* #2, and Miss Victory debuted in Holyoke's *Captain Fearless Comics* #1, the latter's alter ego being the stenographer Joan Wayne (evoking the rugged cowboy actor's name). Although she uses her incredible strength to fight antigovernment forces as Miss Victory, her long-sleeved red, white, and blue costume soon devolves into one approximating a bathing suit.

When Miss Victory moved over to *Captain Aero Comics* in 1943, many of her appearances were drawn by Nina Albright in stories that challenged how women were expected to behave and to dress: one caption announces, "No one suspects Joan Wayne, timid little stenographer on Capitol Hill, to be Miss Victory, firebrand of justice!" ahead of her own declaration, "I've got to ditch this gown and look into this situation as—Miss Victory!"[75] Albright also created the female hero the Commandette ("the female commando!") for *Star Studded Comics* in 1946.[76] As the masked hero the Commandette, stuntwoman Betty Babble was a skilled crimefighter even without any special powers. Artist Pauline Loth also worked on the early appearances of another patriotic superheroine—Miss America (a character who has been reinvented in recent years as the Latinx LGBTQ character America Chavez). Loth, who worked as an animator for Fleisher Studios before doing work for Fawcett and Timely, created the costume for Miss America's initial appearance in 1943's *Marvel Mystery Comics* #49 and drew her solo adventures in 1944's *Miss America Comics* (a series that soon transitioned into a teen humor title featuring Patsy Walker).[77]

Another Timely Comics heroine, Betty Ross, appeared in the first issue of *Captain America Comics* as a government agent investigating a ring of Nazi saboteurs. She was later renamed Betsy Ross (in keeping with the series' patriotic theme) and got her start as Golden Girl in 1948's *Captain America Comics* #66, taking over for a wounded Bucky Barnes as Cap's sidekick. As Ross and Captain America gather by Bucky's hospital bed after he is shot by a criminal named Lavender, Betsy tells Cap that he shouldn't fight alone. "Why not Betsy Ross? A woman to help capture a woman. It might be a good idea! But I'll have to give it some thought," Captain America muses.[78]

But even as one of the top-selling superhero titles of the 1940s began to showcase a new female hero, the story still betrays patriarchal norms in its handling of Golden Girl's origin. While some heroines, such as Red Tornado, subverted traditional ideas about gender identity, the first appearance of Golden Girl reinforced the dominant societal gender roles of the 1940s. When Cap arrives at Ross's home unannounced for an interview about her athletic prowess, he finds her in the middle of washing the dishes, wearing a frilly apron ("We can talk while I'm finishing the dishes!" she tells Cap as he takes a seat in her kitchen). The image of Ross in an apron, dishes in hand, as Captain America weighs whether she is sidekick material is clearly meant to reinforce traditional gender stereotypes while setting up the transition to come when Ross shifts from domestic duties to crime-fighting. Cap quickly seems satisfied enough to let a woman be his partner when she tells him (while holding a dish in her hand!) how she had "won the hundred-meter race in College . . . [and had been] the champion weight-lifter among the girls" as well as "studied

Cap recruits Golden Girl in *Captain America Comics* #66, 1948, Timely Comics.

wrestling and boxing under two former champions." After a few days of rigorous training in which Ross "soon shows a natural aptitude for the dangerous and hard work," the narrator tells us, Golden Girl makes her debut wearing a yellow costume reminiscent of the Silver Scorpion's except for the fact that Ross's miniskirt exposes most of her bare legs.[79]

While she isn't mocked for being a female crime fighter in her first outing, as the Silver Scorpion is, the discourses surrounding Golden Girl's superhero persona are highly conflicting. After scolding her like a child for a mistake she made in their first fight with Lavender, Cap praises Ross in their second battle after she knocks out the villainess. "A good day's work, Betsy! I might never have caught up with them! You were a big help!" says Cap as a police officer takes Lavender away in handcuffs (apparently giving away Golden Girl's real first name in the process). But things get even weirder between Captain America and his new sidekick as they celebrate the victory: Ross moves to embrace Cap, who grabs her wrists to stop her. "Here now! That's no way for a seasoned crime fighter to act!" he warns, before quickly changing his mind and kissing her. "On second thought, this is something I've always wanted to do!" he says, the image of a giant red heart filling the panel with the sound effect "Smack!" inside of it.[80] Cap's conflicted roles as mentor and lover complicate Golden Girl's depiction as a "seasoned" hero capable of success without needing to fulfil the role of love interest. Her evolution from doing domestic chores to punching out baddies in the same story serves to emphasize to

Captain America Comics #66, 1948, Timely Comics.

readers that while she may be replacing Bucky as Cap's right-hand (wo) man, she still upholds traditional gender norms in a postwar era that saw women frequently take over male labor roles during World War II.

The world's most famous superheroine arrived in 1941 when writer William Moulton Marston created Wonder Woman, who debuted in *All Star Comics* #8 before starring in *Sensation Comics* and then her own title series the following year. Marston hoped his character could offer comics readers a more inspiring and commanding vision of female identity: he once said that "comics' greatest offense was their blood-curdling masculinity."[81] In 1943, he wrote in the magazine *The American Scholar*,

> Not even girls want to be girls so long as our feminine archetype lacks force, strength, and power. Not wanting to be girls, they don't want to be tender, submissive, peace-loving as good women are. Women's strong qualities have become despised because of their weakness. The obvious remedy is to create a feminine character with all the strength of Superman plus all the allure of a good and beautiful woman.[82]

Wonder Woman proved to be enormously popular among male readers, who were estimated as being as much as 90 percent of the series' audience.[83] Many of her earliest adventures were penned, although uncredited, by a female writer. Joye Hummel (later Joye Murchison and then Joye

Kelly), worked as Marston's assistant and then ghost writer when he was diagnosed with polio in 1944 and cancer in 1946, staying on the series until his death in 1947. Marston was confident in Hummel's ability to infuse Wonder Woman's stories with his protofeminist beliefs. "He told me that I seemed to have understood his philosophy and how to treat people. He had been trying to find somebody who understood his philosophy and could both write adventure stories and keep that philosophy active in *Wonder Woman.* He really wanted Wonder Woman to be a positive role model for the young readers of the comics," she says.[84]

"Scripts were written in play form—some by me, some by Dr. Marston, some together," says Hummel, who also supervised the initial layouts of the artwork. "Explicit directions were in the script explaining to the artists exactly what to draw, the costumes, the size of panels, the backgrounds. The first layouts were done in pencil and checked by me to make sure they followed the script."[85] The primary artist was Harry George Peter, who had several female assistants helping him with the finished artwork, sometimes completing the penciling over Peter's rough layouts as well as inking the finished pencils. "I think that most of the time Harry did a quick pencil thing," says Hummel, who reviewed all the artwork to ensure "that they had understood what Marston and I had written. . . . Every single thing that he drew had to be done by what we said, and I had to make sure it was done."[86] Like Toni Blum before her, Hummel had creative control over the finished artwork, a rare but powerful role for female comics creators in this era.

The first story written by Hummel, *Wonder Woman* #12 (1945), begins with our hero contemplating the era's gender roles.[87] "Well, here I am back at the old desk again. Sometimes I get so bored being 'Lieutenant Prince,'" she thinks to herself, before further musing about the role that women's clothing plays in their personal identity: "It's funny what clothes do to a girl—just taking off my glasses makes me feel more peppy!"[88] It should be noted that, as a character, Wonder Woman was in fact equally as powerful as most male comic book heroes of the 1930s and 1940s, if not actually much more powerful. In the hands of Marston and Hummel, the character was a symbol of equality in an era that saw many women take over male workplace roles (in the comic book industry and throughout society) as many men were deployed to war overseas. In keeping with the Rosie the Riveter movement, Wonder Woman served as a forceful reminder that women could excel in roles that had always been male-dominated.[89]

Hummel recalls how Marston agreed with this sentiment: "He wanted women to get out there. He felt that women had enormous possibilities within them" and hoped that his character might give women the "real ability to project their strong, positive qualities that would help them to realize how important they were. . . . He wanted them to consider jobs that no woman ever had and feel they'd be right for that job."[90] At a time when women's contributions outside of the home were not largely celebrated, this was a powerfully affirming fact, paralleled by Wonder Woman's strong characterization and sensational adventures. "Dr. Marston didn't want Wonder Woman to be just a female version of one of the male super-heroes," says Hummel. "He wanted her to be an alluring, wise, and loving woman who could stand up to evil while promoting goodness. He liked the word 'alluring.' He didn't mean it as just physically beautiful but to describe a woman with many good attributes."[91]

But while Marston intended her to be a feminist icon, some saw Wonder Woman as a corrupting rather than courageous figure. In his infamous 1954 book examining the comics medium, *Seduction of the Innocent*, the psychiatrist and prominent cultural critic Fredric Wertham considered Wonder Woman to be harmful for both male and female readers. Comparing her to a "horror type" character, he notes that Wonder Woman "is physically very powerful, tortures men, has her own female following, is the cruel, 'phallic' woman. While she is a frightening figure for boys, she is an undesirable ideal for girls, being the exact opposite of what girls are supposed to want to be."[92] Such speculations about the "ideal" nature of femininity would be regularly challenged a few years later as second-wave feminism began to grow in the early 1960s. Prominent feminists such as Gloria Steinem championed the very qualities that Wertham decried about Wonder Woman, seeing her as a feminist role model where others saw an inherently unfeminine figure.[93]

Though many label her the "first" female superhero, many other characters primed readers for Wonder Woman's debut in 1941, from Sheena to Amazona to the Woman in Red to Fantomah, Red Tornado and many more. The debate over who can be called the first superheroine will likely continue to be located in scholarly and fan-based turf wars over genre categorization and the very definition of what a superhero is and is not. But this debate risks overlooking the bigger concern about how women were regularly overshadowed within the comics industry as both characters *and* creators: many challenged what it meant to be a woman in this era, both on the page and in publisher's studios. Challenging the public misconception that Wonder Woman was the first superheroine is only the start of a larger confrontation about how women are treated within comics.

Conclusion

As Wertham and other critics began to make their case against comic books in the late 1940s, superhero titles began to decline and other genres such as crime and horror grew in popularity. Much as *Black Cat Comics* became *Black Cat Mystery*, *Captain America Comics* became *Captain America's Weird Tales* in 1949, dropping Golden Girl altogether as the series shifted to supernatural stories. Wertham's work ultimately helped usher in sweeping changes to the comics industry in the 1950s; although many have decried his beliefs about the psychological impact of comic books on children, he was also a strong advocate for racial equality. He argued against race-based discrimination just two years after *Seduction of the Innocent* in his 1956 book *The Circle of Guilt*—a case study of racial inequalities in the New York legal system.[94] Comics are certainly a forum in which racial stereotypes were (and continue to be) perpetuated, and in turn few heroic characters of color were created in this era. Perhaps, then, despite his concern for what he called the "mental hygiene" of young readers,[95] were he alive today he might be heartened to see that minority female characters have finally been given a spotlight in a medium whose content he so regularly found troubling.

In the last few decades, mainstream publishers like DC and Marvel have attempted to add more women in starring roles to their titles. Marvel now spotlights female characters in many of their most popular titles, developing superheroines such as Jennifer Walters (She-Hulk) and Natasha Romanova (Black Widow) as heroes in their own right. Since 2012, Marvel has continued to launch even more series with women as the title characters, including Kate Bishop (Hawkeye), America Chavez (Miss America), Carol Danvers (Captain Marvel), Jessica Drew (Spider-Woman), Jane Foster (Thor), Doreen Green (Squirrel Girl), Gamora, Jean Grey, Jessica Jones, Kamala Khan (Ms. Marvel), Laura Kinney (X-23/Wolverine), Lunella Lafayette (Moon Girl), Wanda Maximoff (Scarlet Witch), Barbara Morse (Mockingbird), Ororo Munroe (Storm), Gwendolyn Poole (Gwenpool), Betty Ross (Red She-Hulk), Shuri, Gwen Stacy (Spider-Gwen), Neena Thurman (Domino), Nadia Van Dyne (Wasp), Patsy Walker (Hellcat), and Riri Williams (Ironheart). Further, several of these new title characters have been explicitly identified as people of color, marking an important turn toward diversifying the ranks of non-white characters who can headline their own comics.

In 2007 and 2011, DC published two series starring Dinah Drake (Black Canary), a character who also appeared in the series *Birds of Prey* (1999–2014) alongside other female heroes including Huntress,

Lady Blackhawk, and Oracle. In addition to characters like Catwoman, Supergirl, and Wonder Woman, who already had ongoing series in prior decades, DC has launched numerous series starring non-male characters since 2011, including Jessica Cruz (Green Lantern), Barda Free (Big Barda), Barbara Gordon (Batgirl), Honor Guest (Silencer), Koriand'r (Starfire), Selena Kyle (Catwoman), Loma (Shade, the Changing Girl, and Shade, the Changing Woman), Mera, Naomi, Violet Paige (Mother Panic), Harley Quinn, Rachel Roth (Raven), Caroline Sharp (Eternity Girl), and Helena Wayne (Huntress). Sexual diversity has been on the rise as well, with Kate Kane (Batwoman) becoming DC's first lesbian superhero in 2006, followed by the bisexual antiheroine Mother Panic in 2016, as well as the revelation that same year of Wonder Woman's bisexuality.

The recent changes in how diverse identities are represented in comics are tied to contemporary cultural and social shifts regarding how gender, race, and sexuality are understood. Such changes within the pages of comic books should certainly be celebrated. At the same time, it should not be forgotten that though these superheroines opened up new avenues of representation for women to pursue, they also essentially functioned to assimilate women into the ideologies of American nationalism in more active ways. Still, relatively few superheroes in the Golden Age of comics were women (and so very few of those women were anything but cisgender, white Americans), and the female superheroes of the 1930s, 1940s, and 1950s repeatedly challenged gender norms while offering readers of all genders powerful representations of female identity, setting a vital precedent for all the superheroines who followed.

CHAPTER 2

JUNGLE COMICS

Jungle stories were a mainstay of the comic book industry for decades. From the late 1930s through the 1950s, jungle comics had a regular place on newsstands, with most publishers offering at least one such title. Although remembered by many for its male heroes, such as Tarzan and Jungle Jim, the genre was a steady home for strong heroines and even served as one of the most prominent forums for female creators in the Golden Age of comics. The genre's origins stem from Victorian literature, most notably Rudyard Kipling's collection of stories *The Jungle Book* (1894), about a young hero who was raised by wolves, and Joseph Conrad's novella *Heart of Darkness* (1899), about an ivory trader's journey up the Congo River in Africa. Both stories exemplify the ways in which jungle narratives are weighted with the centuries-old processes of imperialism and colonialism,[1] a pattern continuing into the early history of comic books, where the jungle genre flourished. While the jungle was used as a forum for female empowerment in many comics, it was undoubtedly a venue in which harmful colonialist fantasies thrived.[2]

Jungle tales were so widespread in this era that they could often be found alongside superheroes in the pages of popular series. The first issue of *Marvel Comics* featured two different jungle stories in 1939: a tale called "Jungle Terror" and the "Adventures of Ka-Zar the Great." Prior to the comic book format, the 1920s and 1930s also saw numerous pulp magazines devoted to jungle tales, including *Jungle Stories* and *Thrills of the Jungle*.[3] Other mags, such as *South Sea Stories* and *Spicy Adventure Stories*, often highlighted their stories' lush jungle settings. Even the most famous jungle adventurer, Tarzan the Ape Man, got his start in pulp magazines. After publishing his first story, "Under the Moons of Mars," in *The All Story* in 1912, Edgar Rice Burroughs then created Tarzan the following year for the same publication. He continued writing Tarzan stories through the mid-1940s, with several of his tales printed posthumously (in addition to the many new *Tarzan* novels written by different authors that have been commissioned by Burroughs's estate). The character's first film adaptation arrived in 1918, followed by dozens more in the 1930s through 1950s. Their success led to other films starring white jungle heroes, such as *Jungle Jim* (1937), *Jungle Girl* (1941), and *Perils of Nyoka* (1942). There were also two Tarzan radio series, one in the 1930s and the other in the early 1950s, as well as a newspaper comic strip starting in 1929, all demonstrating the multimedia appeal of jungle tales in this era.[4]

Despite the genre's ongoing popularity, "the jungle" was an abstract concept to most readers, bringing to mind images of tropical foliage, wild animals, and native tribes yet lacking in any cultural or geographic specificity. Jungle stories told in novels, pulp magazines, movies, radio plays, and comic books are usually steeped in stereotypes: in short, racism was rampant in jungle stories. The portrayals of indigenous tribespeople rarely rose above the level of ignorant cliché—usually hackneyed, often hateful. Most tales were content to identify their settings as "the African jungle," reducing a whole continent to a single, indistinct locale.

Other stories took place in South America or India (where *The Jungle Book* was set), but the specific venue hardly mattered to most audiences craving an exotic backdrop. These foreign jungle settings were largely interchangeable to most readers in this era; much like the outer space adventures of the science fiction genre, the places and spaces depicted were as vast as they were unknowable. In *Heart of Darkness*, the protagonist, Marlowe, describes his childhood fascination with maps showing "the many blank spaces on the earth" that remained uncharted.[5] Jungle stories readily fulfilled such fascinations for mass audiences across a variety of media in the early twentieth century, much as science fiction storytelling continues to do so today.

This parallel between jungle and sci-fi storytelling is further seen in how Burroughs alternated between both genres throughout his career, publishing ten books in his Barsoom series between 1912 and 1941 (beginning with *A Princess of Mars*) and five books in his Venus series (including *Pirates of Venus*, *Lost on Venus*, and *Escape on Venus*). Similarly, comic book publisher Fiction House found success in the late 1930s and 1940s by offering readers jungle-oriented series like *Jumbo Comics* and *Jungle*

Comics as well as the popular science fiction title *Planet Comics*. But while some publishers used jungle comics as a platform for male heroes, Fiction House was progressive in its regular spotlight on female characters, including Sheena, Camilla, Fantomah, Princess Taj, and Tiger Girl. Jungle tales certainly saw the propagation of colonialist fantasies, but the genre was also a forum for female empowerment.

In addition to the many solo adventures of powerful heroines, jungle stories featured women fighting alongside men as their equals. In Timely Comics' adventures of Trojak the Tiger Man in *Daring Mystery Comics*, the "Tigerish Lord of the Jungle" who was "raised by friendly savages" is aided by Edith Alton, who nurses Trojak back to health after he saves her from a lion.[6] Alton joins Trojak on future adventures, toting a shotgun and drawing her blade as she fights off wild hyenas, builds a log raft, and escapes from spear-toting spies. Similarly, in the Breeze Barton stories from *Daring Mystery Comics*, he fights invading forces in the prehistoric Miracle City alongside Ann Barclay. When Barton defeats the chief of a "savage" tribe of Neanderthal-like warriors, he is "hailed as the new savage chieftain" but is quickly sneak-attacked by his defeated rival. When Ann saves Breeze from drowning, he declares, "You saved me, Ann—we make a good team!" She replies, "Yes! We'll work for civilization—together!"[7]

While Alton and Barclay are presented in these stories as skilled, strong women, the bigger concern surrounding the jungle genre is the problematic notion that these white heroes, heroines, adventurers, and explorers will bring civilization to places populated, broadly, by "natives" and "savages." The primary question isn't necessarily whether there were empowered or empowering representations of women in these comics, but whether women characters and creators contributed to the proliferation of damaging racist stereotypes through their participation in the jungle comics genre. The representations of empowered female characters found in jungle comics cannot be celebrated without also addressing how they bolster the legacy of racist and imperialist ideology. The success and visibility of both female characters and creators in this genre cannot be taken uncritically; what read as empowerment and liberation to some readers in this era no doubt read to others as the same kinds of racism and denial of Black personhood that has always existed in American media. Still, women in jungle comics were not *just* jungle queens (even if those were the more prominent female figures). Stories of Black women fighting back against colonialist settlers and invaders were also occasionally seen during the Golden Age, and although they too were steeped in stereotypes and pejorative representations of non-white characters and cultures, they offer brief glimpses of the kind of Black empowerment that would be seen in comics in later decades.

Jungle Queens

In the current comic book marketplace, few jungle-based titles have had any lasting success. Tarzan has starred in a few miniseries from publishers Dark Horse Comics and Dynamite Entertainment, but the character no longer dominates popular culture the way he did in past decades. Ka-Zar starred in miniseries in 2011 and 2017 at Marvel, but the character has found more success in supporting roles in such series as *Black Panther and the Agents of Wakanda*. Female heroes have fared no better; the cheesecake artist Frank Cho's 2005 *Shanna the She-Devil* miniseries for Marvel served as a forum for his hypersexualized approach to female anatomy, followed by his nearly identical series *Jungle Girl* in 2007 for Dynamite.

Jungle comics were a forum for equally problematic sexual imagery in previous decades: bikini-clad heroines were a major factor in their early success. A 1945 issue of *Fight Comics* even has the jungle queen Tiger Girl swimming naked in a stream before slipping her bikini back on among the trees, foliage strategically covering much of her bare breasts.[8] Other genres moved beyond the regular use of such bawdy imagery in later years, but Cho's work reminds us that jungle comics have not progressed much in this regard.

But despite the genre's steady turn toward gratuitous nudity, it also served as a regular forum for women in starring roles well before other publishers, such as Fawcett and DC, released titles like *Mary Marvel Comics* and *Wonder Woman*. As demonstrated in chapter 1, Sheena, Queen of the Jungle, was a powerful, autonomous, and, perhaps most importantly, *popular* female character whose stories were being published alongside foundational Golden Age characters like Superman, who first appeared mere months before Sheena's American debut. Created by Jerry Iger, Sheena's debut in the British series *Wags* in January 1937 was reprinted in 1938's *Jumbo Comics* #1, where she stayed for the entirety of its 167-issue run until 1953 (while also earning her own eighteen-issue series in 1942). Although the debate over whether she qualifies as a superhero may never be resolved, Sheena deserves to be at the forefront of discussions about comic books' early success, alongside Superman, Batman, and Wonder Woman.

"Tiger Girl," *Fight Comics* #36, 1945, Fiction House.

Sheena's origin story, delivered by a tribal medicine man to two white explorers, claims that she is the daughter of a "learned man" who "wandered into [their] land" and befriended the tribe—while also studying them.[9] When he attempted to leave, the witch doctor cursed him, not wanting him to go, and made Sheena the queen of the tribe. She has lived, it seems, much of her life as the Queen of the Jungle; much like the white goddesses portrayed on screen, she was a friend of the jungle and its people, a figure of the benevolent white savior whose legitimacy is willingly conferred by the natives instead of attained through violence or force.

While stories of vine-swinging men raised or adopted by the jungle were common by the late 1930s, the more immediate reference that Golden Age readers brought with them to comics' jungle queens would have been the popular jungle adventure movies produced in Hollywood in the early years of the decade.[10] Like their filmic counterparts, women in jungle series, such as Sheena and Camilla (who appeared in *Jungle Comics* from 1940 to 1944), were rulers who stalked and protected the jungle alongside its mysterious inhabitants. Such depictions reinforced myths about the vulnerability of white women and made clear their participation in processes of colonialism, but comics shied away from the darkly violent sexual themes that were not uncommon in the jungle films of the early 1930s.[11] For film scholar Rhona J. Berenstein, jungle movies of the early 1930s were overrun with dark and violent sexual themes that, she argues, are about reckoning with white men's guilt over the treatment of Black women throughout history; their "guilt is conferred upon blacks and white women endure terrors historically experienced by black women."[12]

Here, the jungle queens of the Golden Age perform a similar function.

They reinforce the narrative of whiteness as a civilizing and salvational force, but instead of being cast as perpetual victims, they are presented as friends of an unfamiliar world. It is white women's job to act as liaison between white male "explorer" characters and the seemingly "savage tribes" they so easily misunderstand; in short, white women took on a much more active role in the project of racism than they previously had been allowed. In early jungle films, the interstitial role the white goddess played signified the danger and instability of racial boundaries; her proximity to both whiteness and blackness in the jungle "does not guarantee a stable racial membership" that can only be quelled by also casting her as the damsel in distress who must be saved by a white explorer.[13] Jungle queen stories cemented the whiteness—and superiority—of these characters by turning them into saviors and heroines instead of victims. While white men still play an almost omnipresent role, they are typically relegated to marveling at the beauty and power of the jungle queens and often themselves need saving (or, at the very least, guidance). Characters like Sheena retained their status as white goddesses without the stigma or weakness of perpetual victimhood by transforming the dark threat of the jungle into a knowable kingdom over which she can rule. At the same time that these tales cemented that jungle queens could embody and wield their whiteness in the same, often harmful ways men could, they were also some of the first strong female characters seen in the comics industry.

Much as Superman's success soon spawned caped imitators such as Wonder Man and Captain Marvel, Sheena's novelty and popularity also inspired rival jungle queens. When Fiction House launched *Jungle Comics* as a follow-up to *Jumbo Comics* in 1940, it introduced a character who would endure in the new series through 1952: Camilla the Jungle Queen. Although initially appearing as Camilla, Queen of the Lost Empire, in *Jungle Comics* #1—in which she is not a jungle warrior but rather the ruler of a lost civilization "composed of the same Norsemen who went there during the crusades, and who have found the secret of eternal life"[14]—she eventually transitioned to a jungle adventurer much like Sheena after several issues.

While she may not have been the first jungle queen, nor would she be the last, Camilla is an important figure in comics history because of the prominent non-male artists who drew her adventures—including Marcia Snyder, one of the first openly queer comics creators. Snyder drew Camilla (along with Tabu, the Wizard of the Jungle) for *Jungle Comics* between 1944 and 1945, by which point she had been drawing comic books and newspaper strips for at least a decade. As early as 1934 she drew a series of newspaper strips "for a women's page with columns about fashion,

"Camilla," *Jungle Comics* #58, 1944, Fiction House. Art by Marcia Snyder.

child-rearing, gossip, beauty advice, etc."[15] syndicated by King Features, as well as stories combining prose text and illustrations such as "Snappy Stories" and "All-Story Love."

In 1942, Snyder began working for Jack Binder's packaging studio, drawing stories for Fawcett's *Captain Midnight* and *Minute Man*, Parents

Magazine Press's *True Comics*, and "Blackstone" and "Cap Fury" features for Street and Smith Publications. She was then hired by Fiction House in 1944; editor Vince Fago describes that "for $90 a week, I hired Marcia Snyder, an artist who had done newspaper strips. She dressed like a man and lived in Greenwich Village with a girlfriend named Mickey. I never thought about her being a lesbian; I didn't care."[16] Fellow Fiction House artist Lily Renée confirmed that Snyder often wore men's clothing, describing her as "mannish-looking" as well as "very bright" and "a good artist."[17]

Snyder drew for numerous publishers in the 1940s, including work on *Captain America Comics*, *Millie the Model*, and *Miss America* for Timely. Her art regularly matched the tone of the genres she worked in: she often cast the soldiers in her combat tales for *Rangers Comics* in shadows or silhouettes to emphasize the grave business of war, while in *Jungle Comics* she emphasized the muscularity of characters like Camilla and Ka'a'nga, in keeping with their enhanced strength and abilities. Whereas many female artists used male or gender-neutral pseudonyms in this era, Snyder actually signed much of her artwork as "Marcia."[18] As such, she was not only open about her sexuality but also unafraid to make public the fact that she wasn't a male artist.

Snyder's work raises questions about why women at this time were compelled to contribute to genres and industries that bolstered misogynistic ideas about women (much like the popular and highly visible illustrations done by Margaret Brundage for *Weird Tales* in the 1930s and 1940s, discussed in chapter 4). Despite—or perhaps because of—the wild popularity of comics during the Golden Age, stigma was attached to the industry from its inception. Drawing on Erving Goffman's sociological work on social stigma, comics historian Paul Lopes argues that the pop cultural stigma attached to the comics industry and the villainization of it by Fredric Wertham and other critics in the early 1950s has led to a devaluation and pathologizing of the medium and its readers *and* creators that persisted throughout the twentieth century.[19] Though the legitimacy of Wertham's *Seduction of the Innocent* has been rightfully called into question, his arguments about the damage that jungle comics—which he claimed were the most reprehensible of all the genres[20]—could do to developing minds was not entirely off-base, especially given how he calls out the genre's overt racism. Wertham writes,

> While the white people in jungle books are blonde and athletic and shapely, the idea conveyed about the natives is that there are fleeting transitions between apes and humans. I have repeatedly found in my

> studies that this characterization of colored peoples as subhuman, in conjunction with depiction of forceful heroes as blond Nordic supermen, has made a deep—and I believe lasting—impression on young children. And amidst all the violence between slaves, apes and humans in these books are big pictures of lush girls, as nude as the Post Office permits. Even on an adult, the impression of sex plus violence is definite.[21]

Although he later embellishes stories about young people who have been corrupted by jungle comics, the argument Wertham is making here is almost entirely rational, and it helps explain how Golden Age comics became so heavily stigmatized. Lopes cites the popularity of pseudonyms in the comics industry as proof of Goffman's theory that stigma can lead to victimization; he writes that comics artists "agreed to give publishers the rights to their work partly in order to keep their anonymity."[22]

Artists of all genders used pseudonyms when signing their work. There were several female artists, such as Snyder and Claire S. Moe, however, who often published under their given names, which would have immediately identified them as women to most readers. In addition to being in the comic book industry, these artists were *women* and, in certain cases, openly queer or nonnormative in their presentation. By virtue of their very identities, they were more heavily stigmatized than the men who worked in the same industry yet often achieved steady success in their work. In the case of the comics industry, some female artists, like Snyder, may have felt more free to express themselves without fear of repercussions because they were already working within a culturally marginalized space; since the work they were doing was already stigmatized, these artists may have rationalized that the reality of their gender wouldn't hinder their professional success in the way it may have in other industries.

After Snyder left the series, Fran Hopper took over drawing Camilla in the October 1945 through August 1947 issues of *Jungle Comics*. Hopper worked at Fiction House from 1943 to 1948, drawing features in other series such as *Planet Comics* and *Wings Comics* as well as *Patsy Walker* for Timely. Ruth Atkinson, cocreator of Patsy Walker, drew Tabu for *Jungle Comics* in addition to art for other Fiction House titles. *Jungle Comics* was a regular forum not only for female artists but also for African American artist Matt Baker, who worked regularly for Fiction House in the mid- to late 1940s. Baker drew Camilla in 1945 in between Snyder's departure from and Hopper's start on the character, and again between 1948 and 1949. He drew Tiger Girl stories and inked some Sheena stories in this period as well.

Another African American artist, Alvin Hollingsworth, also drew Tiger Girl, along with a different jungle queen named Numa in the pages of Fox Feature Syndicate's *Rulah the Jungle Goddess*. This pattern of Black artists drawing white jungle heroes who reinforced racist stereotypes is certainly problematic. But aside from titles like *All-Negro Comics* and *Negro Romance* created specifically for Black readers, the jungle comic was one of the only genres that offered any kind of role for Black characters in this era, especially Black women, who were portrayed largely in tribal roles or as victims. In *Jungle Comics* #56, Tabu (a white warrior in the vein of Tarzan and Ka-Zar) rescues a young African woman from a group of "marauders" trying to kidnap her.[23] The story was drawn by Ruth Atkinson, who worked on several Tabu tales in 1944. While the plot point in which the young lady is poised to be cooked over a fire as part of a cannibalistic ritual sacrifice was beyond Atkinson's control, she did draw (perhaps under editorial orders) the African woman with flowing, straight hair in conformance with western standards of beauty. The same is true of Lalei, love interest of Waku, Prince of the Bantu, in Timely/Atlas's *Jungle Tales* from 1955. She too has straight, flowing hair and is seemingly drawn by Ogden Whitney as a Caucasian woman who happens to have dark skin. Lalei's voice is literally silenced in her first appearance: in her second and final line of dialogue from *Jungle Tales* #1, she confronts Waku in an effort to save his life, only to be told "Silence, Lalei!" by the Bantu prince.[24] Unlike the commanding white women who were regularly given their own stories in jungle comics, Black women were regularly victimized, misrepresented, and silenced by the genre.

But a starkly different type of characterization is found later in the "Captain Terry Thunder" feature of *Jungle Comics* #56, in which Cpt. Thunder tracks down a slave trader along the Congo River. While in holding in the hull of a paddle steamer, one of the captured Africans makes plans to turn against her captors: "I—who am your Chief's bride, ask you: will you be slaves?! No! Plan with me . . . revolt!"[25] The feminist author and activist bell hooks describes in *Talking Back: Thinking Feminist, Thinking Black* how Black women's voices have not been traditionally valued as worth listening to by men, similar to Lalei being told to keep silent: "Unlike the black male preacher whose speech was to be heard, who was to be listened to, whose words were to be remembered, the voices of black women—giving orders, making threats, fussing—could be tuned out, could become a kind of background music, audible but not acknowledged as significant speech," writes hooks.[26] While Golden Age comics rarely gave Black women any kind of voice—and when they

"Captain Terry Thunder," *Jungle Comics* #56, 1944, Fiction House.

did speak, it was frequently in victimized screams or the pidgin English of imperialist tribal cliché—it is essential to reclaim the rare moments in which they are heard. In "Captain Terry Thunder" the plan to revolt is discovered and the woman is tied to a post to be whipped; notably, artist Richard Case draws her reacting not in fear as the whip cuts through the air but with her brow furrowed in contempt. Her resistance continues as Cpt. Thunder arrives with his troops to arrest the slave trader: "The soldiers cannot take our vengeance from us!" she cries before burning down the boat that had been used as a vehicle for genocide.

As the "orders" and "threats" of the nameless chief's bride are fulfilled through fire, the story offers readers a rare instance of a defiant, persistent and fearless African woman—ideals that Black female activists espoused for more than a century prior to this 1946 comic. As Maria Miller Stewart wrote in 1831 to her fellow "daughters" of Africa: "Possess the spirit of independence. The Americans do, and why should not you? Possess the spirit of men, bold and enterprising, fearless and undaunted. Sue for your rights and privileges. Know the reason you cannot attain them. Weary them with your importunities. You can but die if you make the attempt, and we shall certainly die if you do not."[27]

White jungle queens and kings were regularly used to perpetuate racist colonialist stereotypes of Black men and women throughout the Golden Age of comics. Many publishers overtly highlighted the whiteness of their jungle heroes and heroines, such as in Avon Comics' *White Princess of the Jungle* and Timely/Atlas's "Cliff Mason, White Hunter" stories in *Jungle Tales*, from 1954 to 1955. Far too many stories played upon racist fears about the potential for Black men to kill white people, such as a "Tiger Girl" tale in *Fight Comics* #34. When asked what the pounding drums heard in the distance mean, a tribesman thinks to himself, "Aiee! They say Juju serpent stolen by white men . . . say must kill all those with pale skin!" while the story's narration emphasizes, "Grimly, relentlessly, the drums say kill-kill-KILL!"[28]

Even though malignant stories like these appeared regularly in jungle comics, the genre's widespread legacy is one centered around leopard bikinis, flowing blonde hair and the fearlessness of its beautiful female heroines. The genre's reliance on, and perpetuation of, deeply racist myths and tropes is often glossed over in favor of discussions about how jungle heroines were both sexy *and* strong. It's true that jungle comics, like sci-fi comics, were heavily shaped by non-male creators and defined by non-male characters, but why these genres in particular allowed for the progressive and even subversive involvement of women should be examined more closely. Because of their unfamiliar and seemingly limitless settings, fantasy stories provide fertile ground for creators to experiment with and challenge hegemonic norms; just as often, however, the fantastic is used as an exotic and thrilling new backdrop against which these hegemonic norms can be reproduced in seemingly fresh and exciting (yet still problematic) ways.[29]

Though it's impossible to definitively state why it is that jungle comics were so heavily populated by women in leading roles, the fantasy element that the jungle and its more mysterious inhabitants introduce created a sense of freedom from the boundaries of everyday, contemporary life. Jungle comics turned the expansive and diverse continent of Africa into a homogenous land of exotic animals and uncivilized peoples, so it may have been easier for readers (of any race) without firsthand knowledge of the continent's many countries to believe that white women there could become jungle princesses, queens, and heroines. In 1952, Frantz Fanon theorized that adventurer and jungle comics served as a form of "collective catharsis," an outlet onto which readers could project their collective violent fantasies as a means of maintaining the status quo.[30] With their white heroes and heroines, jungle comics implicitly asked readers of all races to identify *with* whiteness and *against* any and all characters of color. Fanon writes,

> The Wolf, the Devil, the Evil Spirit, the Bad Man, the Savage are always symbolized by Negroes or Indians; since there is always identification with the victor, the little Negro, quite as easily as the little white boy, becomes an explorer, an adventurer, a missionary "who faces the danger of being eaten by the wicked Negroes." . . . The black schoolboy . . . identifies himself with the explorer, the bringer of civilization, the white man who carries truth to savages—an all white truth. There is an identification—that is, the young Negro subjectively adopts a white man's attitude.[31]

In plainer terms, the young Black children reading these comics internalized a vision of themselves—or people like themselves—steeped in white supremacist thought. As beneficial as it may have been for certain readers to see strong, active female characters flitting from vine to vine in their favorite jungle comics, the racism and imperialism inherent in the genre arguably negates the progressiveness of these jungle queens. Nevertheless, the assimilation of white women into the pantheon of power in the United States came at the expense of children and adults of color.

Cross-Genre Adventures: *Slave Girl*, *Cave Girl*, and June Tarpé Mills's *Miss Fury*

Jungle comics thrived in part because they were a forum in which multiple genres regularly collided. While it is tempting to think of jungle comics, superhero books, war comics, fantasy titles, and science fiction as distinct genres with rigid boundaries, in actuality these genres regularly blurred together throughout the Golden Age of comics. This era saw numerous titles that combined genres overtly, such as *Cowboy Love*, *Horrors of War*, *Moon Girl Fights Crime*, *Space Detective*, *Space Western*, and *True War Romances*. Many such combinations were meant to attract readers by their sheer novelty, but this intermingling of genres occurred more subtly as well.

As jungle comics thrived, new variations on the jungle queen character emerged that introduced new themes, settings, and tropes. In 1946, Universal Phoenix Features Syndicate introduced Alani, a.k.a. the South Sea Girl, in the pages of *Seven Seas Comics* #1. Drawn by Matt Baker, Alani was the powerful ruler of several tropical islands in the South Pacific, confronting jungle threats much like those faced by Sheena and Camilla. After appearing in all six issues of *Seven Seas Comics*, Alani's adventures were reprinted by Ajax-Farrell in the 1952 series *Voodoo*, and again in the 1955 series *Vooda*; in each case the text and artwork were altered to transform the character into a jungle princess, first changing her name from Alani to El' Nee and then to the titular Vooda, merging jungle and horror imagery to capitalize on the latter genre's popularity in the early 1950s.

In 1949, Avon Comics published two issues of *Slave Girl Comics* featuring an imperiled white woman named Maru who is sold at various Middle Eastern slave markets. Regularly dressing its female characters in bikinis à la Camilla, Tiger Girl, and their peers, *Slave Girl Comics* was an excuse to offer readers more scantily clad women facing dangerous situations in foreign and exotic locations. While the series mostly features desert locales, the second issue features two backup stories set in different jungles. The first tale, "The Lost Princess," is set "deep in a jungle somewhere in the Middle East" and centers on Princess Tais of the lost city of Neptuna. The second, "The Female Goddess," takes place in "the Peruvian past" about "the lost city of Chicalmo . . . a city of solid, glimmering gold" in which an American woman is mistaken for a goddess by its tribe.[32]

In 1953, another variation of the jungle queen came in the form of *Cave Girl* from Magazine Enterprises, the cover tagline for the first issue inviting readers to "Thrill to the Jungle Savagery" as heroine Carol Mantomer rushes toward two tribesmen with a spear in her hand while a black leopard watches ominously.[33] Her adventures are set in a mysterious realm called the Dawn Lands where prehistoric beasts and beings still live, allowing writer Gardner Fox and artist Bob Powell to add club-wielding Neanderthals to the jungle genre's usual mix of tribal warriors and wild animals. The combination of prehistoric and jungle elements was largely done for the purposes of novelty, coming as it did some fifteen years after Sheena's debut.

The jungle was also used as a backdrop for the adventures of several comic book heroines who were *not* scantily clad jungle queens but instead started out as superheroes or spies. June Tarpé Mills's *Miss Fury* newspaper strip, which was reprinted in comic book form by Timely between 1942 and 1946, transitioned to a jungle setting after the hero's initial fight against crime in an urban context. The city streets, rooftops, and apartment buildings of *Miss Fury*'s initial adventures soon changed as our hero, Marla Drake, travels to Rio de Janeiro, where she is accused of being a spy and arrested. "All this because of a black leopard skin!" she thinks to herself while locked in a cell. Her black outfit is used in the strip's first installment to position her as a costumed crime fighter, and her housekeeper suggests that she wear it to a masquerade party. Drake recounts the origin story for readers as she remains locked up:

"South Sea Girl," *Seven Seas Comics* #1, 1946, Universal Phoenix Features Syndicate.

Somehow, I've had nothing but trouble since my uncle left me the black leopard skin! It had been a witch doctor's ceremonial robe and was regarded as a symbol of justice by the tribe. They claimed it had strange powers and worked miracles . . . though often as blessings in disguise! Hmph! If the things that have happened to me are blessings they certainly have been well disguised!"[34]

Miss Fury, 1942. Written by June Tarpé Mills.

As Drake's adventure in Rio continues, her costume is eventually returned to its original jungle context (albeit on a different continent). After being rescued by a Brazilian woman named Era, Drake aids her fight against the Nazi agents who are preparing to attack the coastline. Slipping off into the jungle while dressed as Miss Fury, Drake is nearly shot with an arrow when local tribesmen believe her to be an animal. On a visual level, Drake's black leopard-skin costume serves a very different function when placed in a tropical setting rather than an urban one. In her earliest adventures, Miss Fury's leather costume is set against the concrete, brick, and asphalt surfaces that encompass her metropolitan surroundings. As she sneaks along rooftops and climbs out of windows, often bathed in shadows cast by moonlight or streetlight, Drake's suit blends in against the dark, hardened textures of her urban confines. When she moves through the jungles of Brazil, however, her leather outfit stands in sharp textural contrast with the lush foliage and natural landscapes. When seen in bright sunlight glistening among the trees rather than lit by car headlights, flashlights, or streetlamps, Miss Fury's costume makes her much more akin to an elegant jungle cat than a prowling cat burglar. When perched atop a giant rock as she surveys a battlefield, Drake looks like a very different "symbol of justice" in a natural jungle setting than in an asphalt jungle—sleek and dignified, rather than hiding in the shadows. Whereas other comics, such as *Cave Girl*, added elements from other genres mostly for the sheer novelty of it, *Miss Fury*'s addition of a costumed crime fighter to a tropical jungle adds new layers to the title character. In combining genres, the narrative potential inherent in the hasty backstory given to her costume in the comic's initial installment becomes fulfilled.

Although jungle comics have proven problematic in how they handle the racial, cultural, and historical representations of their non-white characters, Mills was sensitive in *Miss Fury* to the need for depictions that challenged the traditional and ignorant assumptions about tribal peoples that were reinforced in the genre. In her work for Lloyd and Grace Jacquet at Funnies

Inc., Mills had created the character Jaxon of the Jungle for Centaur's *Prize Comics* in 1940. Using the pen name Edgar Allen Jr., Mills wrote and drew the adventures of white guide Mike Jaxon as he explored the jungles of the Congo for six issues. Her handling of African characters in these stories is as problematic as that seen in so many comics, films, and pulp magazines of this era: members of Jaxon's exploration party speak in pidgin English ("My men scare! Devil pigs attack is evil sign. We go back! / Debbil! Debbil!")[35] while a tribe from the lost city of Tsol are described as an "uneducated, superstitious populace" who, "around by their cruel rules, hold a wild orgy about their human sacrifices."[36] To her credit, however, Mills largely avoids the common pattern of exaggerating the physical features of her Black characters that so many artists of this era perpetuated. Whereas Arnold Hicks's drawings of a "wise native healer" along with members of the "Gemba tribe" in his Trojak tale from 1940's *Daring Mystery Comics* #5 depict Black men with circular faces, wide eyes, and engorged lips (standard tropes of how Africans and African Americans were represented in the minstrel tradition),[37] Mills used relatively realistic anatomy in her artwork and avoided the overt distortions of artists like Hicks.

While Mills does include Brazilian tribesmen dressed in loincloths in *Miss Fury*, she introduces them in a way that confronted the stereotypical depictions of indigenous peoples seen in most jungle comics. As such, we see a very different approach to representation from Mills when she was working on her creator-owned property rather than turning out pages for a company like Funnies Inc., which shopped their material around to various publishers. When an American thief named Fingers pulls his gun on an approaching group of men, he yells in fear, "Holy smoke! Cannibals! Head-huntin' cannibals!" He is quickly corrected by Era, "They are Brazilian Indians, you Yankee idiot! There are many such tribes in the interior! These men are skilled in the use of the blowgun and poison darts . . . they have come to help us!" When Fingers then complains that he can't understand their language ("Wot's he gibberin' about?"), Era picks up a knife and threatens him with it, chastising him for his ignorance.[38] By having a Brazilian woman correct an American man's racist judgments, Mills not only depicts a strong Latina who is unafraid to stand up to a man but also seeks to educate readers by providing specific facts about Brazil's tribes (for example, their regional whereabouts and weapons) rather than the vague generalizations typically seen in how indigenous peoples are represented in jungle comics.

"Mountains and jungles! Jungles and mountains! Nuts to nature—I'll take the city any day!" says Fingers.[39] This contrast between the two settings is key: while Miss Fury is often categorized as a superhero given that she is a costumed crime fighter, her story lines often saw her face off against criminal syndicates, foreign agents, and war criminals rather than superpowered foes, mechanical monsters, or alien invaders. *Miss Fury*, then, was grounded in realistic threats rather than fantastical ones. Her adventures in the Brazilian jungle lasted more than a year in her Sunday comic strip, running longer than the initial city-set story line that began the strip in 1942. While she may not swing from a vine or battle wild animals like Sheena or Camilla, the jungle plays a key part in *Miss Fury* given the tropical setting and indigenous supporting characters. Combining elements of superhero storytelling (e.g., a costumed crime fighter) along with elements of war (Nazi troops, plane and tank battles, etc.) and jungle tales, Mills regularly tested comics' genre boundaries by blending different visual and narrative conventions together in *Miss Fury*.

Mills was so inspired by the storytelling potential of the Brazilian jungle and its people that she returned to it near the end of her career. In 1979, she started a graphic novel about a character who had been central to Miss Fury's adventures in Brazil more than thirty years prior—Jo, "the Brazilian albino Indian."[40] While Jo had aided Miss Fury's fight against Axis forces in the 1940s, Mills sought to tell his origin story in *Albino Jo, the Man with Tigre Eyes*. Chronicling his early life as a child "with a hidden tribe of Amazon Indians in the Brazilian rainforest,"[41] his education at Harvard, and his subsequent return to Brazil, Mills's love of Brazil's people and its culture is clearly seen in this new work. In one scene, Jo chastises a land developer for his plans to level a section of forest for crop planting, responding to the idea that such a move constitutes progress: "That these last irreplaceable rain forests, *teeming* with life and thriving since the dawn of creation, should be obliterated for the growing of crops loaded with insecticides, herbicides and phony fertilizers—that's progress? And the Indians—those that survive civilizados' diseases—are they to be uprooted and herded into compounds? Is this the 'bounteous future' the developers heralded?"[42] The project was never completed, but the fact that Mills was so passionate about her characters, their history, and their culture that she returned to them decades later as the culmination of her career marks her as one of comics' true auteurs.

Lily Renée and Señorita Rio

Like Miss Fury, Señorita Rio's adventure also used the jungle as a backdrop for stories blending together multiple genres in the 1940s. First appearing in 1942's *Fight Comics* #19 from Fiction House, American secret agent

"Señorita Rio," *Fight Comics* #36, 1945, Fiction House. Art by Lily Renée.

Rita Farrar (a.k.a. Consuela Maria Ascencion De Las Vegas, who goes undercover as an actress and singer in Brazil) remained a mainstay of that title through 1951, often setting spy and crime narratives within the jungles of the rainforest. These jungle settings saw the hero fight against Axis spies and other threats among the lush foliage and tropical vegetation: not only were readers offered an exotic environment for Señorita Rio's cross-genre adventures, but these settings allowed for representations of Latin culture rarely seen in comics of this era.

The character was initially drawn by Nick Cardy, and Lily Renée took over in 1944 with issue 34. Renée began drawing for Fiction House in 1942, first working as a background artist and then as penciller on "The Werewolf Hunter" in *Rangers Comics*. She then took over another strong female hero—Jane Martin, who started off as a nurse before becoming a military pilot and secret agent. Renée tried to hide from workplace sexual harassment by keeping to herself at Fiction House ("I was trying to be invisible when I was there," she says), but as her artistic talents became recognized, she soon realized that her male peers resented her success: "They didn't mind if I was there at first, but once you get in competition with somebody, the attitude changes."[43] As the only female artist to draw covers for the publisher, Renée moved quickly from apprentice to leading artist at Fiction House, working on many of their top titles, such as *Fight Comics*, *Planet Comics*, and *Rangers Comics*.[44]

Señorita Rio is a milestone in comics history for being the first Latina character to star in her own feature. While Era, a resistance leader who fought Nazis in her native Brazil, was a strong Latina character in *Miss Fury*, she had only a supporting role (albeit a prominent one) in the strip. Much like Mills did with Era, Renée often drew Señorita Rio in beautiful, ruffled gowns, perhaps inspired by her previous work as a model who wore "elegant dresses" for noted fashion illustrator Jane Turner. Renée was proud of the costumes she drew for her female characters: "I want you to know that I think 'Señorita Rio' and the other women that I drew were the best-dressed women in comic books," she told interviewer Jim Amash.[45]

In her first work on the character, Renée drew Señorita Rio's efforts to stop an Axis saboteur from sinking ships along the Panama Canal. Posing as the victim of a shipwreck, Señorita Rio swims ashore to an island inhabited by "white Indians" who quickly capture her. Leading Farrar (Señorita Rio) through the jungle to a hilltop temple, the natives bring her to their leader, Kokagaran (whose grotesque face has been surgically repaired via skin graft after an explosion, we are told). One of Renée's strengths as an artist was her ability to convincingly draw ugly faces as well as beautiful ones. When we first see Kokagaran's face, its misshapen form is accentuated by the scratchy linework and shading techniques Renée used to add texture and depth to his ugliness. "I've always been extremely conscientious," says Renée about her artwork, "and my pencil work was very detailed."[46] The level of detail frequently seen in Renée's

"Señorita Rio," *Fight Comics* #34, 1944, Fiction House. Art by Lily Renée.

linework predates that of more recent male artists, many of whom are among the most heralded among comics fans and professionals alike.

In *The Education of a Comics Artist*, Arlen Schumer describes how comic book artists of the last few decades of the twentieth century were influenced by Jack Kirby and Neal Adams, who in turn inspired a group of "New Stylists" that were "stylized figure artists," including John Byrne, George Perez, and Walter Simonson along with founding Image Comics artists Todd McFarlane, Marc Silvestri, and Eric Larsen. Simonson, says Schumer, "eschewed realism, substituting a scratchy ink line and stylized drawing," while the early Image artists took "scratchy lines" to new extremes.[47] Renée was a pioneer of this approach, using scratchy linework strategically when needed to add menace to the villainous figures and sinister settings she drew in the "Señorita Rio" stories for *Fight Comics*, "The Lost World" adventures for *Planet Comics*, and "The Werewolf Hunter" tales for *Rangers Comics*.[48] What's more, her renderings of female characters often bear a striking similarity to those of both Byrne and McFarlane, especially those drawn in the 1980s, in which both artists often drew women with long, angular faces and large eyes as well as elongated, jutting legs.[49]

Like Mills, Lily Renée is an important auteur whose work in the early history of comic books deserves more attention. While her work on "The Werewolf Hunter" and in *Planet Comics* demonstrates her heavily stylized art in the horror and sci-fi genres, it is her "Señorita Rio" stories that allowed her to excel in drawing the continuing adventures of a strong Latina hero. Renée left Fiction House in 1948, moving over to St. John Publications, where she drew romance titles as well as the comedic exploits of a famous movie duo in *Abbott and Costello Comics*. She left comics after marrying Randolph Phillips in 1953, focusing on textile designs and then motherhood.[50]

In her penultimate appearance in 1950's *Fight Comics* #68, Consuela Maria Ascencion De Las Vegas dons a cheetah-skin outfit much like Sheena wore, albeit as the star of a circus act rather than as an outright jungle queen. Ruth Roche also wrote at least one installment of the character before later creating the Latin-themed newspaper comic strip *Flamingo* with Matt Baker. With its emphasis on making women of color heroes (and occasionally challenging the conventions of colonialist representations of non-white women that it otherwise typically reinforced in the pages of *Jungle Comics*), along with hiring more women than any other publisher, Fiction House was home to prominent women both in print and behind the scenes. Whereas Renée describes a culture of sexual harassment at its offices in the early 1940s, the workplace atmosphere changed considerably after more women, like Ruth Atkinson, Fran Hopper, and Marcia Snyder, began taking over in creative positions. Penciller George Tuska describes working for Fiction House both before and after serving overseas during World War II, preferring the boys-club environment of the decade's early years to the more restrained working conditions of the mid- to late 1940s: "I went back to Fiction House. It wasn't the same anymore. The fellas were not around. It was mostly girls and older men. We used to kid around a lot, hold a conversation. It was different. It didn't feel right."[51] Rather than work for Fiction House with "girls" instead of "fellas," Tuska chose to do freelance work instead.

As Mitch Maglio writes in *Fiction House: From Pulps to Panel, from Jungles to Space*, "There is no doubt that Fiction House was the first comic book company to commit to the presence of strong female leads in a large percentage of its features," based in large part on owner T. T. Scott's belief that "attractive women sold magazines." The publisher "went for an older audience than the readers of superhero fare, which was largely made up of adolescent boys and young men,"[52] hence the emphasis on "attractive women" beginning with the jungle tales of *Jumbo Comics* and *Jungle Comics* and then in other genres. But while "the fellas" of other publishers might have been strictly the ones to create lurid stories about pretty heroes, the large roster of women who worked for Fiction House (or did work for various packaging companies that were bought by the publisher)—from Roche, Renée, Atkinson, Hopper, and Snyder to writer

Marilyn Mercer and artists Nina Albright, Ann Brewster, Lina Buffolente, and Jean Levander—ensured that the Golden Age of comics had a significant number of stories about women that were created *by* women.

Conclusion

While rarely considered a prominent genre like superhero, crime, or horror comics, jungle titles were a forum throughout the Golden Age of comic books for not only strong female characters but also talented women creators. With so many of the comics analyzed in this chapter produced by Fiction House, it is fair to say that the publisher was one of the most vital to the medium's artistic and cultural growth. Fiction House hired more women than any other comics publisher, and it paid its employees equitably. Renée recalls, for instance, that she received the same Christmas bonus one year as male artist Nick Cardy (enough money, she says, to buy herself a suit, a fur-lined coat, and the ability to buy "everybody wonderful Christmas presents that year").[53] As Trina Robbins puts it,

> Not only did this company employ more women than any other comic publisher . . . but most of their pulp-style action stories either starred or featured strong, beautiful, competent heroines. They were war nurses, aviatrixes, girl detectives, counterspies, and animal skin-clad jungle queens, and they were in command. Guns blazing, daggers unsheathed, sword in hand, they leaped across the pages, ready to take on any villain. And they did not need rescuing.[54]

Though this excerpt rightly highlights the forgotten significance of Fiction House and its heroines in the shaping of Golden Age comics, there is still the less savory reality of the industry to consider—namely, that these empowered, autonomous women were almost exclusively white, and their empowerment, at least for jungle queens, came at the expense of other marginalized individuals. The United States that saw the heyday of the jungle queen in the 1940s was not far removed from the United States that openly celebrated lynchings as community gatherings. As Berenstein points out, jungle films of the early 1930s framed the jungle and its inhabitants as sinister and as direct threats to the innocence of white womanhood.[55] While Golden Age comics perpetuated images of the jungle as an exotic and unknowable place, they recast white women more often as saviors than as victims. This movement away from the explicit and near total representation of Blackness as a sexual, violent threat to delicate white women could be taken as a net positive for racial representation in American popular media, but the lasting damage done by the continued representation of African and Black characters as one-dimensional, seemingly primitive individuals in the comics industry at large cannot be ignored. Whatever positive strides jungle comics made for white female characters must be considered alongside the rampant racist and imperialist ideologies at work within them.

CHAPTER 3

CRIME COMICS

For much of the Golden Age, comics creators such as Charles Biro, Jack Cole, Joe Simon, and Jack Kirby found success with crime tales about mobsters, racketeers, goons, gangsters, and gun molls, many inspired by real-life figures. As superhero comics waned by the late 1940s, this new form of lurid storytelling quickly grew in popularity. But the rise of "true crime" comics brought with it new concerns over how women should be represented in stories centered on violent themes and imagery. Generally created by male writers and artists, many crime comics offered sensationalized stories that positioned women as little more than victims.

But women also played a key role in the early history of the crime genre, as both characters and creators. Policewomen like Toni Blum's Sally O'Neil and Claire S. Moe's crime-reporter Patty O'Day offered readers strong characters who were neither helpless victims nor sinister aggressors, but instead defenders and heroes. At the same time, other crime titles also offered a new take on the female protagonist (and her use of sexuality and violence) in the form of the femme fatale. Best known within Hollywood film noir and in crime novels by authors such as James M. Cain and Dorothy B. Hughes, the femme fatale role depicted women using their sexuality as well as their intellect to get who or what they wanted, no matter the cost. While many critics have read the femme fatale as a patriarchal construct, comics creators often used the character type as a way of exploring how questions of gender and sexuality intersected with themes of power and control in ways that few media did in the mid-century era.[1] Crime comics—a genre that profited off of images of dead female bodies, and that had a strong impact in shaping the cultural reception of comics in mid-century America—contained a range of complicated depictions of women between their pages, some offensive and others empowering. Crime comics are a vital case study of how a revisionist approach to the commonly held beliefs about a genre's origins can offer new insights into whose voices played a key part in that genre's development. By examining a genre's beginnings through new critical lenses and re-reading that history through the frameworks of gendered, racial, and sexual identity, we can upend our assumptions about the characters that helped shape particular themes and tropes and reclaim the forgotten creators whose influential work has been overlooked and marginalized.[2]

The Origins of Crime Comics: Sandra and the Two Sallies; Claire S. Moe and Toni Blum

Historical accounts of how crime comics emerged typically see them as drawing inspiration from the era's real-life newspaper headlines about hardened criminals, convicts, ringleaders, and bootleggers. Most versions of the genre's origins trace its beginnings to 1942's *Crime Does Not Pay* #22 from publisher Lev Gleason and writer/editors Charles Biro and Bob Wood. Its cover contained such taglines as "The First Magazine of Its Kind!" and "True Crime Cases," while an inside editorial proclaimed it "A Completely New Kind of Magazine."[3] Comics fans and historians alike have generally pointed to *Crime Does Not Pay* as the "first crime comic book," as Mike Benton does in *The Comic Book in America*, adding how "the second crime comic book" then followed in 1946 before "there were suddenly thirty-eight crime comics, or fifteen percent of all comic book titles" by 1948.[4]

But much as film noir eventually grew out of the detective and gangster films of 1930s Hollywood, crime comics of the 1940s had precursors of their own, many of them created by women like Claire S. Moe and Toni Blum. The first significant example of police officers battling crooks in comics came with the popular newspaper strip *Dick Tracy* by Chester Gould in 1931. With its literally square-jawed detective hero Dick Tracy serving as a heroic figure of rugged masculinity, the strip featured few women in its early years (besides girlfriend Tess Trueheart) who weren't cast in the victim role, kidnapped or killed by the latest crime boss in the name of serialized entertainment.

Drawing on *Dick Tracy*'s success, many of the earliest comic book publishers created titles about detectives or added crime-oriented features to their books in the mid-1930s. Major Malcolm Wheeler-Nicholson's *New Fun* (the first title from what would eventually become DC Comics, rebranded as *More Fun Comics* after six issues) featured "Sandra of the Secret Service" as the series' lead tale between 1935 and 1938, in *New Fun* #1 through *More Fun* #35, making her DC's first heroine.[5] The feature saw secret agent Sandra McLane battle spies around the world, beginning with the fictional European nation of Gavonia, where she encountered her doppelgänger—the Gavonian princess Yonda. While Charles Flanders is credited as the sole creator, Nicky Wheeler-Nicholson notes that her grandfather Malcom "most likely created the character" and wrote the early scripts: "Flanders is not known for creating characters, especially a woman heroine. . . . Sandra's character is in keeping with the heroines of Wheeler-Nicholson's pulp stories—beautiful, sophisticated, courageous and able to ride, shoot and outsmart a villain."[6]

In *New Fun* #2, Sandra disarms a gunman by throwing a chair at him before knocking the villain out with his own weapon, while in *More Fun* #7 she shoots two Gavonian kidnappers and rescues a pair of male government agents in the process. "You saved our lives, Sandra!" one says. "Nonsense!" she replies modestly, before adding on a practical note, "But say—let's hide this body and skip!"[7] Sandra led off each issue of *New Fun/More Fun* as its opening feature for three years, well before Superman and Batman became the stars of their own anthologies with *Action Comics* and *Detective Comics* in 1938 and 1939, respectively. While *More Fun* also offered the regular adventures of male heroes like Barry O'Neill, Don Drake, and Spike Spalding, Sandra maintained her page-one spot as the first hero in each issue until her final appearance in 1938's *More Fun* #35. Until then, she even held on to her front-runner status despite the series' addition of two different features by eventual Superman creators Jerry Siegel and Joe Shuster—"Doctor Occult" and "Radio Squad." The former first appeared in 1935's *New Fun* #6, while the latter debuted in 1936's *More Fun* #11, but nevertheless Sandra persisted as DC's first leading character through 1938; her saga finally came to an end three months after Superman's success in *Action Comics* #1 transformed the comic book marketplace.

Sandra's adventures were predated by another female crime fighter with ties to DC Comics—Sally the Sleuth. Debuting in the future DC-owner Harry Donenfeld's *Spicy Detective Stories* in 1934, Sally's exploits were told in two-page comics stories for a pulp magazine that otherwise contained mostly prose tales. This was a common tradition in 1930s pulp magazines, complicating our understanding of comics history given that

"Sandra of the Secret Service," *More Fun* #7, 1936, National Allied Publications Inc.

these features were not published in comic books. "Sally the Sleuth" was a pioneering crime comic about a female private eye that has been overlooked due to the limited understanding in comics scholarship about the connections between comic books and other publication formats such as pulp magazines in the early twentieth century. As Tim Hanley points out, Donenfeld's line of pulp mags regularly offered short comics with female heroes in the 1930s:

> The globetrotting "Diana Daw" fought villains and chased treasure in *Spicy Adventure Stories*, "Polly of the Plains" got up to cowboy hijinks in *Spicy Western Stories*, "Marcia of the Movies" had cinematic fun in *Saucy Movie Tales*, and *Spicy Mystery Stories* starred super-powered science fiction heroine "Olga Mesmer, the Girl With the X-Ray Eyes" before she was replaced with "Vera Ray," another cosmically powerful leading lady.[8]

Created by Adolphe Barreaux, Sally's adventures regularly rendered her in various stages of undress (if not fully naked). While titillation was at the heart of Donenfeld's magazines, Sally and her pulp-bred peers were complex figures in how they used their sexuality to actively entrap men, as well as their fists and their guns to take down evildoers. In *The Spectacular Sisterhood of Superwomen*, comics historian Hope Nicholson praises Sally as "one of the original female heroines in comics," noting that even though she often "ended up dressed in a sheer negligee, or was completely naked," Sally "usually managed to conceal a gun on her person, and she saved herself about as often as she needed to be rescued."[9] While she is subjected to sexual violence in many installments, Sally is not merely a passive damsel in distress. Rather, she regularly turns against her captors, punishing the men who sought to sexually exploit her—something few women could dream of doing to the men who abused them in this era (including, of course, comic book publishers like Donenfeld and Archer St. John, who sexually harassed their employees).

The crime genre was a popular one with comics publishers in the mid- to late 1930s. In 1936, Comics Magazine Co. offered a range of tales in *Detective Picture Stories*, including "Egan of the Homicide Squad," "Spurlock and Watkins," "Eddie Brannigan," and "The Police Patrol." In 1937, *Detective Comics* #1 arrived from Major Malcolm Wheeler-Nicholson's National Comics Publications (under its sister company, Detective Comics Inc., both of which were part of a later merger to form what became DC Comics).[10] While issue 27 of *Detective Comics* saw the debut of Batman two years later, the famous series began with the adventures of the harbor policeman Speed Saunders in its first issue, as well as two features created a year before Superman's first appearance by Jerry Siegel and Joe Shuster—"Bart Regan, Spy" and "Slam Bradley."

Centaur Publications followed with *Keen Detective Funnies* in 1938, which included early work by such notable male talents as Jack Cole, Will Eisner, and Joe Simon. Another talented creator who wrote crime tales for Centaur was Claire S. Moe, who came up with the feature "Dean Masters, D.A.," about a district attorney who solves murders and battles gangsters, for *Keen Detective Funnies* in 1939. While sometimes using the pseudonyms Vic Todd and Orville Wells in her work, she also signed many stories "Claire S. Moe," making her one of the earliest women in comics to forego a male pen name.[11]

Moe started her work in the crime genre with a tale called "Pal" about a heroic dog who rescues his owner after an attempted murder, which she wrote and drew for the fifth issue of *Detective Picture Stories* in 1937. She then did several crime stories in 1938 for Centaur's *Amazing Mystery Funnies*, including "The Yellow Terror" (#1), "Stolen Jewels" (#5), and "The Pardon" (#7). For Fox Feature Syndicate, Moe drew the adventures of crime-fighting reporter Patty O'Day for 1939's *Wonder Comics* and *Wonderworld Comics*. In *Wonder Comics* #2 O'Day travels to the Panama Canal and helps capture an Axis spy, and in the rebranded *Wonderworld Comics* #3, she shoots newsreel footage that is used to convict a burglar. Moe casts Patty as a public servant as well as a quick-witted reporter: when thanked for capturing the burglar, O'Day replies, "Nothing at all—we serve the public in any way we can."[12]

Moe then created Penny Wright, about a war correspondent reporter who regularly thwarted Axis spies in Europe with her keen wits and expert jujitsu skills, for Harvey's *Champion Comics* in 1940. While Lois Lane's reporting efforts lasted far longer in *Action Comics* than Wright's three-issue run in *Champion Comics*, Lane's efforts in this era were often a foil for Superman's heroic adventures; Lois often ended up in need of rescue. While Wright didn't gain her own series like Lane did (with

"Dean Masters, D.A.," *Keen Detective Funnies*, vol. 2, #11, Centaur Publications. Art by Claire S. Moe.

1958's *Superman's Girlfriend, Lois Lane*, a title that overtly reinforces male chauvinism), the solo efforts of a female reporter in a starring role at this time are worth heralding. While on assignment in France to track down an espionage ring run by a crooked fortune-teller named Nina in *Champion Comics* #4, Wright is kidnapped, tied up, and "dragged into

"Penny Wright," *Champion Comics* #4, 1940, Harvey Comics. Art by Claire S. Moe.

the vast catacombs beneath the city—where the dregs of the underworld are in hiding." First using the shards of her broken pocket mirror to cut through her rope bonds, Penny escapes by offering her captors a cigarette before thrusting the lit tip into one henchman's eye. When she is followed back to her hotel by another of Nina's spies, she hurls him to the floor with her jujitsu training before knocking him over the head with her typewriter. As the fortune-teller is led away by police, Wright tells her, "Well, Nina, your game is over. Better read your own palm now, your future looks bad!" The police captain thanks Patty for her efforts: "Miss Wright, you American girls certainly have spunk and brains. We are much indebted to you."[13]

Moe continued working in comics throughout much of the 1940s for the packaging houses Funnies Inc. and the Chesler shop, writing and/or drawing stories for titles from Fiction House, Lev Gleason Publications, and MLJ Magazines. She was soon joined by another early crime comics pioneer, Toni Blum, who created the character Sally O'Neil, Policewoman, in Quality Comics' *National Comics* #1 (1940) using the pseudonym Frank Kearn. Sally's first adventure appeared alongside patriotic characters such as Uncle Sam and Yankee Doodle Boy as well as such manly heroes as Paul Bunyan and Prop Powers. Sally was also surrounded by men within her own stories but continually proved to be their better. As a recent police academy graduate, O'Neil joins the force under her father, Sergeant O'Neil, alongside her two older brothers, Pat and Mike. Blum opens Sally's first appearance by describing her as a "two-fisted, sharp-shootin' gal" who is an expert marksman and a jujitsu expert, making her a powerful figure in the war against crime.[14]

Female law enforcement officers were still rare when Blum created Sally O'Neil: while 300 women served as police officers in 220 cities across the United States by 1919 (including the first African American female officer, Gertrude Robinson, hired that year by the Los Angeles Police Department), by 1950 women still comprised only 1 percent of the country's police force.[15] In turn, Blum deftly subverts numerous stereotypes in Sally's first appearance. Going undercover as a socialite to take down a criminal named Big Jim Saponi, Sally infiltrates his gang by flirting with one of his associates, Smilin' Joe Dukes. After accompanying Dukes to several night clubs as he becomes increasingly intoxicated (pouring out her own drinks into a nearby houseplant to maintain her edge), Sally joins Smilin' Joe at his apartment only to fight off his sexual advances. As he grasps at her, Sally fights back, grabbing him by the collar just as Saponi enters the room. "Now I'll take care of you, sister," Saponi barks, pointing his gun at her. Sally's brothers race up the stairs to the apartment, but Sally proves self-sufficient. She grabs the gun, uses her jujitsu training to throw Saponi to the floor, and then fires a warning shot with her own pistol as three henchmen rush toward her. "Everything's under control, boys!" says Sally as Pat and Mike burst into the room. "A sweet job, Sally!" Pat replies. Blum cements Sally's defiance of traditional gender norms in her

"Sally O'Neil, Policewoman," *National Comics* #1, 1940, Quality Comics. Written by Toni Blum.

narration: "Slowly, Big Jim recovers and stares at Sally with unbelieving eyes." In the panel's background, Saponi looks up at Sally while her high-heeled shoes dominate the foreground, visually emphasizing the inversion of power. Holding his head with one hand, he grumbles incredulously, "Licked! By a dame!" In the story's last panel, Sally shoots back, "Don't let the skirt fool you, Saponi! This cop is an O'Neil!"—emphasizing her equality despite the fact that she wears a differently gendered uniform than her male peers.[16]

Blum further upends how 1940s crime comics handled gender roles with her depiction of a female crime boss in *National Comics* #8 when Sally's captain places her undercover as a prison inmate to stop a "notorious woman criminal" named Broadway Flossie, who is going to leave the penitentiary in a few weeks."[17] As her brother drops her off at the prison, he cautions Sally not to underestimate her target just because she's a woman: "Don't think because she's a woman she's not dangerous . . . Broadway Flossie is tougher'n most men, and that's a fact!" he warns. "Sure, but those hard girls always have a soft spot somewhere. . . . I'll play on that and gain her confidence," Sally replies.[18] While this parallel between "hard" and "soft" traits perhaps undermines Flossie's strength, Blum's efforts to inject some complexity into how her female villain's morality is characterized subverts a strictly dualistic approach to femininity.

"Sally O'Neil, Policewoman," *National Comics* #8, 1941, Quality Comics. Written by Toni Blum.

Once they leave prison, Sally joins Flossie's gang: "I have no people, no place to go. I don't know what I'm going to do," Sally tells her. "You just string along with Flossie over here, I'll take care of you!" she promises.[19] Using Sally to lure the witness whose testimony sent Flossie away, the gang starts to suspect our hero's motives. "Listen you . . . if you're double-crossin' Broadway Flossie. . . . After all I was gonna do for you . . . why, you little . . ." says Flossie, slapping Sally across the face. Sally returns the favor, leveling Flossie with a powerful punch to the jaw ("Sally's police training proves too much for Flossie's temper" the narrator slyly tells us as Flossie is knocked down). Flossie is led back to prison, astonished that it was a female officer who caught her: "Well, I'll be. . . . A female copper."[20] Depicted as a tall, attractive blonde, Flossie offers a very different portrait of female villainy (one that anticipates the beauty of the femme fatale) than those encountered by *Dick Tracy* readers throughout the 1940s, with characters like Black Pearl, Mrs. Volts, and Mrs. Pruneface, who are usually older, either homely or outright disfigured women. With the femme fatale figure still in its infancy within American popular culture in 1941, Blum created a beautiful but deadly villain in Flossie well before the trope became commonplace in cinema and comics as the decade progressed.

Sally O'Neil proved to be a popular crime fighter: Blum wrote her adventures through 1942, but the character continued on for several years after her creator left. Sally appeared in every issue of *National Comics* through to its finale in 1949's issue 75—a nine-year run that lasted longer than most of the better-remembered comics with the word "crime" in their titles (including *Crime and Punishment* (1948–1955), *Crime Must Pay the Penalty* (1948–1956), *Crime SuspenStories* (1950–1955), *Real Clue Crime Comics* (1947–1953), and *True Crime Comics* (1947–1949).

The 1940s: Crime Pays

The many stories told by Blum, Moe, and other early comics creators about detectives, criminals, policewomen, and gang leaders in the late 1930s and early 1940s prove that the claim that the crime genre began with *Crime Does Not Pay* in 1942 is false. Much like how Benton calls it the "first crime comic book," Maurice Horn wrote in 1976 that *Crime Does Not Pay* is "usually regarded as the comic book industry's first 'crime' title" in *The World Encyclopedia of Comics*.[21] But early issues of *Crime Does Not Pay* regularly included western tales of history's greatest outlaws, including Billy the Kid and the Dalton Brothers, along with humorous gag strips like "This'll Kill You" and "Conny the Convict." Comedy legend Jimmy Durante even did a feature turn as a sidesplitting sleuth in issue 35, complicating the existing discourse from comics historians about how supposedly serious the series was, as when N. C. Christopher Couch describes *Crime Does Not Pay* as "a dark and violent comic book that seemed to match the postwar mood of lingering disillusionment."[22] For a series that many consider the first true crime comic, *Crime Does Not Pay* frequently contained a range of genres besides the hard-boiled crime tales that most see it as specializing in.

What *is* different about the title is the shift away from heroic protagonists in many of its stories; it instead offers stories about real criminals from the world outside readers' doorsteps and often draws on actual police files, or so readers are told. Issue 22 (actually the series' first issue, after taking over the numbering of the canceled *Silver Streak Comics*), begins with a tale called "Crime Kings—The Real Story Behind Lepke, Mad Dog of the Underworld," which chronicles New York mob boss Louis Buchalter. The first page features a mug shot–like rendering of "Lepke, alias Louis Buchalter" along with an "NYC Police" number board to heighten the perception of realism (as well as the editorial caption "Disgrace to the Human Race #1," further amplifying reader expectations for the scandalous events that follow).[23] Comics historian Dale Jacobs describes how *Crime Does Not Pay* used a "documentary style and purported educational intent" as a way to supposedly "deter readers from a life of crime through examples of where such a life would lead."[24] In their opening editorial, Biro and Wood stress that the comic is "dedicated to the youth of America with the hope that it will make them better, cleaner young citizens."[25] Their stated intent was a sham, of course, designed as a defense against critics by way of framing their lurid tales as edifying instead of injurious.

"Crime Kings," like many of the series' other stories, revolves mainly around men. It begins with Lepke in prison and uses flashbacks to tell its tale, in keeping with recent noir films such as *Stranger on the Third Floor* (1940), *A Woman's Face* (1941), and *I Wake Up Screaming* (1941). But whereas Sally O' Neil stories focus on the procedural steps taken to apprehend criminals and how her actions and instincts lead to an eventual arrest, *Crime Does Not Pay* uses its focus on lawbreakers to highlight acts of severe violence. The extremes of brutality seen with a criminal like Lepke using brass knuckles and throwing acid in victims' faces set the series apart from earlier crime comics. Serving as a template for future stories, "Crime Kings" is a prototypically male-centric tale of criminal enterprise and procedural policework that emphasizes the violent actions of men on both sides of the law.

Women, however, were not prominent characters in most issues, serving mostly as damsels in distress rather than as powerful figures like Flossie. Male gangsters dominated early issues of *Crime Does Not Pay*, including Dutch Schultz (#25), Lucky Luciano (#26), and Pretty Boy Floyd (#27). Women were usually victims on the series' early covers: issue 22 depicts a tommy gun–wielding gangster clutching a woman by the neck during a shoot-out, using her as a human shield as she struggles to get free (a similar scene is found on the cover of issue 35). Another issue (#24) depicts a man pushing a woman's face against a lit stove-burner as her hair goes up in flames, while another (#33) features a young woman kneeling before a man as he raises a butcher's cleaver, about to strike, with the bodies of five dead men hanging from nooses in the background.[26]

While the cover for issue 36 depicts a woman fleeing the police—a gun in each hand and a trail of dead bodies in her wake—no such story appears within the issue. The series offered few accounts of female criminals, often using them to focus on male detectives instead. Issue 39's tale, "Blonde Queen of Crime," tells of the "beautiful Casque D'or, female gang leader of Paris." The narrator uses fiery rhetoric in the opening moments to establish D'or as a powerful force in France's criminal underworld: "For years none knew of her gigantic criminal network and well indeed did she lead her kill-crazed puppets . . . but then an astonishing thing happened and her castle of crime toppled!"[27]

Yet as the story unfolds, the narrative doesn't emphasize D'or's motivations but rather the dutiful efforts of the male police captain who pursues her. "You are blonde and beautiful, Casque. . . . I could have easily loved you—but unfortunately you have sealed your own fate!" says Captain Lapoutre as he arrests her.[28] Other stories centered around women from past decades, like #28's "Wanted—Husband Who Won't Object to Being Murdered," about how Hera Bessarabo stuffed her husband's body in a trunk in 1920, and #44's "Mrs. Bluebeard," set in 1902 and about Belle Gunness's efforts to kill a string of different husbands for their money. But with their historical focus, such stories were never the feature draw of *Crime Does Not Pay*; readers bought the book for its contemporary focus on newsworthy criminals such as Buchalter, Luciano, and Schultz, not the murderers of bygone eras that filled out the back pages.

Its brutal focus on "the evil that men do" paid handsomely: *Crime Does Not Pay* grew from selling two hundred thousand copies per month in 1942 to seven hundred thousand per month by 1945.[29] But while Biro has been given most of the credit for the series' success, many stories were ghostwritten by Virginia Hubbell Bloch, who also wrote issues of *Boy Comics*, *Daredevil Comics*, and other Lev Gleason series. Several of the artists who worked with Biro recall Hubbell Bloch writing the majority of the stories credited to Biro; artist Pete Morisi describes him as an "egomaniac" who "liked to let on that he wrote everything, but he didn't. Ginny Hubbell wrote just about everything that Charlie Biro took credit for."[30]

The success of *Crime Does Not Pay* bred competition, including *Justice*, *Real Clue Crime*, and *True Crime Comics* in 1947. Many of these new titles began to incorporate women more regularly into their story lines to set themselves apart. *True Crime Comics* #2 included the infamous tale "Murder, Morphine and Me," written and drawn by Jack Cole (creator of the popular superhero Plastic Man), about a young drug addict. Controversial both in terms of its shocking imagery and its illicit content, the story was described by Art Spiegelman as having "become notorious as one of the most intense and delirious examples that the lurid genre had to offer."[31] An opening caption announces that the tale is supposedly told by a real-life drug trafficker named Mary Kennedy: "The True Confessions of a Dope Smuggler by Mary Kennedy." The story begins with a full-page collage of her face surrounded by an array of lurid images, including a large syringe,

"Mrs. Bluebeard," *Crime Does Not Pay* #44, 1946, Lev Gleason.

piles of cash, and a deadly shoot-out, along with what appears to be a group of tortured souls burning in Hell. "You can call me a tramp, a bum, but I'm gettin' this off my chest and you're gonna listen, see?" she begins. "I'm gonna tell you the whole ugly truth! About the isle of the dead—the derelicts of the drugs—the murders at the wholesale—and ME in the

"Murder, Morphine and Me," *True Crime Comics* #2, 1947, Magazine Village Inc.

middle! Who was the big boss of it all? You'll never guess, not in a million years," says Mary as one of the flame-stricken, cadaverous bodies tugs on the end of the giant needle.[32]

Panels from the story would soon be widely cited by critics, educators, and lawmakers as an example of the dangers of crime comics.[33] Few

"Murder, Morphine and Me," *True Crime Comics* #2, 1947, Magazine Village Inc.

believed publishers' claims that their crime comics made "better citizens" out of their readers, even when the message was explicit, as when Mary wraps up her tale in the final panel of "Murder, Morphine and Me" by declaring, "Mebbe now I can sleep . . . mebbe not . . . but if my story can show some unthinking souls the foolish folly of crime, I reckon it'll be worth it! Y'unnerstand?"[34] The story's sadism, drug addiction, and shocking abuse (seen in several panels where Mary is smacked repeatedly in the face) made "Murder, Morphine and Me" one of the most infamous stories to be featured in any Golden Age comic. Still, Spiegelman says, "I concede that this isn't Mother Goose, but I find the panel (part of a dream sequence, incidentally) emblematic of the comic book's visceral power to pass the reader's analytical defenses and pierce the brain."[35]

Despite facing a cultural backlash, the crime genre grew rapidly in popularity in the late 1940s. *Headline Comics* rebranded itself from an adventure title starring a group of young heroes called the Junior Rangers to a true crime comic in 1947 with its twenty-third issue. But while still chronicling history's greatest gangsters, such as John Dillinger, Pretty Boy Floyd, and Bugs Moran, *Headline Comics* also frequently included women as criminals, giving them the power to be read as more than just victims. The difference could be seen from the start on the series' covers: usually, either women were the central visual focus on the cover or their actions drove the conflict. Issue 26 sees a woman pointing a pistol at the man who double-crossed her, while issue 27 finds a gun-wielding woman taking charge in an operating room: "Stand back you sawbones!! I'm operating on this copper! . . . Only he won't be alive after I give 'im the lead treatment!" she proclaims.

While *Headline Comics* was also guilty of failing to include stories about the events shown on the cover, the series still offered readers an array of female criminals, such as "Stella Mae Dickson . . . The Bobby Sox Bandit Queen" (#27) and jewel-fencer Monica Bell (#28). The same was true of Simon and Kirby's follow-up series, *Justice Traps the Guilty*, which saw a woman named Kitty Cramer drawn into an insurance fraud racket in "I Was a Come-On Girl for Broken Bones Inc." (#1), mob-associate Cherry Romaine in "Gun Moll" (#2), and getaway driver Belle Munson in "Queen of the Speed-Ball Mob" (#4). When a detective cautions Munson about getting involved with the gang that her late brother also ran with, Munson forcefully asserts her independence: "Don't concern yourself with me, copper! I'm a big girl now—big enough to dispense with a cop playing nurse maid! Peddle that big-brother act elsewhere!" she sneers, Kirby's artwork rendering her face with numerous signals to drive home her point—widened eyes, furrowed brow, bared teeth.[36] While still often the victims of violence at the hands of men, *Headline Comics*' women were just as often the perpetrators of crimes as they were the casualties, allowing them a wider range of identities within the crime genre, much as Blum had done years before.

As crime comics flourished toward the end of the 1940s, Fox Feature Syndicate took Simon and Kirby's emphasis on female criminals a step further by building a new series around them. In 1948, *Crimes by Women* gave a starring role to some of history's most notorious women, beginning with Bonnie Parker. In "Bonnie Parker, Queen of the Gun Molls," the opening narration sets out how she "and her companion Clyde Barrow blazed a trail of blood and murder wherever they went. Only death itself could teach the cigar smoking gun girl the meaning of justice," we are told, as we see Parker shooting out the window of a moving car at two police officers.[37] When Clyde questions her at one point in the narrative, she quickly asserts her dominance: "Can it brother. A gal as tough as I am can do anything. Watch me." As their crime spree continues, the narration makes clear who is in charge: "Next they tried bank robbing. As usual, Bonnie ran the show."[38] Notice how the narrator's rhetoric regularly establishes a reinterpreted history of Bonnie and Clyde: she runs the show, and Barrow is her companion. Most historians believe that the real-life Parker accompanied Barrow in his criminal activities out of her desperate love for him, making her story in *Crimes by Women* a revisionist tale of female empowerment.[39]

The second issue features Belle Gunness, the same serial murderer seen

"Bonnie Parker: Queen of the Gun Molls," *Crimes by Women* #1, 1948, Fox Feature Syndicate.

two years earlier in *Crime Does Not Pay* #44. This time, however, the setting is updated to the modern era rather than the start of the twentieth century; as changes in post–World War II housing patterns led to the rise of suburbia, stories like this one can be read as reflecting tensions about the societal roles expected of women in this era. The tale begins with a caption establishing the location as "The Sorensen house in the Chicago suburbs," with Belle complaining that her husband only ever wants to sit around the house rather than taking her out on the town. "It's about time I got rid of that miserable excuse for a man," Belle says, plotting his demise. "I'll probably ruin my new dress, but it'll be worth it," she rationalizes while preparing to push a planter box onto his head from the second story as he returns home.

"Goodbye forever you lizard . . . Belle, you are about to become a free woman," she thinks to herself before killing her husband.[40] This notion of "freedom," although expressed in murderous terms, echoes the sentiment expressed fifteen years later by Betty Friedan in 1963's *The Feminine Mystique*; she tells of an unacknowledged "yearning" on the part of many women that leads to "the silent question—'Is this all?'"[41] Suburban domesticity was seen by many as the new definition of ideal femininity as

"Belle Gunness, The Monster of Laporte," *Crimes by Women* #2, 1948, Fox Feature Syndicate.

many working women gave up their jobs to returning soldiers, leading to a loss of identity for many women. Friedan describes a missing "independence" and "opportunity" on the part of many mid-century American women, noting how the "suburban housewife" embodied "the dream image of the young American woman and the envy, it was said, of women all over the world."[42] These tensions reverberate in *Crimes by Women*; stories about murderers like Belle Gunness (as well as in many crime and horror tales from EC Comics in the years that followed) played on this new shift in society's expectations about gender roles.

The 1950s: *It Rhymes with Lust* and the Femme Fatale

With such series as *Crimes by Women* expanding the roles played by female characters in the genre, crime comics began telling more extensive stories about women as the 1950s dawned. In turn, comics turned to a character trope that crime films and novels had leaned on heavily throughout the 1940s—the femme fatale. Found in many of Hollywood's most popular film noir efforts, including *The Maltese Falcon* (1941), *Murder My Sweet* (1944), *Mildred Pierce* (1945), and *The Big Sleep* (1946), the femme fatale was embodied by screen stars like Barbara Stanwyck in *Double Indemnity* (1944), Rita Hayworth in *Gilda* (1946), and Lana Turner in *The Postman Always Rings Twice* (1946). Noir narratives regularly depict a male protagonist risking his life or career for a beautiful woman who proves deceptive and/or deadly, with the femme fatale usually tied to themes of risk and betrayal. Often depicted as resilient and resourceful, the femme fatale is just as often rendered manipulative and amoral. Such contradictions have led Julie Grossman to argue in *Rethinking the Femme Fatale in Film Noir* that these fatale characters are marked by far more "complexity" than most commentators acknowledge. The femme fatale, says Grossman, embodies "sexualized and/or highly intelligent and competent women" who deserve to be read in "more nuanced and sympathetic" ways."[43]

One of the most significant examples of comic book noir arrived in 1950 with the publication of *It Rhymes with Lust*. "She was greedy, heartless and calculating. She knew what she wanted and was ready to sacrifice anything to get it," reads the cover caption, alongside an image of a beautiful redhead in a revealing black dress. Described as "An Original Full-Length Novel" on the cover, which also features a banner with the phrase "Picture Novels" across the top, *It Rhymes with Lust* is a prototype of the graphic novel (if not actually the first) and a vital example of how the comics medium handled the femme fatale trope.[44]

Written by Arnold Drake and Leslie Waller, penciled by Matt Baker, inked by Ray Orson, and edited by Marion McDermott for St. John Publications, the book opens with a hapless reporter named Hal Weber clutching a "battered suitcase" and tugging "nervously at his hat brim" while stepping off of a train. He arrives in Copper City to start a new job as editor in chief of a local newspaper, a position offered to him by an old flame named Rust Masson as part of her plan to control the town. The recent widow of a powerful mine owner, Rust uses Hal as a pawn as she seeks to further her own corporate and political fortunes: "Follow him as he weaves through a tangled net of double-cross, dynamite and disaster with a woman who bartered torrid kisses for his soul, a man who spoke with a .38 automatic, and a girl in whose shining eyes he saw reflected the tattered rags of conscience," the narrator proclaims as the story begins.[45]

An early narrative caption spells out Rust's fatale qualities: "Her

Cover of *It Rhymes with Lust*, 1950, St. John Publications.

perfume was heady and seductive. The touch of her fingers arousing. There had always been something irresistible about Rust. He had never been able to put her out of his mind, even after she walked out on him many years ago . . . without saying goodbye."[46] Drake describes *It Rhymes with Lust* as "essentially a 'B film' on paper,"[47] and the dialogue that he and Waller used in crafting their portrayal of Rust as a femme fatale is certainly in line with that found in the best noir B movies, including *Detour* (1945), *My Name Is Julia Ross* (1945), and *Gun Crazy* (1950), all of which revolve around formidable women.

Unable to resist Rust's advances, Hal agrees to help in her illicit political maneuvers despite himself, eventually becoming involved in a murder plot involving one of Masson's rivals, Marcus Jeffers. The narrator tells us,

> He had a nagging suspicion that he was being played with as a cat plays with a mouse. Rust told him what to do, but not *why*. What peculiar power did she still wield over him after all these years? Why

> didn't he just walk out on her? But he knew his desire to be with her again was too strong.[48]

When his conscience finally catches up with him, Weber pens a newspaper exposé outlining Rust's corrupt efforts. Her retaliation proves to be her undoing, as Rust and her gun-toting henchmen try to take control of her angry miners by force: "Power belongs to whoever has the guts to take it! Not to those who whimper and whine and then sit home on election day. We'll rule as long as we live! Do you know how to take control and keep it? With bullets not ballots," she cries from atop a mining bucket high above the restless crowd.[49] But when Jeffers seeks his revenge by turning on the conveyor system, Rust falls to her death. Weber is hailed as a hero for his efforts, while romance blooms between Hal and Rust's step-daughter Audrey: "I don't think I ever loved her," Hal rationalizes to Audrey. "Real love has to be returned. And Rust couldn't love anything but power. She named herself well . . . 'Rust.' It rhymes with lust. The mad lust for power that finally destroyed her. But we've got to forget her now," Hal tells Audrey before they kiss.[50]

Even though Hal becomes an eventual hero, the book revolves around Rust; her actions drive the book's narrative and its central conflicts, and she is the only character featured on the book cover. Much like in *Crimes by Women*, Rust's sexuality is emphasized strongly as a way of luring newsstand readers. But while Baker's artwork consistently depicts Rust as attractive and sensuous, he keeps her hair androgynously short throughout. In one scene, she wears riding pants while clutching a crop as she and Hal embrace, with Baker's shadowy art stripping Rust of traditional feminine signifiers as we view her from behind while they kiss.

The strategic steps that Baker takes in his artwork to position Rust in a way that forces readers to look beyond the gender binary are far more broad-minded than how Charles Biro treated nonnormative gender presentation in the early 1940s. In 1943's *Boy Comics* #9, the youthful hero known as Crimebuster faces a villain called He-She who embodies both male and female attributes, with the left and right halves of their body each containing either feminine or masculine features (i.e., from their left side, He-She looks like a woman, while from the right they look like a man). Biro literally presents the character as being soulless, referring to them with the pronoun "it" several times: "This is the story of a thing—neither man nor woman. A person? Yes! With a soul? No! He or she, call it what you will, lives in these pages and you will have the precious key to the inner secrets of its existence!"[51] Biro's dehumanizing treatment of the gender-fluid villain ("Strip my gears and call me shiftless! It's a . . . a . . .

It Rhymes with Lust, 1950, St. John Publications.

what is it?" Crimebuster cries upon first meeting He-She) is a stark contrast from the ways in which the crime genre frequently allowed for more complex and constructive representations of gender identity.[52] While it is possible that Hubbell Bloch wrote the story, the concept was still likely Biro's, given his editorial role on the series.

While *It Rhymes with Lust* shares many of the same themes as other

"Crimebuster Meets He-She," *Boy Comics* #9, 1943, Comic House Inc.

mid-century crime comics and noir films about women, a key difference separates Rust from other representations of the femme fatale. Unlike most other fatal females, Rust is not scheming simply to avoid punishment or to gain a modicum of power—she already has immense wealth and influence, and seeks to consolidate her power over a town that she already controls. When Jeffers confronts her, Rust quickly puts him in his place: "I own this town, Marcus. I own the mines, the banks, everything. And I own the political machine, too. People have been fooling themselves long enough. *I* boss the machine, I always will. You're through, Marcus . . . all washed up!"[53] With Baker's art adding layers of visual nuance to the representation of Rust's sexuality and the novel-length story affording the room for detailed character development, *It Rhymes with Lust* is a landmark example of how crime comics could potently challenge expectations about the genre's female characters.

One of the most popular crime titles of this era was *Crime SuspenStories* (1950–1955), published by EC Comics. The company was founded as Educational Comics in 1944 by Maxwell Gaines, offering historically based series such as *Picture Stories from Science* and *Picture Stories from the Bible*. But in 1947, Gaines died in a motorboat accident and his son William took over the company; William shifted the focus to more lurid (and better-selling) genres such as crime and horror under the new name Entertaining Comics.[54]

Artist Johnny Craig describes how by the early 1950s, the opportunity to draw female characters in the burgeoning crime genre was of great appeal: "I think at this point my girls, my females were beginning to improve, to look a little prettier. It began to be a pleasure to draw them. I deliberately wrote stories where I could draw one woman rather than have a whole slew of other characters all over the place."[55] As a result, Craig's stories for *Crime SuspenStories* offered readers an array of femme fatale characters, often drawn "prettier" than usual. Many stories in various EC titles also contained sexual innuendoes, albeit subtle ones. Al Feldstein, an artist, writer, and editor for EC Comics, recalls,

> Fiendishly diabolical guys that we were, we were always trying to slip stuff in that the sharpies would see, and maybe we wouldn't get caught. In those days sex was. . . . Tropic of Cancer hadn't been published yet, you know, and there was still a big fuss going on about all that, and so we did suggestive things when we could.[56]

Despite its male artists' intent to slip sex into their stories and to draw pretty girls whenever possible, the working conditions at EC Comics proved much more hospitable to female creators than those of other companies in the period. Unlike Lily Renée's encounters of sexual harassment at Fiction House and St. John Publications, artist Marie Severin recalls the mood at EC Comics being much different. "You felt like you could do your work without someone standing over you. . . . It was a nice atmosphere and you weren't afraid to go to the boss. You felt like you could talk to these people. . . . You had a good rapport," she says.[57] Severin, who worked as a colorist at EC Comics before becoming a penciller and inker at Atlas/Marvel Comics, notes, "I was the only gal [at EC], but they all loved it when I colored their stuff. They didn't see my work as competition, but rather as a complement to theirs."[58]

Crime SuspenStories and its companion title, *Shock SuspenStories*, allowed the crime genre to shift away from emphasizing real-life criminals to presenting stories inspired by noir films and other types of crime fiction. The story "Death's Double-Cross" from *Crime SuspenStories* #1 set the tone for the series, as housewife Ruth Blakely laments her marriage to businessman husband John ("I'll be home late, Ruth! Don't wait up for me! You know how these board meetings are!" he tells her). Echoing Friedan's question "Is this all?," Ruth realizes after two years of wedlock that her identity has been subsumed by her marriage: "To John, I was the perfect wife . . . a picture to grace his luxurious home . . . another of his 'possessions'!"[59] So when she turns to John's twin brother, Ronald, for comfort, the pair plot to murder John and take over his identity. But once the deed has been done, Ruth becomes suspicious about which man is really which, growing increasingly paranoid by the end as she wonders if her new husband is really John and if he is now trying to kill her. In the final panel, Ruth's doubts leave the reader with more questions than answers:

> So you see! I think he's trying to kill me! Of course, these incidents might have been accidents. . . . I don't know! But . . . what can I think! Who am I married to now? Ronnie, who killed my husband . . . then had his mole removed? Or John, who overheard our plan and decided to act first . . . drowned Ronnie, donned a false mole, had it conveniently "removed" . . . and is now trying to punish me by killing me? How can I know? I'm scared I'm sick. . . . I don't know! Do you?[60]

"Death's Double-Cross" offered readers little in the way of overt violence, building psychological tension in its place as a way of offering a more extensive character study in malice and immorality. In *The Dark Night Returns: The Contemporary Resurgence of Crime Comics*, Terrence Wandtke describes the series' recurring focus "on the insatiable greed and stymied desires of its characters" in its "urban and suburban stories of criminal schemes gone horribly wrong, most often plotted by spouses and ordinary people." Rather than historical accounts of notorious gangsters and murderers, the focus in *Crime SuspenStories* is on the everyperson and the innate capacity for evil that lies within. Whereas series like *Crime Does Not Pay* typically stressed the violent actions of their subjects, EC crime stories emphasized the psychological motivations of their characters. Wandtke notes how EC's tradition of twist endings "accentuated the crime but did not always result in capture by the often ineffectual and morally suspect authorities; if the criminals next door were caught, their undoing had much more to do with their own fear and paranoia."[61]

While the crime genre by now lacked the strong voices that creators such as Blum and Moe had provided for their female crime fighters in years past, the addition of series like *Crimes by Women* and the new

"Death's Double-Cross," *Crime SuspenStories* #1, 1950, EC Comics.

psychological focus of EC titles like *Crime SuspenStories* and *Shock SuspenStories* offered readers relatively more nuanced depictions of women than titles like *Crime Does Not Pay* did throughout the 1940s. As lurid and as gruesome as many of EC's stories were, their comics often gave female characters more of a voice than many other crime series of the era.

Even if women were still killed or punished in the end, their characterization was frequently more nuanced, connecting them to current social contexts in a way that series focused on history's greatest gangsters did not. In turn, characters like Ruth in "Death's Double-Cross" could be reinterpreted through the emergent lens of second-wave feminism in the years that followed.

Conclusion

As the genre entered a new decade, crime comics faced a new foe that soon threatened to wipe them out entirely. As crime titles reached their apex in the early 1950s, the genre was increasingly described by cultural critics such as Fredric Wertham as a home for depravity and perversion, becoming closely tied to rising concerns over juvenile delinquency.[62] Comics historian Carol Tilley notes that Wertham was but one of many voices decrying comics in this era: "A mix of teachers, parents, literary critics, librarians, religious leaders, medical personnel, and others weighed in on the value of comics reading."[63] In 1948, Judith Crist's article "Horror in the Nursery" for *Collier's* magazine attacked comic books "which attempt to make violence, sadism and crime attractive, which ignore common morals, which appeal chiefly to the worst in human nature."[64] In chronicling Wertham's efforts to sound the alarm about the dangers of comics in her article, Crist draws specific attention to how women are represented, but in so doing reveals more about how mid-century America envisioned traditional gender roles and the rights of women to determine their own beliefs about sex and sexuality:

> It isn't accidental, researchers claim, that all comic book women are high-chested, full-hipped and given to appearing in any place at any time in abbreviated sarongs or French bathing suits. "There is a deliberate attempt," Dr. Wertham points out, "to emphasize sexual characteristics. Any normal kid is bound to be stimulated by the gorgeous gals. But the destructive thing is that such stimulation is abnormal and unhealthy because the sex desires are mixed with violence."
>
> The comic books' constant emphasis on sexual characteristics, studies have shown, can lead to erotic fixations of all kinds. "For boys," a Lafargue psychiatrist warned, "the results are a perverted ideal of feminine allure. . . . For girls the results are frequently a feeling of inferiority and insufficiency, simply because the adolescent

girl does not have the full bosom and rounded hips of the comic book. Even more dangerous is the adolescent girl's fear of sex and her sometimes resultant frigidity."[65]

From the hyperbole behind sweeping statements about "all comic book women" on display here to the concern that comics might make young women act "frigidly" toward their eventual husbands, Crist's discourses surrounding the role of comics in young women's development are questionable, and at all times uphold Wertham's views on comics as absolute. But Fredric Thrasher, a professor of education at New York University, wrote a scathing critique of Wertham and his peers for the *Journal of Educational Sociology* in 1949 in which he accused anti-comics crusaders of a perpetuating a "fallacy which stems from professional bias or a lack of scientific logic and research, or both." In "The Comics and Delinquency: Cause or Scapegoat," Thrasher writes, "Wertham's dark picture of the influence of comics is more forensic than it is scientific and illustrates a dangerous habit of projecting our social frustrations upon some specific trait of our culture, which becomes a sort of 'whipping boy' for our failure to control the whole gamut of social breakdown."[66] Thrasher saw the moral panic surrounding comic books at the century's midpoint as just one of many that targeted various media throughout prior decades:

> The current alarm over the evil effects of comic books rests upon nothing more substantial than the opinion and conjecture of a number of psychiatrists, lawyers and judges. True, there is a large broadside of criticism from parents who resent the comics in one way or another or whose adult tastes are offended by comics stories and the ways in which they are presented. These are the same types of parents who were once offended by the dime novel, and later by the movies and the radio. Each of these scapegoats for parental and community failures to educate and socialize children has in turn given way to another as reformers have had their interest diverted to new fields in the face of facts that could not be gainsaid.[67]

But Wertham's critique of comics continued to gain strength in the early 1950s, leading to both his testimony before the Senate Subcommittee on Juvenile Delinquency and the publication of *Seduction of the Innocent* in 1954. Gaines also testified, but his exchange with senators about the boundaries of good and bad taste surrounding the cover of *Crime SuspenStories* #22, in which an ax murderer holds the severed head of a woman whose body is laying on the floor, proved especially damning. In *Fredric*

Wertham and the Critique of Mass Culture, Bart Beaty explains, "The negative reaction to this particular exchange harmed the comic book defenders as much or more than anything Wertham testified to, especially as it seemed to prove that comics publishers were out of touch with the concerns of the day."[68]

Later that same year, the Comics Code Authority was established by the Comics Magazine Association of America (CMAA) as a way for publishers to prove to lawmakers and the public alike that these concerns were being taken seriously. In *Seal of Approval: The History of the Comics Code*, comics scholar Amy Kiste Nyberg describes how the code was the "enforcement arm" of the CMAA, designed to give "the appearance of self-regulation" and avoid government regulation of the comics industry.[69] Publishers highlighted the code's official seal on covers or the first page of their titles: Charlton Comics featured a statement at the top of page one alongside the seal, for instance, that read,

> This seal of approval appears only on comics magazines which have been carefully reviewed, prior to publication, by the Comics Code Authority, and found to have met the high standards of morality and good taste required by the Code. The Code Authority operates apart from any individual publisher and exercises independent judgment with respect to Code-compliance. A comic magazine bearing its seal is your assurance of good reading and pictorial material.[70]

Graphic violence and gory imagery were prime targets of the code, as were lust and sexuality. Crime comics were also specifically addressed in the code's rhetoric, with strict limits placed on how criminals could be portrayed and even how large the lettering of the word "crime" could be on the cover.

At EC Comics, Gaines felt that he and his crime/horror titles were being specifically targeted by the CCA, forcing him to try new approaches in his line of books. In turn, sales suffered. As Gaines noted years later, there was a direct correlation between how lurid and outrageous a given issue's cover and content were and how well it sold. "It fell just about the way you could predict: The most shocking books sold the best, and then the next most shocking book sold the next best, and so on."[71] The company only survived by abandoning comics entirely and transitioning its hit humor comic *Mad* into the magazine format, which was not bound by the CCA. Even though the CMAA and the CCA held no legal authority, many distributors required their seals of approval if comics were to reach newsstands. Several publishers canceled titles dealing in murder and the macabre, while others went out of business.

By 1955, most crime comics were gone, and with them the potential for nuanced renderings of female criminals. The Comics Code included specific efforts to curb the sexuality of female characters, including such standards as "All characters shall be depicted in dress reasonably acceptable to society" and "Females shall be drawn realistically without exaggeration of any physical qualities."[72] In the United States, the genre would have to wait several decades to again approach its potential for sophisticated representations of gender and sexuality, as displayed by books like *It Rhymes with Lust*, which proved ahead of its time in both its format and its depiction of female power.

CHAPTER 4

HORROR COMICS

Much like superhero sagas, jungle adventures, and crime thrillers, weird tales of horror and suspense were formative to the development of comics' Golden Age. From the late 1940s through the mid-1950s, dozens of horror comics with titles promising strange, forbidden, terrifying, startling, weird, mysterious, and unusual stories flooded onto the market from nearly every major comic book publisher. Like many comics of this era—especially crime, fantasy, and science fiction titles—horror comics grew out of the tradition of the pulp magazine.[1] The horror comics of the Golden Age, similar to the weird menace mags and shudder pulps of the 1930s and early 1940s, are rife with tales of ghastly ghouls, half-nude damsels, vengeful wives, cheating husbands, sadistic sorcerers (and sorceresses), and all manner of fiends and freaks.

Pulp magazines and comic books were not the first forms of popular media to bring tales of terror to mass audiences. Horror comics, however, made these stories accessible to a wide range of readers (including children) in a way that made the stories both wildly successful and highly criticized.[2] Though it was widely understood that the shudder pulps targeted a more mature audience, with their stories of sexual sadism and gruesome criminality, comics courted a diverse readership—young and old, and of all genders. Most titles avoided directly addressing one segment of an audience or another, and the diversity of advertisements within their pages reveals how many horror comics were aimed at a wide range of demographics.[3] It wasn't uncommon to see lingerie, sequined skating costumes, *How to Become a He-Man* exercise guides and novelty prank toys advertised in the same issue of a comic. While horror titles have long held a poor reputation for featuring unkind representations of women, publishers targeted readers equally, which is part of why the genre drew such heavy criticism. More often than not, these comics retained the more adult aesthetic and themes of the shudder pulps while still catering to adolescent—if not younger—audiences.

Early titles such as *Weird Comics* (a title reminiscent of the popular pulp magazine *Weird Tales*) struggled to walk the line between adult and adolescent interests. The title, published by Fox Feature Syndicate, debuted in 1940, right around the time that the popularity of the pulps began to wane. It ran for twenty issues until its cancellation in 1942, a full six years before the premiere of American Comics Group's *Adventures into the Unknown* (considered by many to be the first true horror comic book). For all twenty issues, *Weird Comics* featured stories about the same recurring cast of characters, a move reminiscent more of superhero titles than of either the shudder pulps or the later, more established horror comics. It's apparent from the covers of each issue alone that *Weird Comics* struggled to find a place for its protohorror stories and noncommittal pulpy aesthetics in the comics industry of the early 1940s. While the first five issues of the series bear cover art featuring half-nude damsels in distress and deformed fiends that wouldn't be out of place in the pages of any of the popular pulps, the covers of the other fifteen issues depict masked men fighting alongside the police.

Although *Weird Comics* ultimately failed to bring horror to a mainstream audience in the early 1940s, the title's female characters are worth examining for the ways in which they reflected and challenged both existing and future character tropes in the horror comics genre. The Sorceress of Zoom is the only female character with her own story title within the series, and she's easily the most complex female character. Her stories, published under the house name Sandra Swift (but likely written by Don Rico, who drew the character and frequently wrote scripts in this era), see the Sorceress of Zoom seeking world domination, pausing to fight the Axis powers, and then taking up her evil ways once again. She is, of course, a beautiful and scantily clad woman, but her magical abilities are emphasized as her ultimate source of power; early in the series, she rarely used her feminine wiles to persuade others to do her bidding, but when *Weird Comics* became more of a superhero title, she created a human alter ego who charms men with her sexuality.

Given the Sorceress' relatively high level of autonomy, the choice to print the Sorceress of Zoom's adventures under the pseudonym Sandra Swift seems puzzling. Publishing stories of a comparably independent woman under a female name lends credence to readings of the character

"Sorceress of Zoom," *Weird Comics* #2, 1940, Fox Feature Syndicate.

as an early pseudofeminist figure in the horror/weird stories realm of the comics industry. However, the reality of her origins (that she was created and written by a man) problematizes that reading. The Sorceress can still be read as a figure of empowerment, but the fact that her creator was a man highlights the unfortunate reality of women artists and writers in the industry. Though their pages may have held tales of women who controlled their own lives, the vast majority of *Weird Comics*' (and most other horror titles') contributors were men.

There were other recurring female characters, too, who occupied important roles in stories that ostensibly revolved around male characters. The Dr. Mortal stories, for instance, supposedly follow the ghastly goings-on of the titular Dr. Mortal, but it is his niece, the sleuthing Marlene, that each story actually follows. Cecelia, a serpent monster turned sidekick, serves alongside the underwater explorer Typhon, and Dr. Bob Warren of the Voodoo Man stories keeps himself surrounded by all manner of women, both monstrous and mortal. Their beauty—or monstrosity, in the case of the native Haitian women in the Voodoo Man stories—is always emphasized, and romance is a near constant plot element, but the women of *Weird Comics* are rarely just one thing, whether helpless, empowered, good, or evil. They aren't straightforward damsels in distress or evil temptresses, even though they're not often terribly complex characters. More so than in many other genres, the horror titles of the Golden Age didn't have much room for characters who could be easily pigeonholed. Many of its characters, regardless of gender, fit into recognizable tropes and categories, but the horror genre also made space for female characters who challenged prevailing notions of traditional femininity and respectability.

Female Horror Creators: June Tarpé Mills and Lily Renée

Although Fox Feature Syndicate may not have created opportunities for female artists and writers of horror tales, there *were* women working within the genre from its inception who helped shape many of its tropes. In fact, the shudder pulps that the horror comics genre grew out of were more hospitable to female creators than many Golden Age publishers were. *Weird Tales* magazine in particular frequently published the work of female artists in the 1930s; illustrator Margaret Brundage created every one of the magazine's cover illustrations from June 1933 to August 1936, and her work continued to appear on the magazine's cover throughout the 1940s. While there were popular female writers who contributed to the pulps, Brundage is one of the more famous and controversial examples of women working in the industry in the 1930s and 1940s. Her illustrations were consistently provocative and sexual, and she wasn't identified as a woman to readers until well into her tenure at *Weird Tales*, when the controversy surrounding her illustrations was already well established.

Brundage wasn't the only contributor to conceal her gender, though. C. L. Moore, one of the most popular female authors to emerge from this particular pulp, carefully concealed her gender from her readers. The tradition of women working in the horror genre under male (or ambiguous) names continued in the early years of the comic book industry. In 1938, June Tarpé Mills began her comics career at Centaur Publications by forgoing her first name, signing her work Tarpé Mills. Her early work spanned a range of genres, in keeping with the "something for everyone" approach found in most comic books of the 1930s. In series such as *Amazing Man Comics* and *Amazing Mystery Funnies*, Centaur offered readers an array of science fiction, superhero, jungle, detective, western, and adventure tales, much like titles from other publishers (including *Action Comics* and *Marvel Comics*) did. Between 1938 and 1939, Mills was the writer/artist on such features as "Diana Deane" in *Funny Pages* and *Star Comics*, "Daredevil Barry Finn" in *Amazing Mystery Funnies*, and "Cat-Man" in *Amazing Man Comics*. Although horror stories weren't common in comics of the 1930s, Mills wrote and drew two early tales of terror: "The Vampire" and "The Ivy Menace."

"The Vampire" follows the narrative template set out in horror films from earlier in the decade, such as *The Vampire Bat* (1933), in which a rural European village is faced with a string of mysterious killings. Mills begins this tale from *Amazing Mystery Funnies* volume 2, issue 2, by setting up a legend about a vampire who supposedly lives in a cave in the mountains near "the peaceful little village of Salano—near the south of Sicily." The vampire, legend has it, "awakens every hundred years to prey upon the villagers for a fresh supply of life-sustaining blood." Before introducing the story's characters, Mills uses two panels that offer readers some familiar imagery: one of a vampire bat, the other of a sinister-looking, caped man with clawlike fingers. "The vampire is said to have the power of returning in either the form of a bat—or in the form of a man," we are told across the two panels. This exposition not only establishes the generic expectations for readers early in the story but also sets the stakes for the twist ending to come.

When two people are found dead, each with a pair of tiny holes in their necks, the village fears the return of the vampire who once stalked their land. While many barricaded themselves indoors at night, one young couple chooses to meet by moonlight—while a vampire bat circles above. When one of the young lovers is found dead the next morning, efforts are mounted to seal up the cave where the vampire is thought to reside. Large stones are used so that "not a single crevice was left unplugged," while a large cross is erected in front of the entrance by some of the townswomen. Further precautions are also taken: "The women had also made crude wreaths of horsehair—said to have the magic power of keeping the vampire away—and these were hung over every door." But despite their efforts, the villagers awake the next day to find a heap of slaughtered sheep and cattle. A woman sobs, "Is nothing safe from this demon? Now our cattle are being killed. . . . I tell you, he'll kill us all; either by taking our life's blood or by starvation. It's the curse of the devil on us and we will be wiped from the face of the earth!"

"The Vampire," *Amazing Mystery Funnies*, vol. 2, #2, 1939, Centaur Publications. Story and art by June Tarpé Mills.

The tale comes to an end as a "ragged old beggar" tries to snatch a woman's baby while she works in a nearby field. "Ah—fresh blood! Young blood!" sneers the sinister-looking beggar, his face bathed in shadows despite the sunny setting. When the police arrive, they notice something peculiar about the man: "Say look at his two front teeth. He has filed them down to look like needle points!" a constable tells us. In the story's final panel, the police captain announces that "the vampire's reign of terror" has ended,

> as it wasn't a vampire at all who committed those crimes! It was the old beggar, who at one time was a highly respected professor at a college in one of the Northern cities of Italy! He had made quite a study of superstitions and legends about vampires until, unfortunately, he went insane and was committed to a sanitarium—where he has been for the last fifteen years! Recently, he escaped and knowing of the

> legend of this village, he made his way to Salano, thinking he was the vampire and hoping that with the blood of youthful victims, he would regain his youth and attain immortality![4]

This lengthy passage of dialogue reframes the story with its surprise ending, a common trope in horror films at the time: *The Mark of the Vampire* (1935), for instance, reveals in the final scene that what we thought were vampires were actually actors. EC Comics later used this strategy in most of its stories across multiple genres; the horror, crime, and science fiction tales that the publisher is best known for regularly finished with a twist. This kind of conclusion is also known as an "O. Henry ending," named after American short story writer William Sydney Porter (who used the pen name O. Henry and specialized in ending his stories with a surprising revelation).[5] Series such as *Tales from the Crypt* and *Vault of Horror* may be better remembered by comics fans and historians, but Tarpé Mills pioneered their hallmark narrative strategy more than ten years before their 1950 debut.

Mills created another horrific tale that would have been at home at EC Comics in 1939: "The Ivy Menace" from *Amazing Man Comics* #6. When a scientist creates an experimental formula "to promote gigantic growth of crops with a minimum of land," his discovery turns disastrous when his cat knocks over the vial and spills "its precious contents down the ivy covered wall" of the old mansion.[6] The ivy quickly grows out of control, its giant vines strangling the scientist as it consumes the house and begins to spread for miles on end. In two panels, Mills draws a giant skeleton looming large over the city skyline, a metaphor for the widespread death caused by the ivy as it buries the entire town and collapses the George Washington Bridge into the Hudson River. Like many films of the 1930s (including 1933's *The Invisible Man* and 1936's *The Invisible Ray*), "The Ivy Menace" blurs the lines between the horror and sci-fi genres. It even evokes Orson Welles's infamous "War of the Worlds" radio broadcast, which panicked many listeners in 1938 into believing that a martian invasion was underway: "A bunch of people must be listening to another 'Worsen Welds' radio dramatization," an officer jokes while fielding phone calls from fearful residents as the ivy grows far and wide, devastating everything in its path.

The story lacks a twist ending, offering readers only a series of shocking events: patients escape from a psychiatric hospital and assault the public, Grand Central Station is overrun with a million people seeking to escape New York City, and "huge skyscrapers collapse as the city's slums lie smothered beneath the seething, twisting plant." The ivy is finally stopped

"The Ivy Menace," *Amazing Man Comics* #6, 1939, Centaur Publications. Story and art by June Tarpé Mills.

by a relentless aircraft bombing campaign, leaving NYC "in ruins while the raging fires reduce it to ashes."[7] The story's bleak tone and alarming imagery—in one panel, an escaped inmate looms over a mother and child with a club in his hand and an ominous smile—anticipates the cross-genre "jolting tales of tension" in the EC series that were at the heart of cultural concerns about the moral impact of comic books on the nation's youth, such as *Shock SuspenStories*. Together, her 1939 efforts "The Ivy Menace" and "The Vampire" make Mills a pioneering creator of horror comics at a time when superhero comics were first learning to fly.

In 1940, Mills left Centaur to begin work on new features for the Eastern Color Printing Company. Along with the adventures of "Mann of India," Mills debuted "The Purple Zombie" in the pages of 1940's *Reg'lar Fellers Heroic Comics* #1. Combining the horror and crime genres (a common pattern in horror films of the early 1940s, as in *Black Friday* [1940] and *The Monster and the Girl* [1941]), "The Purple Zombie" centered around a man brought back to life by a mad scientist. Turning on his master after learning of plans to create an undead army, the Purple Zombie soon stalks the scientist's business partners as he seeks revenge. Unable to be harmed by bullets or electrocution, the Purple Zombie repeatedly strangles his enemies, one of whom attempts to stop him with a fleet of mechanized skeletons. The character appeared in the first twelve issues of *Reg'lar Fellers Heroic Comics*, through 1942, but Mills added new genre combinations as the series progressed by having the Purple Zombie use a time machine to visit different eras (meeting cavemen, Nero, King Richard I, and Sir Francis Drake before landing in the middle of the French Revolution). While it eventually came to resemble *Bill and Ted's Excellent Adventure* (1989) more than the crime-horror hybrid it started off as, "The Purple Zombie" stands as yet another early foray into using comics for tales of terror by a female creator.

Another character often left out of accounts of the horror genre's origins

"The Purple Zombie," *Reg'lar Fellows Heroic Comics* #1, Eastern Color Printing Company. Story and art by June Tarpé Mills.

by comics historians is "The Werewolf Hunter," regularly drawn by Lily Renée for Fiction House's *Rangers Comics*. Like Mills, Renée often used a pen name for her work—sometimes L. Renée, other times merely Reney. "The readers never knew I was a woman. I got a lot of fan mail, especially from soldiers, and they all wrote 'Mr. Renee.' . . . They were always

"The Werewolf Hunter," *Rangers Comics* #16, 1944, Fiction House. Art by Lily Renée.

asking for drawings."[8] In 1943, she took over the series' Werewolf Hunter stories, featuring an occult expert named Armand Broussard who investigated supernatural threats. Under Renée's guidance, the story lines shifted from lycanthropes to a wider range of villains: "I made it into something else," she recalls. "I talked to the writer and convinced him it should be

"The Werewolf Hunter," *Rangers Comics* #19, 1944, Fiction House. Art by Lily Renée.

about magic, where people change into other creatures, not werewolves. . . . 'The Werewolf Hunter' stories were all my ideas," says Renée.[9] The narrative shift allowed her to draw more women in these stories, often powerful villains like Cephalia, princess of the web people, along with a mystical puppeteer named Madame Speszi.

Rangers Comics #19, for example, centers around the uncanny powers of a woman named Magra, who emerges from the flames of Broussard's fireplace to reclaim her children after her husband is shot, staked through the heart, tied to a wooden cross, and burned for being a werewolf. "I am Magra, wife of him they killed with a silver bullet and oaken stake. These are mine—mine alone now and I take them far away. Farewell!" she says, clutching her three children. Magra backs them into the fireplace as the flames consume them, and they disappear. Venturing outside into the snowy countryside, Broussard soon spots "a she-wolf and her three white cubs," who run off into the night. Renée's skills in drawing both beautiful women and dreadful imagery worked in tandem to create some of the horror genre's earliest female-focused phantasmagorias.

While Mills and Renée were pioneer creators of horror-themed comics characters, it wasn't until Avon Comics published the one-off magazine *Eerie* in 1947 that horror comics were fully established as their own genre with their own titles. For much of the 1940s, these kinds of stories were only published as features in other titles and were rarely featured on the cover. Male characters remained prevalent, such as those appearing alongside the Purple Zombie: largely scientists, criminals, and soldiers, indicative of horror's early preoccupation with maintaining strict gender roles. Still, "The Werewolf Hunter" and "The Purple Zombie" were early examples of the increasing popularity of monster and horror narratives in comics, a trend that Mills and Renée were at the forefront of with these stories of a supernatural investigator and an undead, unkillable zombie bent on revenge.

Villainous Vixens

As the early efforts of Mills and Renée gave way to *Eerie*'s publication in 1947, the horror genre experienced a boom that saw the introduction of a wider range of female characters while still remaining firmly centered on men and their stories. For this reason, it's possible to go title by title and separate female characters into neat, identifiable tropes and stereotypes. There are the old crones, damsels, vengeful wives, temptresses, villains, and so forth. In general, the damsels tend to remain in distress, but even the more complex and independent female characters are often undermined. It would be easy to write the entire genre off, then, as antifeminist and misogynistic, and it certainly *is* a deeply problematic genre. To do so, however, would be to deny the complexity of many of these female characters as well as the representational possibilities they may have offered the many women who read horror comics.

When the horror genre fully emerged in the late 1940s, it offered women a chance to see themselves reflected in ways they may not have previously, ways that were more imaginative, messier, darker, and overall less in line with what was expected of the average American woman. While Renée's "Werewolf Hunter" tales offered images of powerful women in supernatural roles, many of the horror comics that followed (especially those from publisher EC Comics) offered readers complex depictions of women in suburban, domestic contexts in place of the gothic-influenced stories of Mills and Renée. Though the horror comics of the Golden Age may not have provided many completely positive female characters for readers to look up to, the representations of women found within them cannot be written off as either totally useless or totally harmful. Female characters who pushed against the confines of traditional gender roles perhaps presented readers with the possibility of rethinking their own place in society. Even though many of these horror comics traded in stereotypes and tropes, the female characters they produced were, for a large majority of readers, something new, different, and exciting. It may not be possible to read the women found in these comics as perfect examples of feminism or empowerment, but they are nevertheless important in the challenge they pose to hegemonic notions of femininity.

Despite the often overwhelming presence of wicked, vengeful women, Golden Age horror comics didn't restrict their representations of evil to female characters alone. Male characters were just as (if not more) likely to commit evil acts than female characters. But this doesn't mean that these were equal-opportunity representations of villainy. Acts of monstrousness perpetuated by women are almost always gendered in ways that those perpetuated by men are not. Male villains are just villains; their evildoing may be a result of greed, jealousy, or lust but is never a natural function or expression of a flawed masculinity. Women, however, seemingly cannot commit acts of monstrousness or evil without said monstrousness being attributed to something inherently broken or wrong with either femininity itself or how that particular character expresses her femininity.

This is not restricted to the horror comics of this era alone, of course. Scholars have long grappled with the demonization of femininity in all forms of media and in society at large. In her analysis of horror movies, feminist film theorist Barbara Creed outlines her concept of the "monstrous-feminine." She theorizes that the term "female monster" is an insufficient descriptor and opts instead for "monstrous-feminine," describing how "the reasons why the monstrous-feminine horrifies her audience are quite different from the reasons why the male monster horrifies his audience. . . . As with all other stereotypes of the feminine, from virgin to whore, she is defined in terms of her sexuality. The phrase 'monstrous-feminine' emphasizes the importance of gender in the construction of her monstrosity."[10]

Though Creed is analyzing cinema, she specifies that some form of the monstrous-feminine is present in every society throughout nearly all of history. On their own, the female characters found in the horror comic books of the Golden Age provide more than enough support for Creed's argument. Similarly, in *The Dread of Difference: Gender and the Horror Film*, Barry Keith Grant writes of "the central importance that themes of gender have had in the horror film,"[11] an idea that is equally true of horror comics. He explains that "the genre has always focused so emphatically on the body as a sight/site of horror, for it has consistently proven 'useful' in addressing the always present but forever shifting dilemmas of difference."[12] As a visual medium, like cinema, comics are another vital site for examining gender representation in the horror genre, especially given that horror comics were far more graphic in their violence than either film or television in this era (at least prior to the rise of the Comics Code in 1954).

The linking of femininity with monstrosity is not a new phenomenon. In *The Monstrous-Feminine*, Creed cites *The Malleus Maleficarum*, a fifteenth-century guide to the identification and condemnation of witches, as centuries-old evidence of the demonization of women. *The Malleus Maleficarum*, commissioned by the Catholic Church and written by Dominican inquisitors Heinrich Kramer and James Sprenger, drew from a variety of sources in order to justify its assertions, including Saint John Chrysostom, to whom they attribute this quote: "What else is a woman but the enemy of friendship, an inescapable punishment, a necessary evil, a natural temptation, a desirable disaster, a danger in the home, a delightful detriment, an evil of nature, painted with nice color?"[13]

While the idea that witchcraft could actually exist is no longer commonly accepted, the hateful notions peddled in *The Malleus Maleficarum* have remained present in various media throughout the ages. Compared to a fifteenth-century witch-hunting guide that contributed to the deaths of innumerable innocent women, the harmful representations of women found in the horror titles of the Golden Age may not seem so serious. And they *aren't* quite as serious, but there is still a shared language of misogyny between the texts that continues to inform how we view women who don't fall neatly in step with social and cultural expectations.

As they evolved out of the early work of Mills and Renée, horror comics became a bastion of bloody tales about women as both victims and killers (but usually the former). But because so many of the women who worked in comics had moved on to other careers by the time horror titles flourished at the end of the 1940s, the genre was in turn built almost exclusively by male creators as titles devoted exclusively to the supernatural hit newsstands. Marilyn Mercer wrote the feature "The Secret Files of Dr. Drew," about a supernatural investigator, for the multigenre series *Rangers Comics* between 1949 and 1951, but her work remains largely neglected because it was not created for a strictly horror title. Fiction House did republish some of Mercer's stories in their short-lived 1952–1953 series *Monster* and *Ghost Comics*, and two of Renée's "Werewolf Hunter" stories were also reprinted in the latter, but the horror genre remains best known for work by male creators at publishers like EC Comics.[14]

In charting the dominant ways in which the horror genre represented women, we can see how the genre took a different path than that forged by Renée and Mills earlier in the decade. One of the first and most successful horror titles was *Adventures into the Unknown*, published from 1948 to 1967 by American Comics Group. The title set an early precedent for female characters in the genre, well before EC began telling crypt-born tales of terror. While many of the female characters in *Adventures into the Unknown* occupied relatively restrictive roles as damsels in distress, sidekicks, or worrying wives/girlfriends, the first few villainous women introduced in the series fall squarely into the category of "desirable disaster," to borrow Saint Chrysostom's phrasing.

A prime example arrived in 1949 with the sixth issue's story "Bat by Night," which tells the story of George Tellier, a student at the Sorbonne who must withdraw from his studies to oversee a castle in the Pyrenees that he has inherited from a distant family member. One of his professors, "a renowned authority of the unknown," offers to visit George, and the two embark on their journey.[15] Once they have settled into the castle, George falls in love with a beautiful young woman named Jeanne, who has long red fingernails. Along with his professor and a servant, George rescues Jeanne from a nasty fall that seemed impossible to survive, and he and Jeanne in turn begin their courtship. Over time, George's castle and the surrounding area are plagued by the presence of a large bat that attacks and kills a number of men. Finally, one night, George looks outside and sees a woman who appears to be Jeanne in an embrace with one of his servants. He rushes outside with his gun, only to discover the servant's lifeless body and the oversize bat. George manages to shoot off

"Bat by Night," *Adventures into the Unknown* #6, 1949, American Comics Group.

one of the bat's talons . . . and it's almost unnecessary to describe the rest. In short, George goes to Jeanne's family home and discovers that it's a long-abandoned, dilapidated castle, realizes that his fiancée is missing one of her talon-like fingernails, confronts her, and eventually kills her by chasing her into a room full of mirrors (which, in the mythology of this story, can kill vampires).

Jeanne's vampiric ways and penchant for murder are framed as only part of what makes her evil. Because Jeanne is only found out because she seduces one of George's servants in a conspicuous location, we're led to understand that her true betrayal is her infidelity, her inability to remain faithful to George, who had rescued her from a near-lethal fall, nursed her back to health, and loved her without exception. Even when presented with evidence of her deception, George dismisses it as nonsense and insists he still loves Jeanne. Even after she dies, George continues to worry about Jeanne, and the characters regard her with sympathy. George's mentor, Professor Gollet, tells George not to think of her any longer, because "she came out of the unknown—and to the unknown she has returned!"[16] While the story treats Jeanne with some sensitivity despite her monstrousness, it's evident that readers aren't meant to pity her. George's sympathetic nature reinforces the idea that he is a sweet, innocent man who has been taken advantage of by an evil, domineering woman.

The fact that Jeanne met her end in a hall of mirrors isn't insignificant, either. George begins to suspect something is awry when he believes he has spotted Jeanne in the arms of another man. Once it is revealed that Jeanne is the giant bat who attacked that man, we understand that it *was* Jeanne whom George saw in a romantic embrace with the man, and that she used her beauty and sexuality to lure him to his death. She used her beauty, too, to keep George's trust. It's only appropriate, then, that she is essentially killed by her reflection. What better way to punish a woman who used her beauty to take advantage of men than by trapping her in a room that reflects that deadly beauty back to her endlessly?

"Bat by Night" is one of many stories in *Adventures into the Unknown* that feature beautiful women transforming into hideous, man-eating monsters. "Shadow of the Panther," published in 1950, tells a similar story with a *Pygmalion*-like twist: the Frankenstein-esque Dr. Robert Lewis creates a "hormone spray" that has the ability to bring animals back from the dead, and he uses it to create the perfect woman.[17] However, the spray transforms the reanimated animals into other beasts when it revives them, and Dr. Lewis has no way of controlling or predicting what kind of transformation will take place. The only constant in his experiments is that the reanimated animals always return to life as more vicious, powerful creatures. To his astonishment, when he attempts to reanimate the corpse of a panther, he finds that he has changed the wild animal into a beautiful woman. Lewis gives the woman, whom he names Mona, lessons on how to act human and quickly falls in love with her. Unbeknownst to Lewis, however, Mona transforms back into a panther under the cover of night and prowls the streets, killing men. Lewis begins to suspect her but puts his fears aside because he loves and trusts her. Days before their marriage, Mona tells Robert, "Cheer up! You're not a condemned man, you're a bridegroom!"[18] When she fails to show up for their wedding, though, Lewis goes to find Mona, only to realize that she's still the panther she was when he first gassed her. The story ends with Mona disappearing after killing her bridegroom.

Like Jeanne in "Bat by Night," Mona's monstrousness is made worse by her betrayal of her loving, trusting fiancé. It's a far bleaker and far more interesting story, however, because it doesn't end with the evil safely contained. Mona murders Lewis and escapes. There is no reference to her being captured by law enforcement officials or turned in by neighbors; Mona gets away with her crime and is left free to roam the streets, looking for her next target. Though their plots are essentially the same and they trade in the same nefarious shape-shifting woman trope, "Bat by Night" and "Shadow of the Panther" are radically different in how they contend with that particular kind of evil. While death is the only option for Jeanne in "Bat by Night," Mona is allowed to escape into the world. And while it is implied that Jeanne comes from a long line of vampires, Mona never chose to be reincarnated as a panther woman; the story acknowledges as much by admitting that Lewis "dared to plumb the forbidden secrets of life [and] death."[19] Nevertheless, she is condemned to live out her life as a hybrid monster with an unquenchable thirst for the blood of

"Shadow of the Panther," *Adventures into the Unknown* #9, 1950, American Comics Group.

men. Despite this, Mona is ultimately free from anyone's control once her bridegroom is dead. Unlike "Bat by Night," "Shadow of the Panther" seems to understand on some level that women aren't toys to be played with or specimens to be experimented on. While one story disciplines the monstrous-feminine, the other allows it to roam free.

Adventures into the Unknown was far from the only title to feature tales of beautiful women either transforming into murderous creatures or using their feminine desirability to lure men to their deaths. *Witches Tales*, published by Harvey Comics from 1951 to 1954, published a number of similar stories, such as "Curse of the Statue" (#7) in which a woman murders her husband before turning into a statue, and "The Witch Who Wore White" (#8), in which a young hospice nurse worships the devil. Avon Comics' *Witchcraft* (1952–1953) also published a few such tales, including the story "The Red Spider" from issue 3 about a beautiful woman who takes the form of a mythological red spider and lures men to the house she shares with her equally murderous husband. *Web of Mystery*, published by Ace Magazines from 1951 to 1955, offered a story called "Mark of the Sinister Cat" in issue 7 about a woman who attempts to use her ability to transform into a cat to infiltrate the happy home of a young married couple and seduce the husband. Though only a handful of the innumerable tales of women transforming into beasts, these stories are representative of how the horror titles of the Golden Age dealt with unruly women: they dehumanized them.

In all of these stories, the female characters' monstrousness is both inextricably linked to and hidden by incredible beauty and sex appeal. Their ability to transform into some kind of animal or supernatural being with magical abilities serves to strip them of their humanity; womanhood is devalued and undermined in most horror titles, while the act of making women literally inhuman largely serves to make them inaccessible and unsympathetic. Even characters whose monstrousness is not of their own design, such as Mona in "Shadow of the Panther," are denied much sympathy. She, like so many of the women in this particular type of story, slinks off into the night, never brought to justice and never given the chance to speak in defense of her actions. Her beauty and strength aren't enough to save her, and though her maker is punished for attempting to play god, it is Mona who is branded as a "beast" and "killer."

Still, it is noteworthy that many of these stories allowed for the possibility of an uncontained and evil woman walking away from the scene of her crimes without (major) consequence. Law enforcement, punishment, and discipline are near omnipresent themes in many horror stories, especially those that feature women exercising their own autonomy. Stories such as "Shadow of the Panther" and "The Witch Who Wore White" may not have painted their female antagonists as admirable beings, but these women were ultimately empowered to slink off into the night to pursue their own desires.

Angry Old Women, Wicked Witches, and Young Wives

The authors of *The Malleus Maleficarum* also cite the Roman philosopher Cicero's assertion that "the basis for all the faults of women is greed."[20] Horror comics did little to combat this idea. In addition to villainizing beautiful young women, they frequently portrayed aging women as greedy, vengeful monsters. While these women were often just run-of-the-mill murderers seeking to get revenge on their no-good husbands, witches and hag-types were also common. Like their younger, half-girl, half-monster sisters, though these aging women were sometimes married, sometimes bitter and single, and sometimes supernatural beings, they were depicted as being motivated by only a few things. Greed and bitterness are the common threads tying all of these kinds of stories together. Readers are never allowed to forget that men—or the absence of men and romance—are at the center of every woman's life. Female evildoers are rarely allowed to simply commit acts of monstrosity for their own sake. There is always something that has been stolen from them or something they're lusting after, something that they need to complete or some lack inside of them that drives them to commit murder or toy with monsters.

The idea of some kind of feminine "lack" is by no means unique to the Golden Age's horror comics. The feminist scholar and filmmaker Laura Mulvey writes in her seminal essay "Visual Pleasure and Narrative Cinema" that "an idea of woman stands as lynch pin to the system: it is her lack that produces the phallus as a symbolic presence, it is her desire to make good the lack that the phallus signifies."[21] This lack, which, in psychoanalytic terms, all woman have, is understood and received as "a threat of castration and hence unpleasure."[22] Though this notion of a lack comes directly from psychoanalysis, an in-depth knowledge of psychoanalytic theory isn't necessary to understand how monstrous female characters are figured as a source of castration anxiety and abjection. As Creed points out, characters representing the monstrous-feminine are often depicted as incomplete women who are driven to evil to settle some score or recover something that has been either lost or stolen from them. They rarely pursue evil just because they feel like it or want to. Villainous women push against social expectations and traditional gender roles and therefore present a threat to those invested in maintaining those gender roles. These women, then, represent a "collapse of gender boundaries and the uncanny feeling associated with a familiar/unfamiliar place [that] disturbs the boundary which marks out the known and knowable."[23]

On that note, it's entirely understandable that the horror comics of this era found new ways to tell familiar tales of bitter old women. And for many contemporary horror and comics fans, the EC Comics' trio of horror anthology series introduced in 1950 has come to define the Golden Age, thanks in part to the prominent role played by crone-like women. EC introduced *The Crypt of Terror*, quickly renamed *Tales from the Crypt*, in 1950. That same year, it released *The Haunt of Fear* and *The Vault of Horror*, though *Tales from the Crypt* remains the most popular of the trio due in large part to the multitude of film and television adaptations of the series, which began in the 1970s. Both *Haunt* and *Vault* were critical, however, to the overall success of EC's horror anthologies.

Tales' Crypt-Keeper is, naturally, the most enduring character of any EC series, but he was joined by two other horror hosts, *The Vault of Horror*'s Vault-Keeper and *The Haunt of Fear*'s Old Witch. Together, the three were known as the GhouLunatics, and they frequently made appearances in each other's titles. Despite the Crypt-Keeper's durability, the Old Witch appeared across the three titles with the most frequency. Born of a beautiful vampire named Elicia and a werewolf named Zorgo, the Old Witch is just one (highly visible) example of the old crone or hag trope that horror comic books of the Golden Age so often utilized.[24]

The Old Witch is simultaneously one of the less complex *and* less stereotypical hag characters from the Golden Age. As a comic book host, she had the first and final word in any story she introduced in any of the EC titles, but she also lacked any real complexity or dimension. She would pop in and out of the narrative, taunting her readers and asking them to second-guess whatever conclusion they'd arrived at about what a story's twist might be. And she did this in every story. For an old crone figure in the horror genre in the Golden Age, her position of relative power, visibility, and intelligence is unique. Older women were rarely represented with much generosity in *any* genre during the Golden Age, but horror comics were especially unkind in their treatment of aging women. Earlier humor titles of the Golden Age established older women as the butt of cruel jokes centered on the loss of their youth, their envy of younger women's beauty, and a general bitterness attributed to their advanced age.

Horror comics took the generally negative attitude toward older women in comics and literalized it, turning these women into all manner of monsters and murderers. Since horror titles didn't usually feature recurring characters aside from the hosts who introduced each story, the Old Witch serves as one of the most frequent female faces seen in horror comics. Drawn exclusively by male artists, including Johnny Craig, Jack Davis, Graham Ingels, Joe Orlando, and Wally Wood, the Old Witch's face was an ugly, haggard one regardless of who worked on her; with her rotten teeth, bloodshot lazy eye, and wart-covered, heavily wrinkled skin, the Old Witch's face was one of the most recurrent images of women in comics' Golden Age.

They weren't always witches, though. Sometimes the horror genre's female characters were not human at all, but rather possessed objects. In the story "Bridegroom, Come Back" (*This Magazine Is Haunted* #18, 1951), drawn by Steve Ditko, a wedding dress haunted by the spirit of a long-dead bride seeks revenge against her murderous groom. The sentient dress, purchased from a pawnshop, realizes that its new owner's fiancé is the same man who murdered the original wearer. On the new couple's wedding night, the murdered bride exacts her revenge. The story plays with the tropes of both the old, haggard witch and the beautiful, young wife, marrying them in a bizarre tale of revenge and love. The story ends with the narrator, the possessed wedding dress, exclaiming that it is happy because now it "shall be worn for all eternity!!"[25] While it's clear that the murdered woman is getting her revenge, her identity as a (newly) married woman is also clearly important to her. The narrative ultimately isn't much different from many of the other revenge tales told in horror comics, but the supernatural and romance elements highlight that women characters always remain anchored to their femininity and traditional gender roles, even in death and murder.

Despite these more complex supernatural stories, however, EC (although it's *far* from the only publisher to do so) also churned out a number of revenge and murder stories that portrayed older women as cruel and mentally unstable. "Hook, Line, and Stinker!" (*The Vault of Horror* #26, 1952) and "Hail and Heart-y!" (*Crime SuspenStories* #15, 1952) are two examples of the vengeful wife trope. The specifics of the two stories are fairly different, but they each end with women getting revenge on their husbands—or, in the case of "Hook, Line, and Stinker," fiancé—for their wrongdoing by murdering them. After murdering their useless men, the women are happy—unhinged, but happy. And they are always, always caught. Even when women are allowed to exercise some amount of power and autonomy in their lives, punishment and the supremacy of the law are always ensured. Unlike the beautiful half-monster, half-woman whose power comes primarily from her ability to hide her monstrosity behind her beauty, the aging and undesirable women in these tales of revenge are almost always found out.

The Vault of Horror tale "One Good Turn" (#31, 1953) is an interesting variant of how these killer women are punished. Here, an old woman named Jennifer comes home every night and tells her bedridden husband, Edwin, about the work she does every day to make others happy. She is shown, over and over, consoling the downtrodden and fixing their lives, "making them so happy" by murdering them. At the end of the story, it's revealed that Edwin was long ago "made happy" by Jennifer and a cup of cyanide-laced hot chocolate.[26] There is an extended scene with two detectives who have discovered Jennifer's secret and, presumably, will see to it that she is punished. The actual presence of law enforcement in these stories isn't entirely unheard of, but much of the time the stories end with the women being discovered by a neighbor or a maid; in this case, because

"One Good Turn," *Vault of Horror* #31, 1953, EC Comics.

Jennifer performs more than her fair allotment of murder, actual agents of the law are shown discovering her secret.

In nearly all of these stories about old women, their power is their anger and their ability to exact their revenge. Once that anger has dissipated and they've gotten to confront the source of their frustrations, all of their power is taken from them. Though they are portrayed as formidable threats to the weak men in their lives, once their jealousy or revenge-motivated monstrosity is complete, they become senile, blithering old women, ready to be carted off to jail or an asylum. It is only the supernatural, magically imbued crones, hags, witches, and ghosts that retain any sort of power for themselves, but their crimes are presented with even less sympathy than the old wives'. That they are able to retain some intelligence and autonomy even as they commit heinous crimes—as in the 1952 *Shock SuspenStories* story "Sugar 'n Spice 'n . . ." which tells a twisted Hansel and Gretel–type tale, or the aforementioned "Bridegroom, Come Back"—is a sign of ultimate evil, not strength. Often, analogous male characters are portrayed as geniuses who, time and again, escape the law and trick those around them into becoming their prey. For the most part, women are only given one chance to be evil, and once they've crossed over to that side, they are marked indelibly by their betrayal of humanity.

It wasn't just older women whose marriages were falling apart. Younger married women were often portrayed as gold diggers, social climbers, or self-absorbed fools who inadvertently drive their husbands to death, and buzzkills standing in the way of their husband's ambitions. Regardless of which kind of wife a woman is, the husband, as always, ends up dead. There is no such thing as a healthy marriage in the horror titles of the Golden Age. Marriage, it seems, is almost always a death sentence. Unsurprisingly, World War II had seen a dramatic increase in marriages, many of which ended in divorce. By the late 1940s, one in three married couples were divorced.[27] It's not surprising, then, that narratives about marriage often painted it in a deadly light. The beautiful young women depicted in these stories differ from those discussed in the first section, though, because they are motivated by their own jealousy, greed, and stupidity. Whereas women who have the ability to shape-shift and disappear into the night retain both their monstrousness and their sexuality, the vengeance-seeking wives here must trade their beauty and femininity for a grotesque kind of power. When beauty and sexuality are no longer a woman's primary source of power, and domesticity—even a twisted, toxic kind of domesticity—becomes her domain, her power comes from her ability to control her husband. Often, when she loses (or is in danger of losing) that power, her options are murder or be murdered.

The 1952 *Tales from the Crypt* story "Squash . . . Anyone?" (#32) tells the story of a married couple who perform with a traveling circus. The husband, Milo, is an elephant trainer. His beautiful wife, René, is, naturally, his death-defying assistant. During the act, *she* lies on the ground and places her head under the highly trained (by her husband) elephant's foot. *She* places herself in the path of death for the sake of her husband. And even though she is a selfless character, René becomes the victim of a murder plot. Milo, who has been cheating on her with another woman, cooks up a scheme to have the elephant, Emma, "accidentally" slip during their act and crush his wife to death. Of course, this means that he must also sacrifice the elephant, as it will undoubtedly be put to death for the "accident."[28] René dies, the elephant is put down, and Milo and his new wife, Leeta, travel the country with the circus and their new elephant. A year later, they return to the town where the murder took place and perform the same act. Not content to let her husband get away with murder, a miraculously reanimated (albeit decaying) René, riding atop Emma's rotting body, bursts into the circus tent. Both Milo and Leeta are trampled to death by the corpses of their victims. The story ends with René and Emma, having gotten vengeance for their deaths, melting into a putrid puddle on the floor of the tent in front of a shocked crowd.

"Squash . . . Anyone?" isn't a story about a cheating, greedy, jealous wife. It's not a story about a gold-digger or a witch or a shape-shifter who lures men to their deaths. It's a story about a loving wife who puts herself in harm's way on a daily basis for the sake of her husband's livelihood. And she's still murdered. She still melts away into a powerless puddle of nothing when her sole purpose in the afterlife—to avenge her and Emma's wrongful deaths—is completed. These narratives, while not uncommon, don't appear as frequently as narratives of infidelity and gold-digging. Still, that these kinds of stories exist alongside each other and show their vastly different female protagonists performing incredibly similar kinds of brutal acts exposes a process of homogenization of female characters. In this process, no female character, regardless of how just or unjust her actions are, is allowed to escape her story without repercussions.

Conclusion

As their popularity grew, horror comics received a great amount of cultural criticism from those outside of the comic book industry. The most famous of these concerns arrived in Frederic Wertham's *Seduction of the Innocent* and its claim that juvenile delinquency was directly correlated with comic book consumption. Wertham targeted a number of the more sordid comics genres, but horror received extra attention. EC Comics, of course, was decried by Wertham and his supporters for the especially graphic and gruesome depictions of murder and monstrousness in its books. As comics scholar Qiana Whitted notes, EC Comics "helped to usher in the mid-twentieth-century debates over the social function of art into mainstream comic books" thanks to the social uproar over the horror genre's ghastly stories.[29]

Ironically, many of the most gruesome images were toned down, quite literally, by EC's lone female creator—colorist Marie Severin. Artist Johnny Craig recalls how when Severin encountered a page of artwork that she felt was particularly grisly, "she went dark" with her coloring so as to obscure a given panel's imagery.[30] Fellow artist Al Feldstein describes how the publisher "left it to Marie and her creativity" in terms of how to color artists' work, even when she served as a de-facto "censor" as well as "the conscience of EC":

> She was a young Catholic girl and she had specific limitations as to how far she would go, and if we went farther than she wanted to go, she would kind of object and tone down some of the stuff that we did. Once in while she would paint an entire panel blue so you could hardly see the details of the gore we were putting in.[31]

Despite Severin's efforts, Wertham painted all of EC's books with the same blood-stained brush. Often, he used over-the-top and ridiculous examples of children copying violent crimes they saw in comics to hammer home his point, such as: "When, for example, a young child hangs himself and beneath the dead child is found an open comic book luridly describing and depicting a hanging (as has happened in a number of cases), the mechanics of the relationship between have to be investigated."[32] Wertham provided no evidence that this kind of violent child suicide had ever happened, much less on multiple occasions. As the comics historian Carol Tilley notes, *Seduction of the Innocent* "included numerous falsifications and distortions," and "Wertham edited and altered children's statements and clinical presentations to make his rhetorical position more compelling to readers."[33]

It wasn't just the images and characters within comic books that he had issues with, though. He objected to the array of objects advertised in them, too, such as the women's undergarments, diet pills, personal massagers, and romance magazine subscriptions that were hawked alongside full-page ads for knives, BB guns, and other weapons and toys aimed at young children (particularly boys). While his concerns may have been overblown and misdirected, they weren't always entirely off base. He criticized the comic book industry for its glorification of racism, anti-Semitism, and violence against women. About the horror genre in particular, Wertham worried that children would develop sleep disorders (which, he posited, would damage the child for life) from reading scary stories before bedtime. Worse than sleep disorders, though, was the violence he alleged children would learn from horror titles. He lumped crime and horror comics into the same category, writing, "If they have a revulsion against it [violence], crime comics turn this revulsion into indifference. If they have a subconscious liking for it, comic books will reinforce it, give it form by teaching appropriate methods and furnish the rationalization that it is what every 'big shot' does."[34]

But in this analysis of the social and cultural effects of comic books, the alarmist and totalitarian methods Wertham used did not account for how the comics he examined were as much a reflection of society as society was a reflection of comic books. Cultural norms and expectations are not established overnight or because a child reads a violent comic. We learn these behaviors over a lifetime and from every type of media we consume. Wertham wasn't inherently wrong for questioning the effect these representations could have on readers, but his anger and criticism *was* misplaced. As Feldstein describes it, Wertham's efforts were capitalized on by larger social and political forces:

> Estes Kefauver wanted to be President, and he started a Senate investigation into organized crime in America. As part of this investigation committee, there was a subcommittee on juvenile delinquency which was getting to be a problem for young parents that had come back from the war and were used to having the Army tell them what to do.
>
> They wanted people to tell them how to bring up their kids, which is why [pediatrician Dr. Benjamin] Spock did so well with his book [1946's *The Common Sense Book of Baby and Child Care*]. So they all wanted a little help with this thing, they wanted some sort of guidance. Of course it went overboard, and the Senate Subcommittee investigating juvenile delinquency took on the comics because they had this self-appointed expert named Wertham. Of course this was like the end of our Golden Era, as it was, because we suddenly became these terrible people who were doing these awful things. All we were doing was entertaining.[35]

Ultimately, the industry chose to self-regulate instead of potentially facing government censorship. The Comics Code Authority was formed in 1954, the same year the vast majority of horror titles disappeared from newsstands. This, of course, was no coincidence. The Comics Code specifically forbade depictions of explicit violence; most supernatural creatures; any excessive gore, bloodshed, or sexuality; and (most damning of all) the use of the words "horror" or "terror" in comic titles. This was devastating to the genre, and many publishers chose to completely cancel their horror titles (like EC) or sell them off to other publishers to use them as they pleased (as Fawcett did when it sold the majority of its less savory titles to Charlton).[36] The titles that managed to comply with the code did so by focusing more on mystery, sci-fi, superhero, and fantasy narratives. But as Nyberg explains, the years of "bad publicity" generated by Wertham and the Senate hearings drove down sales, leading several publishers to go out of business by mid-decade: Ace Magazines, Avon Comics Group, Comic Media, Eastern Color Printing Co., EC Comics, Fiction House, Quality Comics Group, Star Publications, Sterling Comics, and United Features.[37]

The creation of the CCA almost entirely obliterated horror comics by the mid-1950s. While many might say that this move wasn't much of a loss for female characters, given how the genre traded in stereotypes and tropes, horror comics *did* offer female readers of the period something outside of the norm. Although these stories almost never end with an autonomous, empowered woman walking away from a horrific situation unmarred, within their narratives women are often allowed to exercise different types of power and agency—ones that are often tied directly to their femininity. Once those stories end, of course, the women are typically left dead and/or disgraced in some way.

Still, these kinds of roles *were* something different, often allowing women to display their sexuality in ways that emphasized their own pleasure and needs. Horror comics also allowed women to act in ways that prioritized their desires in life, even though punishment or retribution of some sort was essentially a given. Since the genre was so quickly undone by the Comics Code in the mid-1950s, this potential to offer more challenging portrayals of women as the decade continued went unfilled. But from the genre's unheralded origins in the work of Mills and Renée to how female bodies were represented in ways that were alternately both injurious and challenging, stories told *by* and *about* women were central to the evolution of horror comics.

CHAPTER 5

WESTERN COMICS

Although no longer a prominent genre in the modern comics landscape, the western was one of the most popular throughout most of the Golden Age. Once the cowboy emerged as a central figure in popular culture in the first half of the twentieth century (first in pulp stories, then in films, and eventually on television), western comics became a widespread forum for thrilling tales of sheriffs, cowpunchers, bandits, ranchers, and outlaws—men and women alike. The comics historian Maurice Horn notes that over one hundred western titles emerged in the late 1940s and into the 1950s.[1] Western heroes regularly replaced caped ones on newsstands as superhero titles began to wane in this period, with female characters proving central to the genre's early success despite that it is best remembered for its male cowboys.

Western comics dominated the output of some publishers: in the early 1950s, for instance, around two-thirds of Fawcett Comics' regular line of titles were westerns. Fawcett published four superhero titles revolving around Captain Marvel (*Whiz Comics*, *Captain Marvel Adventures*, *Captain Marvel Jr.*, and *The Marvel Family*), the superhero anthology *Master Comics*, *Fawcett's Funny Animals*, the adventures of *Nyoka the Jungle Girl*, and sporadic titles based on television shows like *Captain Video*. Overshadowing these other genres was the long list of western comics Fawcett regularly released: *Bill Boyd Western*, *Bob Colt Western*, *Gabby Hayes Western*, *Hopalong Cassidy*, *Ken Maynard Western*, *Lash LaRue Western*, *Monte Hale Western*, *Rocky Lane Western*, *Rod Cameron Western*, *Six-Gun Heroes*, *Smiley Burnette Western*, *Tex Ritter Western*, *Tom*

Mix Western, and *Western Hero*. Women are glaringly absent from this lengthy line of gunslingers, a symptom of how the western was an overwhelmingly male-dominated genre within popular culture overall in this era.[2] Film scholar Jesús Ángel González notes that in cinema, "classic westerns used to be a fundamentally male genre where women were either absent or secondary characters."[3]

Despite how many western comics centered around male heroes, the genre actually allowed a range of different roles for female characters, although not right away. Several titles combined the western and romance genres in an obvious appeal to female readers, such as *Cowboy Love*, *Cowgirl Romances*, *Range Romances*, *Real West Romances*, *Western Love*, and *Western Love Trails*. But numerous adventure-oriented titles aimed at readers of all genders regularly included women among the ranks of their feature characters as the genre progressed into the late 1940s. The emphasis on women within the genre parallels the ways in which non-male authors played a significant role in the development of western novels. As Victoria Lamont demonstrates in *Westerns: A Women's History*, the work of authors such as Emma Ghent Curtis, B. M. Bower, and Francis McElrath shows us how fictional tales about sheriffs and settlers were not solely the domain of male writers.[4] While western comics didn't see as many women creators as other genres in this era, the proliferation of women as starring characters in what many have assumed is a male-dominated type of storytelling is a testament to how a feminist re-reading of a genre's history can change many of our most basic assumptions about it.[5]

Western comics appeared on newsstands within a few years of the comic book format's debut in the mid-1930s. Most anthology titles featured at least one cowboy among their ranks, such as Chuck Dawson in *Action Comics*, Lightnin' and the Lone Rider in *Famous Funnies*, and Wilton of the West in *Jumbo Comics*.[6] Titles devoted solely to western characters began in 1937 with *Western Picture Stories*, *Star Ranger*, and *Western Action Thrillers*. The latter featured tales of real-life figures like Buffalo Bill alongside fictional heroes like Laramie Joe, the Texas Kid, and Two Gun Thompson, while *Western Picture Stories* saw such characters as Buck Bush, Tex Maverick, and "Wild Tex" Martin. *Star Ranger* was also full of various short stories, some adventurous and many humorous. But like other western series from this decade, there were few tales that featured women in any kind of supporting role, let alone as protagonists. There was the rare sighting of a settler's wife or daughter (many of whom were kidnapped), but overall, one could get the sense in reading early western comics that there were hardly any women inhabiting the Old West at all!

The absence of women in these first western titles was so glaring that it prompted one creator to write a poem about it. In *Star Ranger* #6, the writer/artist Fred Guardineer offered up a one-page poem titled "The Cowgirl":

We often write about the West
And cowboys on the range,
But why we never write about
The cowgirl is most strange.
This hardy girl can do most things
That all the cowboys do—
She rides the toughest bucking bronc
And shoots both fast and true.
Activity keeps her in form
While sunshine tans her face,
In all the history of the West
The cowgirl has her place.

The poem features three panels depicting a blonde cowgirl: she first surveys the open range on horseback, then shoots a wolf at full gallop, and finally relaxes with a drink back at the ranch while a young, guitar-wielding cowboy serenades her. Guardineer clearly positions the cowgirl as a complex figure, one who challenges our expectations of labor and gender roles within the history of the American West. But this strong persona was rarely seen in the pages of early comic book westerns. Instead, women were often used as comic relief, when they weren't being used as plot devices in need of rescue by male protagonists.

One of the first recurring female western characters was Tenderfoot Mary, who appeared in *Star Ranger* (and its follow-up, *Star Ranger Funnies*) in one-page gags between 1937 and 1939. Newly arrived in a small town, Mary is mocked by the locals for her ignorance about life outside of a big city: "That city gal sure don't know nothin'. She thinks a range is something you cook on," says one of the townsfolk. "She told me she always thought cowboys only ride cows," says another. They are then dumbfounded when Mary comes over to ask the group of men, "Will one of you boys lend me a branding iron. I want to do up a couple of shirts."[7] Other gags find her convinced that male cows provide condensed milk, declining an oyster cocktail from her date because she doesn't drink alcohol, and declaring her complete indifference toward mathematics.

As one of the first regular female characters, Tenderfoot Mary's foibles were just as silly as *Star Ranger*'s comedic male characters, such as

"The Cowgirl," *Star Ranger* #6, 1937, Centaur Publications.

Sam Hill, Okie Doke, Jess Phoolin, and Tenderfoot Joe. Yet while these male jesters were balanced with a range of masculine character types in the early years of western comics, there were few alternatives to counter the foolishness of Tenderfoot Mary (aside from the occasional wife or

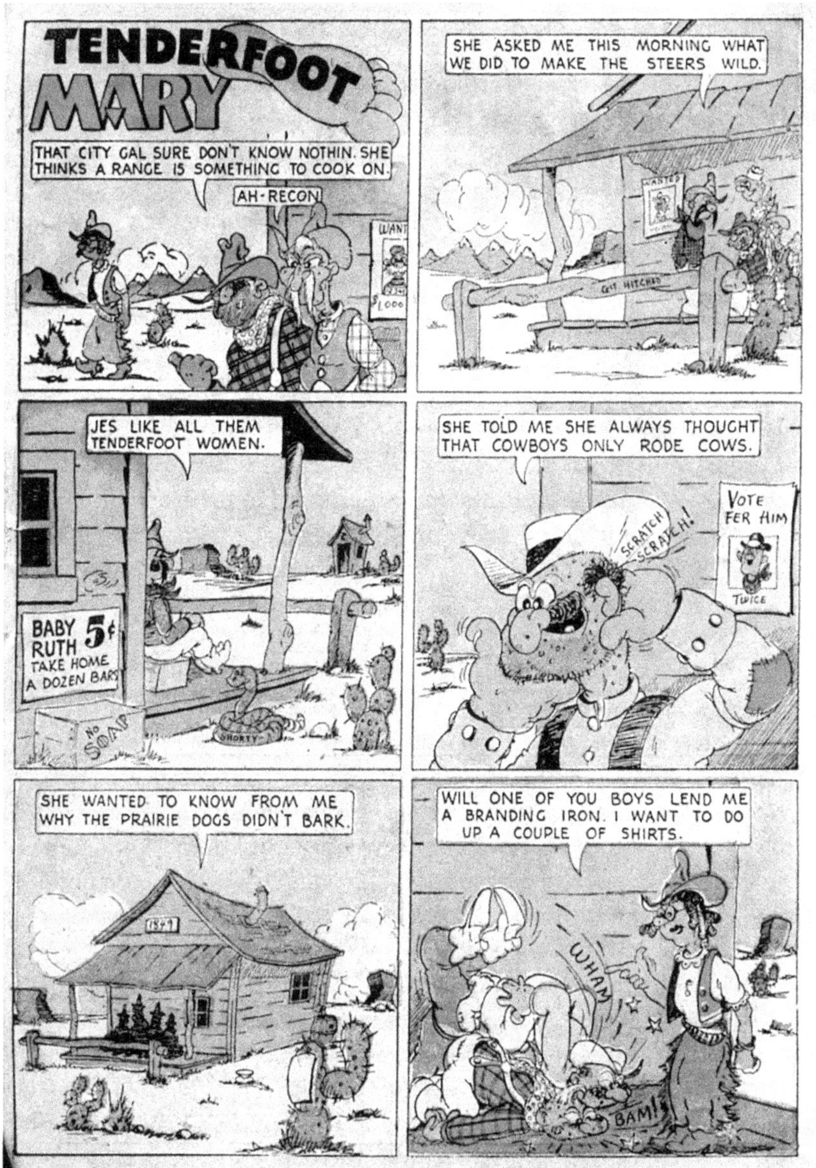

"Tenderfoot Mary," *Star Ranger* #2, 1937, Centaur Publications.

girlfriend in need of rescue). One masked vigilante named the Crimson Outlaw appeared in six issues of *Jumbo Comics* between 1939 and 1940, but she was a rare exception. The "hardy" cowgirl of Guardineer's poem would not appear in comics with any regularity for several more years.

Cowgirls

The number of western comics on newsstands began to increase in the early 1940s as titles based on famous movie cowboys grew in popularity. Gene Autry received his own book in 1941, followed by Hopalong Cassidy in 1943 and Roy Rogers in 1944 (first as single-issues in both the Dell *Four Color* and Western Publishing *March of Comics* series, and finally his own title in 1948). Silent-film cowboy Tom Mix starred in a line of promotional comics from pet food company Ralston Purina, despite the star's death in 1940. The success of these titles led a surge in western anthologies as the decade progressed, starting with *Cow Puncher Comics* in 1947. By 1948, a torrent of titles hit the market, including *Blazing West*, *Dead Eye Western*, *Real Western Hero*, *The Westerner*, *Western Adventure Comics*, *Western Fighters*, *Western Killers*, and *Western Thrillers*.

On the surface, many of these titles perpetuated the trope of damsels in distress that superhero comics and pulp magazines before them specialized in. The cover of the second issue of *Cow Puncher Comics* features a buxom young woman tied to a post (with her blouse torn to reveal most of her chest and her skirt bunched to reveal her thighs) as two men fight in the background. Similarly, the third issue's cover features a woman whose dress has been torn in the front to reveal most of her breasts. A cowboy races toward her on horseback, hoping to save her before a gang of masked outlaws arrive.

This emphasis on sexualizing women extended into the stories as well, with the debut of the "ace backwoods woman" Kit West in *Cow Puncher* #1 finding her dressed in a very short skirt and a blouse whose neckline plunges down well toward her navel.[8] West's outfit is so revealing that the artist regularly adds shadows around her breasts and upper thighs to hide just how much of her body is actually exposed. The story even uses her bare legs as a central plot point in order to justify showing them up close. When a Wyandotte warrior sees Kit spying on his tribe, he fires an arrow at her: "First, to tame those pretty white limbs!"[9] The next panel shows a close-up of the arrow whizzing toward Kit's bare thighs, offering other pleasures to male readers besides the dangerous actions depicted. The arrow pierces straight through her leg, allowing subsequent panels to dwell on her bare thighs as she struggles with her injury.

Placing women in danger was a common trope around which Golden Age western comics built their narratives. Often this meant women were restrained, slapped, punched, cut, and killed, all in the name of providing character motivation for male heroes coming to the rescue (or out for revenge). In the second issue of *Cow Puncher*, a rancher's daughter named

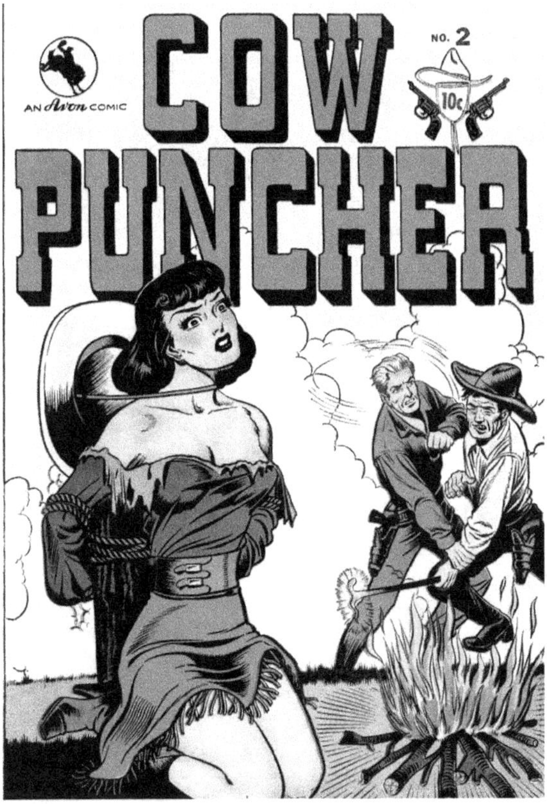

Cover of *Cow Puncher Comics* #2, 1947, Avon Comics.

Marilyn is blackmailed into marrying a murderer named Buck Roper in order to save her father. When she later confronts Buck with the truth and calls off the wedding, he has his men kidnap her: "Rustlin' dames is a darn sight more fun than rustlin' cows!" one says. One of the men pistol-whips her with the handle of his gun: "Maybe *this'll* make her act like a lady!" Tied to a chair, she is then assaulted by Buck: "So, you don't want to be the Queen of Eden? You're gonna regret that decision, Marilyn, after a couple of kisses!" Marilyn bites him as he kisses her, drawing blood. "I warned you not to take advantage of me!" she yells. Buck retaliates by punching her in the face: "Maybe you'll like this kind of kissing better!!" "That's the stuff, boss! Clip 'er again!" yells one of Buck's henchmen.[10] She is soon rescued by the town's pastor (who is also a gunslinger).

The story does allow Marilyn one moment of self-preservation: while lying on the floor still tied to the chair, she aids in her own escape by kicking Buck. This causes him to drop his gun, giving the pastor an opening to save the day. Despite her intervention, the story is a common example of how western comics used women as plot devices to be rescued by male

"Kit West," *Cow Puncher Comics* #1, 1947, Avon Comics.

characters—but not before having any number of violent acts committed against them.

While women were often portrayed as victims and sex objects in western comics, many powerful examples of strong female heroes could also be found within their pages. Foremost among such heroines was Dale

Evans, the frequent on-screen partner (and off-screen wife) of film and television cowboy Roy Rogers. Film historian Peter Stanfield notes how Rogers's screen career was helped by his partnership with Evans: "Rogers made his reputation in the years after 1943 when he teamed up with Dale Evans, who allowed his films to focus in a novel manner on domestic intrigue."[11] Evans had appeared in supporting roles in films of various genres for a few years before first teaming up with Rogers in *The Cowboy and the Senorita* (1944). After that, they appeared regularly together in westerns from Republic Pictures and then on television in six seasons of *The Roy Rogers* show starting in 1951.

In 1948, Evans earned her own series from DC, *Dale Evans Comics*, which lasted twenty-four issues through 1952. Licensing restrictions placed limits on how closely the comic could follow her on-screen adventures: Roy Rogers did not appear, given that he had his own series at Dell, and Evans did not ride her horse Buttercup but instead ones named Pal and Soda. Her adventures veered toward the absurd at times: one issue finds her shooting at a gang of outlaws while riding a kangaroo; another sees her trade in her horse for an elephant named Rajah.[12] But with few women headlining their western comics, Evans's four-color adventures were popular with her fans at a time when DC's roster of superhero titles frequently gave way to western series.

The series even included a feature called "Dale Evans' Roundup," supposedly written by her (but more likely by a publicist), in which she shares personal and professional updates. In issue 4 she recounts a recent vacation she and Rogers took to Lake Henshaw: "[We were] near San Diego, California, with our house trailer, five dogs, guns and fishing tackle. We planned to rough it. It was to be strictly cowboy all the way!" The last day of the trip, she notes, they were joined by Carl Switzer, the actor who played Alfalfa in the *Our Gang* films. She also assures readers that she performs her own stunts in her movies: "Unlike some other actresses, I scorn the use of doubles. I prefer to depend on my own riding ability to carry me through some of the more demanding and risky scenes."[13] In issue 18, she offers details about Roy's and her move to a new house, including the various steps involved in packing their belongings ("Roy had to find some particularly heavy boxes in which to pack his guns and fishing equipment"). She also describes working on a new film called *South of Caliente* (1951), which she notes was her first time back on set in a year.[14]

Like those of other western films stars of this period, Evans's comic book was a way to maintain her star persona with fans between on-screen adventures (her first issue, for instance, sees her producer send her to a town called Greedy Gulch to work as a substitute teacher as research for a new film role).[15] Jim McArdle drew most of Dale's adventures in the DC series (some sources list Suzie Day as an artist on early issues, but little is known about her),[16] although the series is now prized by Golden Age comics collectors largely because of backup stories about a male hero named Sierra Smith drawn by celebrated artist Alex Toth. When the book ended in 1952, Dell soon picked up the rights to publish a new series called *Queen of the West, Dale Evans*, which ran from 1953 until 1959.

The appeal of western heroines was also seen in the various series starring Annie Oakley, the famous sharpshooter who performed as part of Buffalo Bill's Wild West show. Born Phoebe Ann Moses, Oakley was so accurate with a rifle that she earned the nickname Little Sure Shot from the Lakota chief Sitting Bull, who befriended her after his victory at the Battle of Little Big Horn. As a major historical figure (and one whose name and likeness were covered under public domain copyright law), Oakley was used by several comics publishers throughout the Golden Age, with sales helped by three seasons of the *Annie Oakley* television series (1954–1957) starring Gail Davis. Dell featured Oakley in numerous issues of *Four Color* between 1952 and 1959, while Atlas included her in 1948's *Two-Gun Kid* #3 along with two issues of *Wild Western* in 1955. Charlton made her a recurring character in its *Cowboy Western* series between 1948 and 1957, and again in *Six-Gun Heroes* beginning in 1958.

Atlas gave Oakley her own series in 1948 (though it lasted only four issues) and again in 1955 to capitalize on the success of the television series. The first issue of her Atlas series is an anomaly among female-led western comics in its attempt to appeal to fans of both cowgirls and the "cheesecake" subgenre of Good Girl art. The cover depicts a shotgun-toting Oakley in mid-stride, her skirt flapping upward to reveal much of her calves and thigh. "I wonder why the men in this town shy away from me the way they do?" she exclaims while looking at the reader and as numerous men look aghast, the joke being that she has just used her gun to create the outline of a cowboy with bullets on the side of a building.

The covers to issues 3 and 4 both show lovestruck men doting over Oakley, with hearts literally encircling their heads to give the reader a visual symbol of their infatuation. The first four issues of the series were drawn by Christopher Rule, who had previously worked as an inker on *Patsy Walker* and also drew that character in the 1954 series *Girl's Life*. He also worked on issues of such 1940s and 1950s romance titles as *Gay Comics*, *Joker Comics*, *Junior Miss*, *Love Tales*, and *Wendy Parker Comics*, most of which also included male characters with hearts regularly floating around their heads. When Atlas assigned him to *Annie Oakley*, it must have seemed only natural to make Oakley a love object for the series' male characters.

But while the first four issues presented Oakley as a tough-but-tender cowgirl prone to romantic misadventures and love triangles alongside scenes in which she saves the day, when Atlas brought the series back in 1955, the tone shifted from playfully lovestruck to one that was more often straight-up adventure mixed with melodrama. Whereas issue 3 finds Annie and her rival, Sally, vying to see who looks better in a bathing suit at the local swimming hole ("It takes certain kind of wimmen to look good while swimmen! And my gal Annie has what it takes!" sings Tex, the object of both women's affection), issue 6 finds Annie preventing a crooked landowner from seizing the deed to a ranch, and issue 7 sees her battle a duo dressed as Spanish conquistadors in search of buried treasure.

Along with this shift in tone comes a very different art style, one that foregoes Rule's curvy, more cartoonish depictions of women. Whereas Rule's backgrounds within many panels are often blank or contain minimal elements, later issues of the series regularly place Annie against the rugged landscapes of her various outdoor adventures, given how the story lines move her beyond the ranch (and its local watering hole). With Rule gone, the narrative scope of Oakley's adventures greatly increased, turning her into a hero who takes action—catching bank robbers, foiling bandits, and the like—rather than a mere love interest for male characters. While issue 4 sees Annie and Sally competing to earn enough money to be the first to buy a fur coat, issue 10 finds Oakley demonstrating her skills as a sharpshooter when she appears as the main attraction at the Buena Vista rodeo. She is then challenged by Frank Butler, a member of Buffalo Bill's Wild West Show, and after beating him she earns a place in the famous show itself. Rule used Oakley to tell stories with conflicts that were largely interchangeable with the other romance comics he worked on, while subsequent issues developed the character further by allowing her to move beyond the love triangle and become the star performer that she is best known for being in real life.

A significantly different version of Oakley is found in her books from Dell, whose westerns were distinctly less violent in keeping with the publisher's stated intent in the 1950s to make its books a more wholesome alternative to those that drew criticism for their lurid qualities. The motto "Dell Comics Are Good Comics" was featured in each issue starting in 1954, and the publisher offered a "Pledge to Parents" in 1955 that its books were "clean" and "not injurious to anyone."[17] In turn, Dell's characterization of Oakley is a far cry from Rule's cheesecake rendition: rather than sporting a dress that regularly flaps up to reveal her thighs, Annie wears a fully buttoned shirt and long pants (with nary a bathing suit in sight). Her first issue in 1952 begins in medias res, with Oakley and her brother Tagg herding cattle across their ranch only to discover that one of their steers has a mysterious mark branded on its side. Whereas Atlas introduced Annie by focusing on how the men in town reacted to her, Dell immediately placed Oakley on equal footing with other comic book cowboys by launching straight into an adventure worthy of her wit and skill. Dell made Oakley a cowgirl equal to her male counterparts without resorting to the gender stereotypes that pervaded her early Atlas issues.

Ranch Owners and Sheriffs

While cowgirl comics offered readers daring tales of range-riding heroines, women regularly played other roles in western titles, often occupying prominent positions within society revolving around land ownership and law enforcement. Women were historically well represented among land owners after Abraham Lincoln signed the Homestead Act in 1962 (which allowed settlers to claim 160 acres of land). By the early 1900s, one in five homesteaders were women—many of them immigrants—who enjoyed new opportunities for personal autonomy.[18] But despite such gains, depictions of women as independent landowners, let alone as a female cattle-ranch owner, are rare in popular culture. One such character was Wilma West, who starred in Trojan Magazines' *Western Crime Busters* beginning in 1950. Inheriting her father's ranch after he dies, West manages both the property's day-to-day operations and its finances. She regularly enlists the help of her trusted ranch hand, the aging Sonora Sam, who rescues her on multiple occasions after she is tied up by the stories' villain. Despite being described as a "brave, lovely daughter of the cow country," West's bravery often ends with her abduction and subsequent salvation at the hands of male villains and heroes.[19]

One female ranch owner who reversed these tropes was Boots Bradley, debuting in 1947's *Cow Puncher Comics* #2. While the series regularly featured women in peril being tied up and smacked around by male aggressors, Bradley was a complex character who defied traditional gender roles in several ways. While the opening narration refers to her as a "rootin', shootin' cactus beauty," Bradley is in fact the sole female ranch owner of the fictional Sunburst Valley. As a landowner who supervises a team of male employees, Boots Bradley's societal role is one of relative power and status within her community. The fact that she doesn't act or speak in traditionally feminine ways in the story sees her further challenge gender roles of the period. When her ranch hand, Kansas, tells her that the town has a new schoolteacher, Bradley is furious: "Cuss! As the only woman ranch owner in Sunburst Valley, that means I'll be obliged to entertain . . . that'll put off work on the North fence, and until that boundary is established, Rattler Flint will continue to graze his cattle in our land . . . cuss!" she exclaims. While comics in this era couldn't have their characters say actual curse words, the substitution of "cuss" for expletives allows the writer to show how Bradley defies our expectations about how women should speak. "Wish I was a man, Kansas," adds Bradley. The grizzled ranch hand replies, "Ye wouldn't make a likely lookin' one, Boots."[20]

Begrudgingly, she prepares her ranch for a dance that night only to learn that the new schoolteacher is a man named Wilson, further defying gender expectations. When Flint's gang captures the teacher (binding his wrists as he hangs from a tree branch), Boots rides off to the rescue, lassoing one of them: "The first one who moves will get my initials tattooed on 'em . . . in hot lead!"[21] Not only does having a female hero ride to the rescue of a kidnapped man reverse the common trope of western narratives, but the fact that he is bound with rope shows that *Cow Puncher*'s tendency toward bondage imagery in its stories was not limited just to female victims.

After rescuing the teacher, he and Bradley ride home together as the sun sets. "Do you know, Boots," says the teacher, "you're the first girl that ever took me home . . . and I like it." Boots replies, "Easily known you're a stranger in these here parts, Wilson . . . your direction is all mixed up . . . *you're* taking *me* home!"[22] Bradley is clearly in control of her blossoming relationship with the teacher, with Wilson's admission that he enjoys being tamed by a woman coinciding with his recent bondage framing him as submissive. The issue's advertisements are geared toward men (selling leather billfold wallets and a body-building guide, among other things), but Bradley's sly correction of gender roles in their courtship as she insists that Wilson is in charge of the situation is clearly meant as a knowing wink to readers who have been conditioned to see men as the dominant gender.

Another dominant social role fulfilled by women in many western comics was that of sheriff. While female sheriffs appeared in occasional episodes of television series such as *Hopalong Cassidy* and *The Gene Autry Show*,[23] along with a few B-movie westerns such as *Target* (1952) and *The Gunslinger* (1956), placing women in leadership roles typically held by men constituted a novelty gimmick for viewers who had been watching western stars like Autry and Hopalong for many years. In contrast, female sheriffs could be found very early in the history of western comic books, frequently appearing alongside male sheriffs as the genre took off in the late 1940s. When Ace Magazines launched its first western series—*Western Adventure Comics*—in 1948, the first issue featured a female sheriff in addition to such male heroes as Bud Steele and Duke Buckland.

The first glimpse of Sheriff Sal, a.k.a. Sally Starr, has her standing in the middle of town, both guns drawn and blazing as she stares directly at the reader. The opening image deliberately establishes Sal as a woman of action so that readers do not underestimate her once they learn how she became sheriff: "When the frontier town of Red Dog elected Sally Starr its sheriff, mocking laughter rang out from canyon wall to grazing land, and echoed across the western ranges! A girl sheriff! What a jest!" states the narrator. The story begins by making Sally a figure of ridicule in order to soon subvert such mockery. When a "delegation of business men and ranchers" decide to appoint Sally Starr as the town sheriff, she gladly accepts. "The town is plenty peaceful and yuh won't have trouble," one well-to-do gentleman in a top hat promises her. But while having a badge pinned on her chest, she is informed, "Only reason we're offering it to yuh, Sally, is that the town's so doggone peace-loving that no *man* wants it!" "Oh! So that's why you're giving it to a woman!" replies Sally.[24] News of Sheriff Sal's appointment leads to widespread mockery: "Reckon the females of Red Dog lead the men folks around by the nose! Ha! Ha!" "A silly schoolmarm for sheriff! Ha! Ha! Ha!" An outlaw named Nueces Callan decides to take advantage of the situation, figuring that the town's bank will prove an easy target: "Reckon they've had plenty of time to put ready cash in that bank, and no *gal* sheriff is goin' to stop me from gettin' it!"[25]

The story's reversal of the genre's traditional gender roles also extends to making a supporting male character a lovestruck admirer: "Maybe Sally will marry me, if we can get her to give up this crazy job!" rancher Flash Gannon thinks to himself. "If yuh'd quit we could get hitched!" he tells Sal, an offer she does not respond to. Rather than jump into marriage with the first man who shows an interest in her, Sal captures the outlaw with the help of a rancher's wife: "I reckon with the help of womenfolk like Mrs. Vicks here, a girl sheriff will be able to keep law and order in Red Dog after all!" she proclaims in the story's final panel as a group of men look dumbfounded.[26]

Her second appearance finds all former mockery replaced with jealousy and disbelief. The opening narration tells us, "A slip of a girl wears the sheriff's badge in frontier town of Red Dog. The men folk, however, are secretly jealous of her, and feel no 'fee-male' can be a good lawman!" When a stranger comes to town looking for the sheriff, he is taken aback by Sal: "Hey! You're a gal sheriff!" She shoots back, "That's right! And

"Sheriff Sal," *Western Adventures* #1, 1948, Ace Magazines.

just as good as a *man* sheriff any day!"[27] Each issue finds the townsfolk calling for Sal's resignation, only to watch her arrest the various ne'er-do-wells that the men are unable to capture. Sal also regularly fights off Flash Gannon's requests that she quit her dangerous line of work and marry him. When she finally agrees to marriage only if she can remain sheriff, he withdraws his offer: "Well, someday you'll give it all up, honey . . . an' I'll be waiting for you!"[28] Both Boots Bradley and Sheriff Sal provided readers with strong examples of how not all women followed traditional courtship models, sometimes choosing a career over marriage.

Joining Sal as a bearer of the badge was Two-Gun Lil in the pages of Quality Comics' *Crack Western*. Just as Sheriff Sal appears in the first issue of *Western Adventure Comics*, so too does Two-Gun Lil make her debut in the first issue of *Crack Western*. True to her moniker, the series makes the point that firearms are not a tool for men alone—and mocks the men who assume so. Her first appearance begins with narration stating, "'Keep shootin,' honey,' Sheriff Sam Peters told his beautiful daughter, Lil! 'Some day those six-guns may turn out to be the only friends you got!' So little Lil played with guns before she played with dolls—and when the terrible day of vengeance came, she was ready!" When Lil tries her hand at a carnival booth, she's told by the operator, "Guns ain't for ladies!" Her date further warns her, "Be careful, Lil! You have no idea how heavy and loud they are!" In turn, Lil proceeds to shoot down all of the booth's tin cans, proclaiming "Phooey! I cut my first teeth on the barrel of a Colt .44!"[29] Western comics regularly demonstrate that the ability to commit violent acts—whether in the name of justice or vengeance—is not innately masculine.

Lil is persuaded to run for sheriff after returning to her childhood home of Sage City. While away at college in Boston, she receives a telegram saying that her father has been killed by "bushwhackers." Vowing revenge, she returns to Sage City to stop a gambler named Garson Cade (who, we learn, murdered her father). When he discovers Lil's mission of revenge, Cade and his men tie her up, start a fire in her room, and ignite a bundle of dynamite for good measure.

"These men always figure a gal will be too paralyzed with fright to use her head!" says Lil after they leave, as she picks up the dynamite with her feet and tosses it out a nearby window. Using a piece of broken glass to cut through her restraints, Lil vows to kill her captor: "Now Mr. Garson Cade is in for a shock . . . and it's bound to prove fatal!" After she forces a confession about her father's murder, the deputy sheriff promises that Cade will be hanged for his crimes. For her efforts Lil is greeted by townsfolk carrying a banner declaring "Two-Gun Lil for Sheriff / Vote For Lil Peters / She Cleaned Up Sage City."

Whereas Sheriff Sal was regularly challenged in her role, Lil's tenure as the head of the town's law enforcement is openly embraced by its residents. Lil's role as sheriff is born out of a quest for personal vengeance, but her gender isn't the same issue as it was for Red Dog's townsfolk when Sal proved equally proficient at her job. Historian Elizabeth Jameson describes how women of the American West were subject to hypocritical judgments about whether their behavior was good or bad, moral or immoral: "The stereotypes inhabited a public masculinity that offered women no way to win. The good women were not man enough for the West. The best stayed hidden in domestic seclusion, far from the public arenas where history was made. Those who, like good men, were sexual, competent, self-reliant, active, and adventurous became, by definition, bad women."[30] Sheriff Sal poked fun at such judgments, while

"Two-Gun Lil," *Crack Western* #63, 1949, Quality Comics.

Two-Gun Lil and Boots Bradley defied them. At their best, Golden Age western comics became a forum for tales of powerful women in prominent societal roles. They also allowed female heroes to utterly emasculate men, such as in *Crack Western* #64 when Two-Gun Lil responds to a male villain who is reaching for a shotgun. Lil shoots the barrel of his gun, scolding him as she would a small child: "Mustn't touch! Might burn little hands!"[31] The women who ran ranches and protected towns in these comics regularly challenged gender stereotypes of the western genre in alternately overt, playful, and critical ways that women in other media rarely did.

Outlaws

Much like how female sheriffs arose early on in the western comics boom of the late 1940s, women outlaws were also offered up as the genre expanded. Fox Feature Syndicate launched several titles that regularly offered tales of female fugitives, marauders, and outlaws in 1948, such as *Western Thrillers*, *Western True Crimes*, and *Women Outlaws*. The first issue of *Western True Crimes* features a story entitled "Kiss of Death Kate," which opens with some hair-raising, even rhapsodic rhetoric about its title character:

> Purty as a rose an' deadly as a rattler!—That's what the miners, barkeeps and gamblers on Virginia City whispered about Kate Cardell who'd come up from California to grab her share of gaiety and gold in the Nevada boom town, but Kate found there was no sweet

> chivalry to excuse cold-blooded killing, as the shadow of the noose grew closer to her neck, she threw a kiss to the hangman and spurred the sheriff's sorrel into a race against whistling death![32]

She dies not at the end of a rope but while escaping on horseback, shot by a member of the sheriff's posse who mistook her for a man after she dressed in the stolen clothes of a cowboy she leaves for dead. The fact that she dies in men's clothing is just one example—albeit a visually blatant one—of how female outlaws subverted standard representations of gender in western comics.

Although the first issue of *Western Thrillers* boasts the tagline "Bad Men of the Wild West" on its cover, the outlaws it features are exclusively female in its three stories: "The Saga of Velvet Rose and Her Dance of Death," "Two Gun Sal—Poison in Pigtails," and "Striker Sisters—The Murderous Farmer's Daughters?" Other publishers soon followed. Atlas debuted a character named Tricky Min in *Western Outlaws*, while Magazine Enterprises offered readers a masked female bandit in *Tim Holt* called the Black Phantom (which one character in the story awkwardly describes as "the most deadly shemale of 'em all!").[33] While starting off robbing stagecoaches in her first appearance, Black Phantom returns as a hero in later issues and even becomes the town deputy and a sidekick to the hero, the Red Mask.[34]

Distinctions between supposedly good and supposedly bad women were frequently tested in these tales devoted to famous and fictional bandits, rustlers, and killers. Historian Sarah Barringer Gordon notes, "The legal landscape of the West, one might say, changed as much in the nineteenth century as the physical landscape."[35] The boundaries of what was legal and illegal shifted across both territories and the passing decades, but western comics generally adhered to mid-twentieth-century distinctions of right and wrong, virtue and vice.

The western genre was often considered a relatively wholesome one across various media in this era: William J. Devlin describes, for example, a "traditional western framework that contained innocent and wholesome westerns struggling to live out the American dream, typical villains driven by greed and power, and the heroes who fought for what is right."[36] But not everyone agreed that western comics were a better alternative to the crime, horror, and superhero titles that were condemned by cultural critics in the Golden Age. In *Seduction of the Innocent*, Frederic Wertham describes how the western genre is not as innocent as many believed: "What about the 'wholesome' adventure stories, the 'Westerns,' for example? The vast majority, if not all Western comic books are crime comic books. They describe all kinds of crime and brutality." He cites what he refers to as a "liberal magazine, *The Reporter*," and its 1951 article about what draws children to comics. "Children are charmed by the comic books because in them they can follow 'the fortunes of cowhands and mice.' That is how we deceive ourselves and others," writes Wertham. "'Cowhands' do occur in western comics; but Western comics are mostly just crime comics in a Western setting."[37]

Wertham was concerned not only with how western comics were apparently just a different breed of crime comics but also with how they subverted traditional images of women. *Seduction* contains sixteen pages of images in the middle of the book, many serving as stand-alone examples that are not analyzed elsewhere by Wertham. One such image comes from the first issue of *Women Outlaws*, the Fox series whose cover announces its emphasis on "True Stories of Famous Western Gun Gals." Wertham uses a single panel depicting a casino/saloon owner and cattle rustler by the name of "Cattle Kate" Maxwell (a real-life figure whose actual name was Ellen "Ella" Watson). In the image, Kate rushes forward, wearing a low-cut dress, while a single word balloon has her yelling, "Lousy!!! Filthy!!! I'll tear ya . . ." Wertham offers only the following caption as our sole context for understanding the panel: "Giving children an image of American womanhood." Presumably, Wertham took issue with the character's stern language and the threat of violence uttered, coupled with how her outfit becomes more revealing as she leans forward to rush toward the reader. His caption is highly sarcastic; "American womanhood," then, is supposedly well mannered, nonviolent, and demure.

But the panel Wertham chose to critique how comics portray womanhood is, not surprisingly, taken out of context within the story's larger dynamics, as well as the real-life circumstances around the very moment in Cattle Kate's life that Wertham snidely critiques. While not visible in this panel, Kate's arms are bound behind her back after being caught by a rancher named Al Booth, whose cattle she and her partner, Jim Averill, were stealing. Booth offers Jim and Kate the chance to leave town for their crimes but then quickly decides to "take justice into [his] own hands" as he and his men prepare two nooses. Both are hung from the same tree by the lynch mob; "strung her up like a prize turkey!" exclaims Booth. This picture of "American womanhood" that Wertham uses is an image of persecution, of legal injustice, and of imminent death. It is also an image of resistance, of a woman fighting back against a man playing judge, jury, and executioner.

There's more to Kate's story: at the start of the narrative, she arrives in Carbondale, Wyoming, to set up a gambling house but is quickly

The full context of the panel featuring Cattle Kate saying "Lousy! Filthy! I'll tear ya . . ." used by Fredric Wertham in *Seduction of the Innocent* (1954). From *Women Outlaws* #1, 1948, Fox Feature Syndicate.

confronted by townsfolk who seek to prey on her. After hanging a sign to announce her grand opening, she is forced to reject an unwelcome sexual advance: "Glad to meet ya, Kate . . . Zeb's my moniker. Me and you's gonna be good fr . . . Hey!" In the midst of telling Kate how "friendly" he plans to be, she knocks Zeb to the ground with the handle of her revolver because he put his hands on her. "Get ya dirty hands off me, ya filthy lobo! Don'tcha know how to act when yer with a lady?" she yells, adding, "Lissen, th' rest o' ya cowpokes. . . . Kate Maxwell don't take no pushin' aroun' from no one, see!" By labeling Zeb a "lobo," she calls him out as a predator ("lobo" being the Spanish word for wolf). Kate constantly stands up to men behaving badly, using force when necessary to avoid being taken advantage of.

The opening narration describes Kate as "the wildest woman in the west" with a "fiery temper," a "ruthless tigress of the gambling table" who "dealt cards from the bottom of the deck with the best of them," a vicious murderer, and a "beautiful bandit who reigned supreme as 'the queen of the rustlers!'"[38] The problem with all of this sensational rhetoric is that it describes the wrong woman. Historians found that the legend of Cattle Kate was based on two different women, one a homesteader named Ellen Watson and the other a prostitute named Kate Maxwell. The story in *Women Outlaws* that Wertham draws on conflates the two identities, making Kate Maxwell an alias of Ellen Watson. Lori Van Pelt explains that the confusion stems from how "newspapers carrying reports of the lynching confused [Watson] at first with a prostitute, Kate Maxwell, from Bessemer Bend, more than twenty miles from Ellen Watson's homestead

"Cattle Kate," *Women Outlaws* #1, 1948, Fox Feature Syndicate.

claim. Because Ellen had been accused of rustling cattle, newspapers affixed the moniker Cattle Kate, and the name stuck."[39] In reality, Watson was accused of stealing cattle by ranchers who had repeatedly attempted to buy the land that she acquired legally through a squatter's rights claim under the Preemption Act in 1886. Three years later, the ranchers hired a

Cattle Kate sets up shop in *Women Outlaws* #1, 1948, Fox Feature Syndicate.

posse to kill Watson and her husband, James Averill. Both were hanged from the same tree, where their bodies remained for two days.[40]

Women Outlaws certainly perpetuates the falsehoods behind the legend of Cattle Kate. But Wertham's use of a single panel, taken entirely out of context from the story's terrible events, is even more injurious in how he seeks to turn Ella Watson—a woman who died tragically—into a symbol of everything that American women supposedly should not be. When he writes that the panel gives young readers "an image of American womanhood," what he really means is that women should not speak out in anger, they should never threaten acts of violence, they should not fight back, and they should never resist—even in the face of injustice, and even at the hands of men who want them dead. Wertham considered Watson's dialogue—"Lousy!!! Filthy!!! I'll tear ya . . ."—to be improper, hostile, and unfeminine. But given how this moment shows us a woman facing death who *does* fight back and who *does* resist her executioners, we should reclaim this line as a new interpretation of American womanhood:

as persisting, unflinching, fearless. *Seduction of the Innocent* ultimately helped undercut the popularity of crime and horror comics by the mid-1950s, with those two genres suffering most under the creation of the Comics Code Authority. The ways in which Wertham vehemently targeted female characters for being too dominant, too spirited, and too unlike his limited conception of "womanhood" must also be remembered as part of his legacy.

Women of Color

While western comics featured more women in strong roles than most genres of the Golden Age did, it is vital to note which groups of women are noticeably absent from such tales. Women of color, especially Black women and Asian women, are almost entirely unseen in the pages of western comics. Hispanic women are featured on occasion but rarely in more than a brief, supporting role—frequently as caregivers for white characters. Dell's first Annie Oakley comic, for example, finds her seeking the aid of an older Mexican woman named Maria who, we're told, "used to do housework" for a local cattle rancher. She appears in only three panels: in the first we find her on her knees doing laundry at a creek; in the second she is carrying her laundry basket back to what Oakley describes as her "shack"; finally, she literally takes Annie's injured brother under her arm, promising to take care of him until a doctor arrives.[41]

A similar pattern is found in *Western True Stories* #15, which gives us a character named Señorita Manriquez in one mere panel. She is described by the narrator as "an old flame" of an outlaw, who "furnishes refuge and care" for his injured partner. When asked if there is any hope for the man, Manriquez replies, "He will die, Senor. Eet ees gangrene."[42] These two Hispanic women are marginal to each story, used only to protect one male character and pronounce another's death. In each case, they exist only to serve the needs of narratives centered around white characters.

Historian Elizabeth Jameson notes that when studying women's history in the American West, it is vital to consider exactly which groups of women form the center of any historical narrative: "A history focused not on the West itself, but on the people who sojourned or settled there, raises essential questions about women, the West, and the nineteenth century. *Which* women?" Jameson describes how such diverse groups as the "hispanas, indias, mestizas of Northern New Spain"; the "Lakota, Cree and Blackfoot women of the northern plains"; the "African American Exodusters who migrated West after the Civil War"; and the "Mormon women" of Utah would have gone through radically different experiences in the nineteenth century, including "periods of changing gender options" for some groups but not others. "Which women, whose story, should open this history?" she asks.

Indeed, the stories told about women in western comics of the Golden Age are typically about a narrow range of women: protagonists are almost always white, and most are either teenagers or in early adulthood. Many are from well-off families who own ranches. Whereas other genres often featured women of a wide range of ages and social classes, western comics offered much more limited roles for female characters. To be both a woman *and* a hero for comics readers in this era came with certain restrictions about which kinds of women could fulfill such a role.

In turn, Jameson describes how "'Western women' as a collectivity shatter into distinct individuals and groups whose histories do not always touch."[43] She argues that the history of American settlers in the nineteenth century has been "recast by many historians as the histories of conquest and colonization." She writes,

> From women's perspectives they also become intimate encounters that, on one end of the spectrum, added rape and sexual exploitation to the violence of conquest, and, at the other, resulted in intimate cultural exchanges and new mestizo and métis people. Those relationships, involving people of different races, cultures and classes, as well as different genders, can only be understood if we understand them from the perspective of all the actors.[44]

There was certainly a limited number of races, cultures, and classes represented by the women who gained starring roles in western comics. Even when their stories turned to indigenous peoples from first nations tribes, comics creators frequently inserted white characters. Firehair, for one, first appeared as a supporting feature in Fiction House's *Rangers Comics* between 1945 and 1952, and had her own title, *Firehair Comics*, from 1948 to 1952. When she is injured and her father killed during an attack by white men posing as members of the Dakota tribe, Lynn Cabot is taken in by the Dakotas and is trained to become a warrior. In turn, she confronts the attackers and clears the tribe's name of wrongdoing. She remains with the Dakotas after proving to be their strongest and fiercest fighter, given the name Firehair by the tribe for her flaming red locks.

She is welcomed into the tribe by their chief, Tehama, and quickly becomes the tribe's leading warrior. In the first issue of *Firehair Comics*,

Chief Tehama is warned by the tribe's healer, Two Horns, that his "smoke signs show death and danger around her." When Firehair bests a rival at archery and then knocks her into the river when accused of cheating, Tehama proudly exclaims, "Hah! I say death and danger for those who dare to oppose our warrior maiden, Firehair!"[45] The series regularly reminded readers that a female hero could be the equal of men. As Firehair and the chief's son, Little Ax, race to find a herd of wild horses, she comments about the gendered optics of her riding a horse and his running on foot: "The teepees will laugh, Little Ax, to see the sister ride while the brother goes afoot." Little Ax defiantly responds, "Bah! Who cares for the giggles of fools?"[46]

Make no mistake, Firehair is a strong female character, and the fact that her popularity within the pages of *Rangers Comics* led to her own solo series is notable. Relatively few women headlined their own series in this era, let alone within the western genre. But as a white character who becomes a leading warrior within a native tribe, Firehair still embodies a colonialist fantasy in which a white hero is trained by an indigenous group (and their community is transformed by the white hero's presence in the process).[47]

Still, a few powerful attempts were made at telling stories about indigenous women in Golden Age westerns, even if they remain little known. Beginning in 1948 with the second issue of Fiction House's *Indians*, Starlight became the first indigenous female character to regularly star in a non-comedic American comic book, appearing through issue 8 of the series; there were various gag strips with comedic characters, but Starlight offered a serious, dramatic alternative to such mockeries. Her first appearance opens with narration describing just how different Starlight is as a character: "Maidens should be modest . . . maidens should be gentle and shy—content to cook and weave for the meat killers . . . but the heart that beat in Starlight's breast was tuned to the windigo winds . . . to the hunt and the chase and the danger drums!"[48] In *The Spectacular Sisterhood of Superwomen*, Hope Nicholson notes that the series "was praised by Indigenous readers as a step in the right direction, citing that the stories featured Indigenous characters as human beings instead of murderous madmen."[49]

Starlight's first story opens with her resisting the domestic role expected of her within the Huron tribe: "Behold the day is bright and warm—more hunters leave to stalk the deer . . . but we sit in sweltering huts, tending pots and babies . . . are we slaves? I can hunt as well as any brave! I can wing my arrows."[50] By the end she rescues a captured tribe member,

"Starlight," *Indians* #2, 1950, Fiction House.

wrestling a tomahawk from the hands of a Mohawk chieftain. Some 1950s readers may have considered an adventure like this fantastical, but in reality, native American women were frequently warriors. Historian John P. McWilliams describes Apache tribeswomen: "Unlike some misconceived stereotypes, the women of the Apache were not passive observers of what went on around them, or what affected their lives, their families, their culture, their way of life, or their People. Apache women were known to fight beside their warrior men, often at their husband's side."[51]

While Starlight didn't debut until the second issue of *Indians*, she was preceded in the first issue by another strong female character named Red Fawn. Described as a "young maiden" of the Tawonki tribe, Red Fawn is a preadolescent girl who, we are told, "cared naught for woman's work, instead she yearned to roam the plains with the stalkers of the deer." Much like Starlight, she decries the limitations placed on her potential: "Pah! Is our lot to be nothing but cooking, sewing and making wigwams?"[52] Sneaking away to hunt in secret, by the end of her adventure Red Fawn not only uses her bow to kill an eagle but also captures the leader of a rival tribe's "Comanche raiders." Taking pride in her efforts, she ends by declaring, "Aye, Red Fawn is a *great* hunter!" with a knowing glance at the reader.[53] Starlight and Red Fawn offered readers positive examples of indigenous women who were the equal of (and often more skilled than) their male counterparts. While many western comics resorted to stereotypes of Native American characters, there was a clear attempt by Fiction House to make *Indians* a forum for more nuanced characterizations of indigenous peoples.

A similar effort can be found in the Dell series *The Chief* (later renamed *Indian Chief*) with the character Moon Maiden. Issues 2 and 3 tell the tale of White Wolf, a Pawnee tribesman who marries the daughter of an Onondaga chief. When White Wolf is excluded from the Iroquois tribe's hunting and trapping activities, Moon Maiden offers to mentor her new spouse: "I will teach my husband *all* the Onondaga's secrets of the trap line and the hunt!"[54] She teaches him how to build a shelter and fire in the snow, how to avoid being seen by enemies, where to best set snares to trap game, and how to bait a bear trap. When White Wolf tries to fight off a wolverine stealing their bait, he ends up caught under the heavy logs of the bear trap. Following her missing husband's trail, Moon Maiden rescues him, builds a fire, and treats his wounds, saving his life. Unlike the brief appearance of Latina caregivers in many western comics, series such as *Indians* and *The Chief* devoted ample space to showing the depths of their female characters' knowledge and abilities rather than reducing them to stock characters meant only to advance the plot. "Your skill—and your love—have already brought me back from death, Moon Maiden!" says White Wolf.[55]

The third issue sees their story continue, with Moon Maiden having helped White Wolf to trap many animals for their fur throughout the winter. When her husband sets out to catch more game, she mocks him playfully: "In case you don't bring home a deer, I will go to the lake and

Moon Maiden in *The Chief* #2, 1951, Dell Comics.

catch some fat trout through the ice!" White Wolf fires back, "Laughing at me, are you, saucy girl?" But while Moon Maiden is ice fishing, she is captured by a group of Abenaki hunters, who steal her pelts and then attempt to kidnap her: "Woman stealers! Don't touch me with your dirty hands, or . . ." she warns while drawing her knife. Overpowering her, the hunters set out to return to their Abenaki tribe, where Moon Maiden will be forced into domestic service: "March girl! From now on you will keep an Abenaki house!" Resisting her fate, Moon Maiden taunts her captors when they make camp for the night and demand that she cooks her fish for them. "The Abenaki is such a poor hunter that he steals a woman's catch of trout! Pah!," she sneers, before adding defiantly, "It will be your last meal! Death follows closely on your trail, Abenaki!"[56]

Like other women in western comics, Moon Maiden actively resists her captors, fighting back while skillfully escaping the literal ties that bind her. Using her foot to secure an ember from the campfire, Moon Maiden first burns and then trips one of the warriors just as her husband arrives and begins to fight. After Moon Maiden saves White Wolf's life from an unseen attacker, the couple subdues the Abenaki warriors and forces them to carry the stolen pelts home. But Moon Maiden ultimately offers her assailants forgiveness rather than death of servitude: "I have said that I would not keep house for the Abenaki—and I will not have them in *our* house, my husband! Can't you let them go?"[57]

Starlight, Red Fawn, and Moon Maiden offered readers far more complex characterizations than most women of color were afforded in the Golden Age of comics. Historian Kimberly Moore Buchanan notes that indigenous women are usually "regarded and portrayed as mere supporting characters" in American history, "but among many tribes there were those who defied the stereotype of the drudging squaw."[58] The same is seen in western comics, as powerful characters like Moon Maiden prove to us. While the genre offered relatively few opportunities for women of color to become heroes, those that did emerge are powerful examples of women as valiant warriors who were equal to—or better than—any man.

Conclusion

Ultimately, western comics are mostly remembered for their male heroes, especially those who also had long runs in B movies and on television, such as Gene Autry, Tim Holt, Hopalong Cassidy, Lash LaRue, and Roy Rogers. Comics series with manly titles like *Ben Bowie and His Mountain Men* reflect how the western genre regularly emphasized masculinity, despite a few cowgirls such as Annie Oakley and Dale Evans earning their own titles. Many female characters, however, played supporting roles, either as fodder to advance the narratives of male characters or as part of anthology titles with a range of (usually male) characters. Starlight, Moon Maiden, Kit West, Sheriff Sal, Wilma West, Black Phantom, Boots Bradley, and Two-Gun Lil were all strong characters, but without their own titles most have been largely forgotten.

At the same time, few female creators worked on western comics for very long, further cementing the western as a mostly male genre. As owner of Orbit Publications, Ray Herman likely wrote at least some stories for *The Westerner* (which often featured the masked outlaw Calamity Kate), given how much remains uncredited on that series and how often she wrote for her company's other titles. Some fan websites credit Pauline Loth as drawing western comics at Better Publications in 1950, but the exact titles and issues remain unknown.[59] The Kit West stories in issues

4 through 6 of *Cow Puncher* (as well as *Geronimo* issues 2 and 3) were illustrated by Jill Elgin, who had drawn *The Black Cat* for Harvey Comics earlier in the 1940s. She also drew a handful of stories for issues of *Crack Western*, *Wild Bill Hickock*, and *Colt Western Library*. Ruth Roche created the villainous character Ace of Spades, a masked outlaw who appeared in *Phantom Lady* #20 in 1948 (though was never seen again).

While Fiction House does credit a writer named Ann Adams as the creator of Starlight and another named Emila Jayne as the creator of a character called Orphan of the Storm in *Indians*, neither appears to have written anything else for that publisher or any other, making it likely that both were pseudonyms. While Roche wrote under several pen names for Fiction House, including Rod Roche, Agnes Wilson, Miss Thorpe, and Miss Adams, it's unknown whether she was indeed the same Ann Adams who created Starlight.[60] While other genres saw creators such as Ruth Atkinson, Toni Blum, Fran Hopper, Lily Renée, and Marcia Snyder write or draw costumed heroes, daring adventurers, jungle warriors, frightful creatures, romantic couples, and outer space explorers, relatively few western comics were created by women.

While the genre appears to be a largely masculine one on the surface, western comics were steadily enjoyed by both men and women in the 1940s and 1950s. The letters to the editor section of *Cow Puncher Comics* regularly printed letters from female readers. In issue 3, a reader named Andrea writes, "I have bought almost all the books on the news stands and I think Cow Puncher is one of the best," while the secretary of a "comic club" for local "boys and girls" in Wilton, North Carolina, named Imogene tells of how *Cow Puncher* is in high demand: "By the time we have all read it the copies are in shreds. *We think it's swell!*"[61] Similarly, the fourth issue contains a letter from a reader named Anna describing how she has the series "saved at the corner newsstand" so she never misses an issue.[62] In turn, advertisements in western comics frequently targeted both male and female readers. One issue of *Firehair Comics*, for instance, featured back-to-back ads for bodybuilding courses ("Let's go, pal! I'll prove I can make YOU too an 'all-around' He-Man *fast*—or it won't cost you a cent") and mail-order dresses ("Mothers—Housewives—here's an amazing new plan! Gorgeous dresses for you without paying 1¢").[63]

While Fred Guardineer's 1937 poem celebrating cowgirls was an anomaly in 1930s western comics, by the late 1940s it was commonplace to find female characters riding the range. Although Wertham condemned female outlaws like Cattle Kate, other characters, such as the sheriff Sally Starr and the ranch owner Boots Bradley, proved that female gunslingers could hold their own alongside their male counterparts, both within their own series and on newsstands. Dale Evans enjoyed more than ten years' worth of issues, outlasting characters in several other genres in the process. Westerns may be commonly considered a male genre, but Golden Age comics saw fearless female heroes regularly challenge the belief that men made the best buckaroos, wranglers, and cowpunchers.

CHAPTER 6

TITLE CHARACTERS

In 1957, Stan Lee and Martin Goodman faced a crisis. After a distribution deal for their line of Timely/Atlas comics fell through, the respective editor in chief and owner of what would soon become Marvel Comics were forced to strike a deal with Independent News, a company owned by their main rival, DC Comics. As part of the deal, Goodman and Lee could produce no more than eight comics a month, which led to their existing line of titles being slashed drastically and most staffers being fired.[1] Titles from a range of genres were canceled, including the fantasy/horror series *Marvel Tales* and westerns such as *Outlaw Kid*, *Rawhide Kid*, *Ringo Kid*, *Western Kid*, and *Wild Westerns*. But three series remained safe: *Millie the Model*, *Patsy Walker*, and *Patsy and Hedy*, which had long ranked among Timely/Atlas's top sellers.

Even as Lee and Goodman rebranded Marvel as a superhero publisher in the early 1960s, they still couldn't cancel their female characters while building a new brand of costumed heroes with *The Fantastic Four*, *The Amazing Spider-Man*, *The Incredible Hulk*, and *The Avengers*. No matter how many new superheroes Marvel introduced in the early 1960s, *Millie*, *Patsy*, and *Patsy and Hedy* remained three of the eight Marvel titles available on newsstands. Even when Independent News allowed Marvel to expand its line to a maximum of fourteen titles per month in 1963, Patsy and her pals continued their veteran presence.[2] While Marvel Comics may be best remembered now for how it birthed a new line of powerful superheroes, the company was only able to reinvent itself thanks to the steady success of its powerhouse young female characters.

Comics like *Patsy Walker* and *Millie the Model* offered fans a different, more personal form of engagement than did comics in other genres, often fostering a sense of community among readers. In the first issue of the comic book adaptation of the 1950s television and radio program *My Little Margie*, for instance, the titular character describes in a direct address to her readers the idiosyncratic, intimate nature of comic readership. "For here," Margie writes, "I have only one person in my audience at a time. YOU." In this letter, Margie implores her readers to share with her any and all of the stories they want to see her and her pals in; to write her often, as she'll be "dying to hear from [them]"; and, of course, to tune in to her television program of the same name. The purpose of the comic book here—as opposed to television, radio, or the newspaper, all of which court mass audiences, appeal to the thousands, and address the entire family—is to appease the individual reader and create some semblance of friendship. Margie isn't just a character you read about; she is your confidant, your pen pal, and your personal entertainment. She wants to listen to *your* ideas, and she wants to use them.

For the women of the 1930s, 1940s, and 1950s, the idea that they might actually be seen, listened to, or taken seriously by anyone in an industry as male-oriented as comic books would have been novel. *My Little Margie* was only one of dozens of Golden Age titles aimed at women and girls in the hopes of providing a different kind of comics reading experience. What's more, such books offered many women creators a chance to provide new types of characters to teenage and young girls who read comics, including Gladys Parker's Mopsy, among other characters.

Female comics fans were more prevalent than many assume. By the mid-1940s, studies showed that young girls made up a large proportion of overall readers and continued to read comics well into their teenage years. A 1944 study found that 91 percent of girls age six to eleven regularly read comics, not far behind the 95 percent of boys the same age who were also comic book readers. Most girls continued reading comics as teenagers: 81 percent of those age twelve to seventeen as compared to 87 percent of boys. While the drop-off in readership was steep after the teenage years, 28 percent of adult woman age thirty and under still read comics in 1944. After age thirty, the number of regular readers dropped to just 12 percent, but an additional 10 percent of women declared themselves as "occasional readers."[3]

While men made up a higher proportion of readers in each age category, millions of women across the country read comics, and the range of titles that catered to them grew steadily throughout the 1940s. As the decade progressed, most publishers recognized the need for titles targeted specifically to women and girls, as well as comics that all genders

My Little Margie #1, 1954, Charlton Comics.

would enjoy equally. The teen comic was one such result. While such titles are often considered part of the humor genre (and they are indeed humorous!), their teenage concerns, revolving around life and love, are vastly different from the challenges faced by protagonists in other types of humor comics.[4] The struggles faced by animals such as Donald Duck in

Walt Disney's Comics and Stories or by younger girls such as Little Lulu are not the same as those that Millie, Patsy, Hedy, and Margie encounter. Teen comics often combined the humor and melodrama genres in a way that allowed readers transitionary titles as they aged out of funny animal books and that also served as a bridge to more adult-oriented romance comics by the end of the 1940s.

The majority of Golden Age teen comic taxonomies began in 1941 with the arrival of a certain redhead and his two rivaling girlfriends in issue 22 of MLJ Magazines' *Pep Comics*. The teen comic craze, integral to the industry's growth throughout the 1940s, was jump-started by the first appearances of Archie Andrews, Jughead Jones, and Betty Cooper (followed by Veronica Lodge four issues later in 1942). Although Betty and Veronica were part of the *Archie Comics* crew from the very beginning, they didn't get their own title until 1950; even then, they are qualified as *Archie's Girls Betty and Veronica*. Betty and Veronica's thirty-seven-year run long outlasted every single female title character that came both before and after them, but their boy-centric adventures did not define the first wave of women with their own comics.

The first notable female title characters arrived in the 1940s with the career girl comics, which had roots (like so many other female-led titles of this era) in newspaper comic strips. Beginning with Russ Westover's *Tillie the Toiler* strip, which debuted in 1921, the career girl comic made a return in the mid-1940s with such Timely Comics titles as *Tessie the Typist* (1944–1949), *Millie the Model* (1945–1973), and *Nellie the Nurse* (1945–1952). Few of the stories involving the career girls, however, have anything to do with actual work pertaining to their career. The office (or the catwalk, or the hospital) is simply the stage upon which each character performs her various farces and follies.

The second major—and arguably the defining—group of female title characters are the teens. As the comics historian and cartoonist Trina Robbins notes in *From Girls to Grrrlz*, the *Archie* craze inspired a number of clones that never quite reached the popularity or charm of the originals.[5] They did, however, signal a massive boom in teen comics that, despite the assumed male audience of comic books at the time, turned out to be primarily female titles. There is the requisite *Archie's Girls Betty and Veronica*, but there are also numerous other teen girl titles at this time: *Patsy Walker* (1945–1965, Timely/Atlas/Marvel Comics), *Suzie* (1945–1954, MLJ Magazine/Archie Comics), *Margie* (1946–1949, Timely Comics), *Candy* (1947–1956, Quality Comics), *Penny* (1947–1949, Avon Comics), *Rusty* (1947–1949, Timely Comics), *Jeanie* (1947–1949, Timely Comics), *Cindy* (1947–1950, Timely/Atlas Comics), *Sunny* (1947–1948,

Fox Feature Syndicate), *Vicky* (1948–1949, Ace Magazines), *Meet Corliss Archer* (1948, Fox Feature Syndicate), *Kathy* (1949–1955, Standard Comics), *Katy Keene* (1949–1961, MLJ Magazines/Archie Comics), *Ginger* (1951–1954, MLJ Magazines/Archie Comics), *Mazie* (1952–1954, Nation-Wide Publishing; 1955–1958, Harvey Comics), *Wendy Parker* (1953–1954, Atlas Comics), *Lucy, the Real Gone Gal* (1953–1954, St. John Publications), *My Little Margie* (1954–1964, Charlton Comics), and so on.

Many of these lasted for a decade or more, while others saw only a handful of issues or changed titles midway through their run. Like the career girl comics, teen titles mainly focus on romance, humor, and general hijinks. Where they are distinct is in the appearance of each characters' family members, classmates, and teachers, as well as the school-specific shenanigans they frequently get into.

Around the same time in the late 1940s and early 1950s came the third (and perhaps most difficult to categorize) wave of female title characters. They are often older, and their narratives explore marginally more mature themes, in terms of both sexual content and general subject matter. The women in these comics are still young and beautiful, but distinct from both the teen title characters *and* the career girls, characterized neither as specific working women nor as students. Though they may have jobs, their careers are rarely the focus of their comics. And if they are students, their studies are eclipsed by more important matters, such as boyfriends and fashion. Instead, they return to the same humor and romance themes that every female title comic book circles around, but with a more nuanced approach to romance and sexuality, since these characters are no longer teens. Books like *Dixie Dugan* (1941–1949, Columbia Comics; 1951–1954, Prize Comics), *Dotty* (subtitled *Dotty and Her Boyfriends*; 1948–1949, Ace Magazines), *Boots and Her Buddies* (1948–1949, Standard Comics; 1955–1956, Argo Publications), and *Torchy* (1949–1950, Quality Comics) chronicle the lives of unmarried women as they attempt to find well-paying jobs and lasting romance, both of which lead them into more trouble than good. However, *Dotty*, *Boots*, *Dixie*, and *Torchy* are exemplary of just how diverse the titles falling under the loose "leading ladies" heading really were. While Dixie always seems to have some job or another and pays little mind to showing off her sexuality, Torchy is a shiftless—though exceedingly nice and empathetic—sex kitten whose days are spent on whatever scheme she has been dragged into by those around her. Likewise, Dotty's and Boots's lives revolve around romance and friendship, but Dotty focuses more on her career and Boots on her future family.

Other titles that fall into the category of leading ladies include *Flyin' Jenny* (1946, Pentagon Publishing Co.), *Hedy De Vine* (1947–1949, Timely Comics), *Starlet O'Hara in Hollywood* (1948–1949, Standard Comics), *Mopsy* (1949–1953, St. John Publications), *Miss Beverly Hills of Hollywood* (1949–1950, DC Comics), *Miss Melody Lane of Broadway* (1950, DC Comics), *Canteen Kate* (1952, St. John Publications), and *Meet Miss Pepper* (1954, St. John Publications). As their titles indicate, the women in this category range from test pilots to aspiring actresses to school teachers. What they all have in common, however, is that they are always the most beautiful women in every room (or panel) they enter and always eager and willing to help those around them. And whether they dress provocatively, flirt, or otherwise put themselves "on display," they are consistently objectified by the male characters in their stories. Beauty, kindness, and sexual desirability are mandatory characteristics across all the female title character comics of the Golden Age. Intelligence, work ethic, and personal autonomy are often secondary to many of these characters' desirability and need to please others.

Though a pattern emerges in the female-led titles of the Golden Age, these categories are not rigid. Many titles span categories or defy categorization altogether. Likewise, the hypersexualization and fetishization of female characters is consistent across all three categories of title characters. Whether she is a working girl, a teenager, or a grown woman, these characters are often seen in various stages of undress, up-close shots of their stockinged legs, or other tantalizing displays. This isn't to suggest, though, that many of these same characters are not *also* often empowered, liberated, independent, or what we might consider feminist. Empowerment and disempowerment are not mutually exclusive concepts when it comes to discussing female title characters, nor are race, sexuality, gender, and class. The female title characters of the Golden Age frequently display an inherent complexity and resistance to categorization.

Working Women: Career Girl Comics in the 1940s

Tillie the Toiler, created by Russ Westover and distributed to newspapers by King Features Syndicate, is often thought to be the first in this particular working girl tradition, with its initial run as a daily strip lasting from 1921 through 1959. In 1941, *Tillie* was reprinted as a series of fourteen title issues by Dell Comics, lasting through 1949. Tillie first appeared as a prominent office girl with her own strip in the wake of World War I, when more women than ever had begun working outside the home, and

Cover of *Tillie the Toiler* (*Dell Four Color*) #195, 1948, Dell Publishing.

reemerged in comic book form when the United States entered World War II, a time when women were once again called to take up prominent workplace roles. Most of the career girls arose in the mid-1940s from Timely Comics, mirroring Tillie's postwar trajectory. With titles such as *Tessie the Typist*, *Millie the Model*, and *Nellie the Nurse*, career girl comics made clear that they were about working women and ostensibly constructed the basic narrative of each story around the woman's profession. Though their alliterative titles tie character to career, the working girls' stories follow the same romance and humor formula as the majority of the other titles aimed at women and girls.

Even though she is not the first working girl on the comic strip circuit, Tillie's arrival in 1921, and her reprinted comic book rebirth in 1941, highlight the significance of the shifting cultural, social, and political conditions surrounding both the production and consumption of comic books. Throughout the 1920s, *Tillie* and other comics featuring working women played a key role in integrating the working girl into the American cultural landscape. In his 1947 book dedicated to comic strips, *The*

Comics, Coulton Waugh writes, "Tillie had accepted her position with no sense of 'See how daring I am.' While she got into trouble, it was never because of fighting off the evil attentions of her employer. These object lessons helped to make it difficult for the mothers of would-be Tillies to complain that a business career was immoral."[6] It's frustrating that Waugh sees no conflict between (a) commending *Tillie* for its role in shifting cultural attitudes toward working women and (b) praising the character for lacking any kind of revolutionary spirit. But he *does* get at the heart of a key feature of the career girl comic: her ability to affect real-life, often wartime, change, or, at the very least, to help American society cope with postwar cultural and social changes.

Tessie the Typist, *Millie the Model*, and *Nellie the Nurse* all appeared, like *Tillie the Toiler*, during a period of great social upheaval in the United States. Like Tillie, Tessie, Millie, and Nellie use the pages of their comics to urge their readers to get acquainted with the working woman, and even to become one themselves. The first issue of *Tessie the Typist* (1944) features a panel depicting Tessie speaking directly to her audience: "Seriously, though, girls. Uncle Sam needs a lot of women workers . . . so if you can take a job to relieve some man to fight—do it! Remember, every job done by a woman is a war job!"[7] While such serious and straightforward excursions away from the actual story are rare for *Tessie the Typist*, which is invested much more in slapstick than in social change, the fact that *Tessie*'s creators felt it their duty to urge their audience to "do their part" is significant. *Tessie* is, by all appearances, very much in line with the standard humor and romance formula of other titles aimed at teenagers, but the character's status as a career girl bestows upon her a certain sense of responsibility.

That sense of responsibility doesn't stop Tessie from getting involved in all manner of wacky (and, frankly, weird) to-dos. Her boyfriend, Skidsy, is often somehow made the victim of Tessie's misadventures, and it is primarily their romantic and professional ups and downs that we follow over *Tessie*'s twenty-three-issue run. It seems to be a career girl tradition that any character who joins the workforce must leave her brain behind; both Tillie and Tessie spend more time worrying about romance and their appearances than about their jobs. The implication is perhaps that the only palatable woman outside of the home is the woman who does not do much to challenge the dominant social order. Both Tillie and Tessie, like the majority of the women and girls with their own comics in this period, do little to challenge the stereotype that women and girls are obsessed with their looks and their boyfriend's success, and are unconcerned with intelligence and hard work.

Cover of *Nellie the Nurse* #21, 1949, Timely Comics.

Nellie the Nurse, which ran for thirty-six issues between 1945 and 1952, was slightly more popular than *Tessie* and seemed, initially, to be moving away from the formulaic slapstick comedy that the likes of *Tillie* and *Tessie* offered. Although early issues of *Nellie* still feature the titular Nellie Nelson fussing over her clothes and appearance, their narratives and individual stories are more intimately involved with Nellie's profession than is typical of other career girl comics. Even when *Nellie* is removed from the hospital setting, some mishap always brings the story back around to her medical expertise. Nellie's friends and supporting characters are her fellow hospital employees Snazzy and Speed, and though both are male there is no excessive flirting or sexual tension. The art style, too, of these earlier issues is more detailed and complex than that of its predecessors. Each panel is intricate and full of visual information; the world of *Nellie the Nurse* has a certain amount of sophistication and fullness that its contemporaries don't always capture. Nellie herself is also spared the overt hypersexualization that the majority of Golden Age women characters are subjected to. Although it is clear she is a classic beauty, her clothing, behavior, and sense of humor are modest and demure. The message is clear: Nellie, unlike previous career girls, is no empty-headed good girl; she is a competent, professional, good-hearted woman.

As time wears on, however, Nellie's competence and professionalism dissipate at an alarming rate. By issue 12 in 1948, a third of the way through the title's original run, Nellie has lost nearly every semblance of the competent caregiver identity she once possessed. Before *Nellie* can narratively announce its departure from its previous, more serious subject matter, the new, bolder art does so. While the cover bears the same *Nellie the Nurse* title as previous issues, the artwork both inside and out immediately reveals that this is not the Nellie we have previously known. The series' art credits remain largely unknown, but the colors are brighter, the panels are simpler, the backgrounds are less detailed, and Nellie is curvier. Her adventures began, at this point, to fall more in line with what one would expect of a straightforward humor title.

The first story in issue 12 sees Nellie and her hospital friends learning from a French lecturer that "for ze good of mankind, we must give vent to our inhibitions!" All the female characters are shown resolving to make the objects of their affections their own. Nellie vows to "fix that two-timing, chiseling minx, Pam! And get Snazzy Wilks" for herself; Pam likewise promises to "pull that scheming Nellie Nelson's hair out and get Snazzy" for her own. The male characters, in contrast, shed themselves of their inhibitions by grabbing the nearest woman and kissing her. As time wore on and *Nellie the Nurse* moved further into its run, its art style and narrative antics only grew more cartoonish and farcical. After seven years of increasingly sexualized and dumbed-down stories, *Nellie* finally came to an end in October 1952.

Millie the Model was published in the winter of 1945 alongside *Nellie the Nurse* but far outlasted it with a twenty-eight-year, 207-issue run. Cocreated by Ruth Atkinson, *Millie* was also the only career girl whose first appearance was in her *own* title comic book, as opposed to being a backup feature in another title. This is significant given that female title characters were still a new phenomenon in 1945, and *Millie the Model* proved that they could be more than successful. With Millie and Patsy Walker, a character Atkinson also cocreated, the artist originated two enduring women whose multi-decade success outlasted nearly every other character—superpowered or not—that began in the 1940s. A *Millie the Model* spin-off series called *A Date with Millie* began in 1956, but it was temporarily canceled in 1957 in the wake of Goodman's new distribution

Cover of *Millie the Model* #25, 1950, Timely Comics.

deal with Independent News. The new series was brought back in 1959, with its name changed to *Life with Millie* in 1960 and then finally *Modeling with Millie* in 1963, and ran through 1967.

Atkinson previously had been an art director at Fiction House, where powerful female characters were common.[8] Seeking more time to draw her own work rather than supervise that of others, she left Fiction House to work as a freelance artist.[9] With her first freelance assignments for Stan Lee at Timely, Atkinson cocreated two characters who played a pivotal part in the company's success—and survival—as the market shifted in the late 1950s and early 1960s.

Part of Millie's appeal also stemmed from the fact that, unlike *Nellie*, *Millie* never pretends to be much more than a vehicle for low-stakes laughs and attractively drawn characters. Millie Collins is a small-town girl who moves to New York City to fulfill her dream of becoming a model. There she works, plays, dates—all the usual things that the average American might imagine a successful—but still hardworking—young model might do. In most ways, from the art style to the sense of humor,

Millie the Model was unremarkable, but this didn't keep her from becoming Marvel's longest-running humor title.

Out of all the career girl comics, *Millie the Model* thrived well past the end of the 1940s because it so closely resembled and assimilated itself into the teen trend. From the mid-1940s into the early 1950s, teen girl titles flourished within the comics industry, and Millie's easy approach to dating, fashion, and friendship fell in with the teen crowd in a way that the other career girls could not.

Teens Take Over: The Teen Title Boom of the Postwar Era

Comic book scholars and historians often locate the beginning of the teen comics craze with the arrival of Archie Andrews and his pals in issue 22 of *Pep Comics* in 1941, the same year the United States officially joined World War II.[10] Though the comics industry had much to say about the war, teens and GIs alike began to look for something more innocent to escape into: enter the teen comic, with its innocence and good-natured humor.

Teenagers were not identified as a distinct demographic until at least the 1920s, when college-age youth became a marketing target. By the 1930s, high schoolers were seen as "reliable consumers," with teenaged girls in particular being thought of as "a discrete social group with purchasing power" and "important arbiters of clothing, beauty products, music, and movies—consumers with decided opinions and preferences."[11] Public awareness of this trend grew with the 1944 debut of *Seventeen* magazine, but comic books with lead female characters had been around for several years by then. While few comics historians have delved into the role played by female comics fans, titles targeted to girls thrived during the 1940s.

Coulton Waugh describes how the teenage title boom was driven by superhero fatigue and a thirst for normalcy:

> Why, in the name of a free republic, is all this hooding necessary? True, these people are always on the side of right, of democracy; but democracy's justice does not need to mask itself. From the picture point of view—and this means a great deal in comics—such hooded people suggest the Ku Klux Klan more than anything else, the very reverse of the process of democratic law. Protests of many kinds, from many sources have poured in, to the point where at last a

> change is taking place. . . . The big news of the moment is not the emergence of a new supercreature; it is the growing popularity of the gay, animal comic book of the general Walt Disney type, and the various titles devoted to teen-age interests.[12]

That Waugh identifies the teen comic as a major force in the 1940s is significant, given that he spends only one chapter discussing actual comic books. Even more notable is how he situates himself as the representative of a larger contemporary social attitude that regarded teen comics as a chance for the comic book industry to redeem itself. Never mind that *Archie* made its debut in 1941 alongside the very masked figures he rails against, and never mind that Waugh believed teen comics to be "very normal and healthy as a rule."[13] The teen comics of the Golden Age were often neither "normal" nor "healthy," but they were ubiquitous and frequently difficult to tell apart. And as the Golden Age marched on, public opinion on comic books shifted from optimism to alarmism.

Before comics were plagued by moral panic about their sexuality and juvenile delinquency, Archie, Jughead, Betty, and Veronica were busy setting the example for what a proper teen comic should be like in *Pep Comics*. By 1946, MLJ Publications, which was founded in 1939, renamed itself Archie Comics, given that Archie had been promoted to permanent cover status alongside the superhero the Shield on *Pep*'s covers. The Shield was usually shown expressing his love for Archie in some way—declaring him the winner of a boxing match ("Archie, you're always a knock-out!"), carving a giant snow sculpture of him, or kicking a football resembling him ("I always get a big kick out of Archie!").

Betty and Veronica also made it on the cover of *Pep* by 1944, and in 1950 they finally received their own title, *Archie's Girls Betty and Veronica*, which ran 347 issues through 1987. While they *are* two of the most well-known and lasting characters (let alone *women characters)* of the Golden Age, as they first appear in print Betty and Veronica are not much different from the average good girl of the time. Both are boy-crazy, manipulative, and often more than a little lacking in intelligence (to their credit, however, they are both incredibly generous spirits, given that Archie Andrews has never done much to earn their attention or respect). So while the contents of *Pep* are good, wholesome fun, Betty and Veronica are just two in a long line of female characters who perpetuate harmful, sexist notions of femininity. Despite current iterations of Betty and Veronica being more intelligent, mature, and invested in activism, the original *Betty and Veronica* title paints them as little more than a rivaling blonde and brunette who would stop at almost nothing to win the affection of a mediocre boy. If you're looking for feminism and progressive ideology in the Golden Age, there are better characters to look to.

Patsy Walker is one such character who provided a stronger example of the average American girl. Nearly every female title character of the Golden Age began her comic book career as a supporting character in a backup feature within a general teen humor comic or girls' magazine. She was almost always either the girlfriend of some unremarkable male title character or the eye candy in the background. *Patsy Walker*, which originated as a feature in Timely's superheroine title turned girls' magazine *Miss America*, is an early example of a (non-Archie Comics) female title character who experienced lasting success. Patsy premiered as the backup feature in *Miss America*, a title that made a somewhat meandering journey. It began as the patriotic teen superhero Miss America's title comic in 1944, but by its second issue had transformed into a girls' magazine offering dating tips and fashion advice, and featuring pictures of (supposedly) real high school girls on the cover. Many of these early covers were drawn by Louise Alton, who also did the illustrations accompanying some of the series' prose stories. In addition to drawing covers for *Miss America*, *Patsy Walker*, *Junior Miss*, and *Mitzi's Romances*, Alton worked as a commercial artist and a children's book illustrator before becoming a painter.

By 1945, Patsy received her own feature from Timely, lasting until 1965. All the while, she remained a part of *Miss America* magazine, which later transformed into *Patsy Walker Starring in . . . Miss America* in 1951. In addition to both *Patsy Walker* and *Miss America*, Patsy went on to star in several other titles focusing on different aspects of her life, from friendship to dating to fashion, including *Patsy and Hedy* and *Patsy and Her Pals*. Though Patsy Walker exists as a character to this day within the Marvel Universe (rebranded from the every-girl ideal to the superhero Hellcat), she was *the* force to be reckoned with at Timely Comics in the 1940s. Few people remember that Patsy Walker was actually one of Timely's top sellers alongside *Captain America Comics*, meaning that more people read about Patsy's love life than about the adventures of most of the publisher's superheroes.

If Patsy's primary appeal was her normalcy, common sense, and confidence, then it makes sense that her popularity skyrocketed. It makes even more sense that she would fit in alongside dating tips, life advice, and special interest columns in a magazine targeting the average American teenage girl, and yet even more sense that the magazine would go on to make her its primary feature. Trina Robbins calls Patsy "a female

Cover of *Patsy Walker* #1, 1945, Timely Comics.

variant of Archie" with a penchant for poetry who was "as smart as she was pretty."[14] Many of *Patsy Walker*'s stories, like *Betty and Veronica*'s, revolve around boys and fashion, and Patsy *does* have a heel in the form of the dark-haired Hedy Wolfe, but there is a depth and sweetness to Patsy that sets her apart from much of the slapstick comedy of the teen genre. And although not necessarily a realistic example of the average teenager, Patsy's good looks, romantic success, and style coupled with her intelligence and can-do attitude would have undoubtedly appealed to masses of teen girls hoping to have their cake and eat it too. Her well-rounded characterization likely explains, too, why *Patsy Walker* lasted so much longer than any of the other teen girl comics Timely introduced during the Golden Age. Among them are *Margie* (1946–1949, fifteen issues), *Rusty* (1947–1949, nine issues), *Jeanie* (1947–1949, fifteen issues), *Cindy* (1947–1950, twelve issues), and the blatant, college-age *Patsy* knock-off *Wendy Parker* (1953–1954, eight issues). Still, Timely Comics dominated

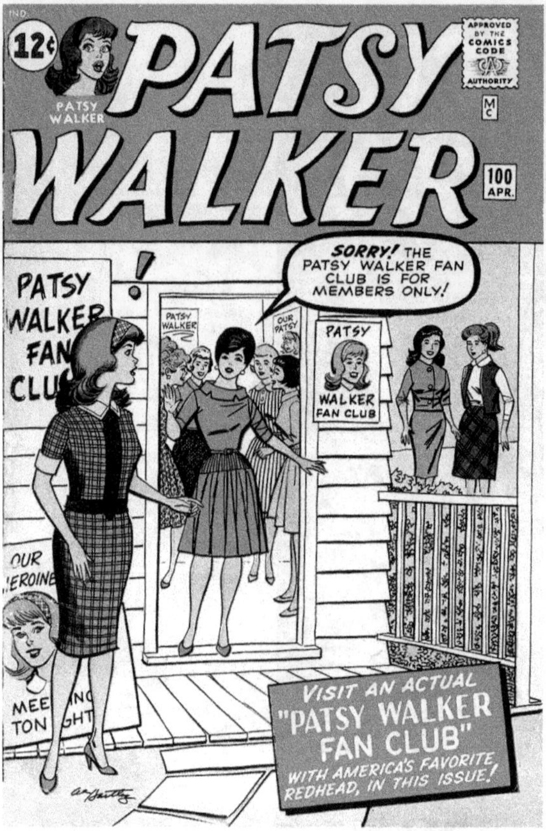

Cover of *Patsy Walker* #100, 1962, Marvel Comics.

the teen market through the Golden Age, and Patsy stood at the helm for most of it.

While Patsy was the reigning queen of teen titles at Timely throughout this period, Katy Keene was Archie Comics' answer to her. She first appeared in 1945, in issue 5 of *Wilbur Comics*, and hopped around from title to title throughout the 1940s. Finally, in 1949, she gained her own sixty-two-issue title, which ran until 1961. Like Patsy, Katy's popularity spawned a number of spin-off titles, such as *Katy Keene Fashion Book* and *Katy Keene Pin-Up Parade*. Katy was not known as much for her intellect as for her beauty and glamorous movie star lifestyle, but she was never stuffy or sleazy.

Much of *Katy Keene*'s legacy centers around the amount of fan interaction Katy had with her readers. Like most comics at the time, *Katy Keene* included paper dolls, pin-ups, and fan-designed fashions, but what made it remarkable, and *popular*, was the sheer number of things one could do to interact with both Katy and her creator, Bill Woggon, who seemed to foster real relationships with his readers. Not only does the first story in the debut issue of *Katy Keene* feature Katy lounging about reading fan letters congratulating her on getting her own title magazine (wearing an outfit and hairstyle designed by Katy Keene superfan Janet Lehmann, age fourteen, of Burbank, California), but it also features a full-page spread from everyone at Archie Comics congratulating both Katy and Woggon on *Katy Keene*'s success. She was beloved both by fans and within the industry, in no small part because of Woggon's dedication to maintaining the character-fan relationship. Whereas Patsy might have been the average teen girl's ideal, Katy was the populist's character, always accessible and always graceful.

Miss America magazine also invited readers to engage with the series' characters, creators, and fellow fans in many different ways. There was the column "Miss America Speaks," in which the editors published what they referred to as "ideas, suggestions, little bits of interesting news and chatter . . . straight from your many, many letters," in one issue and as "your own 'exchange-mart'—where you can offer original ideas, suggestions, opinions" in another issue.[15] Readers were offered one dollar for each excerpt published, which sometimes included their photographs; examples included fashion tips, advice with recipes, movie star sightings, and household tips, along with occasional praise from overseas readers in South Africa, Australia, and elsewhere.

There was also an advice column called "For Girls Only!" in which readers could seek answers to their most pressing personal problems (almost always about boys!). Both this advice column and the Miss America Speaks feature were dropped by the early 1950s, but readers could participate in different ways throughout the decade. Patsy Walker's solo title featured a section called "Patsy Walker's Fashion Page," for which readers submitted designs for dresses, paper dolls, and other creations. Later issues also embedded readers' clothing designs directly into the stories themselves, crediting readers within various panels for their creations. In some cases, the clothing was part of a regular story line, while in other instances there were short stories built specifically around the various clothes submitted by readers in which she tried on different outfits.

The reader-submitted designs also helped Timely's artists stay up to date on the latest fashion trends. While some artists enjoyed drawing women's clothing, others acknowledged it as a weak spot in their work: Al Jaffee notes that while fellow artist Chris Rule "knew better than anyone at Timely about putting women into clothing that had credibility," he had more difficulty drawing women's outfits. "I used to draw the same dress over and over again. I wouldn't know one dress from another," says

Katy Keene #1, 1949, Archie Comic Publications.

Jaffee. He would show reader's designs to his wife for help choosing, but "Chris could make up high-style fashion on his own," he recalls.[16]

Both the "Fashion Page" section and the use of reader designs within Patsy's stories continued into the 1960s, but as Marvel made the shift to new superheroes such as Spider-Man, Thor, and the Fantastic Four in the early part of the decade, Patsy began to offer readers something different: the chance to design her new hairstyles. A new section called "Patsy's Crowning Glory" saw Patsy try out new hairdos that the editors tell us were "selected from the hundreds of clever designs" sent in by readers. Only the "loveliest and most original," we are told, made the cut.[17]

There were a number of teen titles that were not quite as wholesome as *Patsy Walker*, *Katy Keene*, and their innumerable clones. While true pin-ups and cheesecake illustrations were commonplace in titles featuring slightly older characters and aimed at older audiences (both male and female), it was rarer to see high school–age characters drawn in this manner. While the majority of teen comics restricted sexualized, pin-up illustrations to their covers or selected pages sprinkled throughout—see *Katy Keene*, or even the Lily Renée–illustrated *Lucy, the Real Gone Gal*—other titles made their teen characters' sexuality and objectification a more central part of each narrative. *Sunny* (1947–1948, Fox Feature Syndicate) and *Meet Corliss Archer* (1948, Fox Feature Syndicate) feature the quintessential examples of the oversexualized schoolgirl in teen comics. Like the majority of the female teen title characters, they live at home with their parents, go to school, quibble with classmates over boys, and get into various kinds of mischief. Unlike their peers, they do all of this in tight sweaters, bullet bras, and thigh-high stockings with seams running up the back. For the modern reader, it's jarring to see a character asking her parents' permission to go to the movies in one panel and then sitting in front of a vanity in her lingerie in the next.

These kinds of sexualized representations were not at all uncommon in the title comics aimed at more general audiences, both adult and young adult alike, but the characters were always clearly *adults*, even if they were infantilized and made to look dumb. *Sunny* and *Meet Corliss Archer*, however, displayed their fifteen- and sixteen-year-old protagonists in all manner of sexualized scenarios, from shots of Sunny in the bathtub to panels filled with nothing but her high-heeled, stockinged legs, and images of Corliss undressing. It's difficult to imagine the intended adult male target audience of these images willingly purchasing a title so clearly aimed at teenage girls, and comics like *Sunny* and *Meet Corliss Archer* stand as representations of both the dearth of female creators in the comic industry at the time and the often confusing (and confused) attempts publishers made to appeal to wider audiences.

Part of the comic book industry's attempt to capitalize on as many markets as possible were titles that spanned a multitude of media platforms, like *Meet Corliss Archer*. Creator F. Hugh Herbert introduced Corliss Archer in a series of short stories published in a magazine, then took her to the stage in his 1943 play *Kiss and Tell*, which was then adapted into a film starring Shirley Temple in 1945. The *Meet Corliss Archer* radio program also began in 1943 and ran through 1956. *Corliss Archer* was then adapted into two live television performances in 1951 and 1952, a television series from 1954 to 1955, and yet another live television performance in 1956. But before Corliss took her act to television, Fox Feature Syndicate published *Meet Corliss Archer* for three issues in 1948, hoping to capitalize off of the runaway success of Corliss across the stage, screen, and radio.

Corliss Archer wasn't the only teen girl to get the multimedia treatment in the 1940s, however; *A Date with Judy* and *My Little Margie* were two programs that began on the radio and wound their way through film, television, and, of course, comics. *A Date with Judy*, which premiered on the radio in 1941 and ran through 1950, was first published as a comic book in 1947 by National Periodical Publications (later DC Comics) and ran until 1960, with a total of seventy-nine issues. *My Little Margie* ran from 1952 to 1955 as a radio program, and its comic adaptation was published by Charlton Comics from 1954 to 1964 for fifty-four issues.

The feminist media scholar Mary Celeste Kearney sees the "transmedia exploitation" of titles such as *Meet Corliss Archer*, *A Date with Judy*, and *My Little Margie* as part of a wider cultural appeal to the figure of the "bobby soxer," who represented the larger, emerging teen girl market. In the 1940s and 1950s, the bobby soxer teenage girl is figured as both a "negative force of social disruption" and a "positive force of social transformation," which makes her an appealing new demographic, Kearney writes, to the entertainment industry during a "promising, but uncertain, socioeconomic period."[18] In terms of content, these titles differed little from the rest of the teen girl title comics and contributed, perhaps, to the oversaturation of the bobby soxer/teen girl market and the eventual decline of media (including comic books) specifically made for young women.

Leading Ladies

The leading ladies that fronted titles such as *Dixie Dugan*, *Dotty*, *Boots and Her Buddies*, *Mopsy*, and *Torchy* appealed to a wider audience than the average teen character. While teen titles concerned themselves with the dramas of dating in high school and living under one's parents' thumb, these other titles contained themes that were more immediately accessible to older audiences. Whereas teen comics were restricted on some level to narratives centered on high school happenings, the leading ladies of these more adult-oriented books were free—though freedom was a relative concept for women in the 1940s and 1950s—to embark on any number of adventures. Those adventures were typically related to the pursuit of a husband or a career in show business, but the characters were nonetheless allowed to move beyond the hallways of their high schools or their parents' front yards. By appealing to the grown-up ambitions of teenage readers, as well as to those already facing the everyday joys and struggles of the workforce and/or domestic life, these leading ladies were often created with slightly older female comics fans in mind (nearly one-quarter of adult women identified themselves as either "regular" or "occasional" comics readers, keep in mind).[19]

For characters like Boots Ruggles of *Boots and Her Buddies*, being able to move narratively beyond the constraints of youth meant getting married to her star-crossed sweetheart and starting a family, but for Torchy Todd (of *Torchy*), it meant having the freedom to cavort with whomever she pleased, whenever she pleased. Other leading ladies, such as *Flyin' Jenny* and *Canteen Kate*, chased men and adventure in far-off foreign countries, while working women like *Hedy De Vine* and *Starlet O'Hara in Hollywood* pursued fame and fortune on American soil. These characters are difficult to categorize precisely because of the diversity of their subject matter, though they can be collected together by their desire to tackle the issues of adulthood and maturation (romance, parenthood, employment) that earlier teen comics often avoided exploring in any meaningful way.

This does not mean that these comics were devoid of humor or mischief, of course. In most cases, humor was a defining factor for these books, second only to the beauty or sexual appeal of the title character. *Boots and Her Buddies* and *Torchy* are both exemplary of the varying ways in which the comics that fall into this category utilized humor and adult subject matter relevant to their more mature audiences. Both titles began as newspaper comic strips (as is common of female title characters), though *Boots* has a significantly longer history than *Torchy*. Boots Ruggles debuted in creator Edgar Martin's 1921 comic strip *Girls* (Newspaper Enterprise Association) which became *Boots and Her Buddies* in 1924. Martin's strip ran from 1924 to 1968, but the two separate *Boots* comic books were published, respectively, by Standard Comics from 1948 to 1949 and Argo Publications from 1955 to 1956. Though comic strip fans would have primarily known Boots as a curvaceous college girl with numerous boyfriends, the five issues of *Boots* published by Standard Comics follow her journey into a more structured version of adulthood. In a story that would have been relatable to many unmarried young women at the time, the first issue of *Boots and Her Buddies* sees her struggling to reconcile the happiness she feels as she watches two of her close friends marry with the disappointment she feels about her own unwed status. Any serious emotional exploration is undercut, though, by jokes about how Boots's friend Horace makes a less-than-adequate groom, the unusual airplane wedding they are determined to have, and the housekeeper Opal's rotund size ("Perhaps we can find a trailer for you!").

Standard Comics' *Boots* series made a habit of approaching more mature subject matter, dramatizing it, and then softening everything with humor. When Boots believes that she is on the verge of losing her beau, Rod, to an old girlfriend of his, the ex-flame reveals that she only wants Rod and his wealth for a publicity stunt to boost her acting career. The story ends with Boots and Rod's engagement. Similarly, the last issue of the series contains stories about Rod struggling to adapt to fatherhood and Boots taking their son on a solo trip to the country, where she receives a letter from a neighbor alleging that Rod has been spotted around town with an attractive young woman. The issue, of course, ends with Rod explaining that the young woman was nothing but a business associate and a declaration of his undying love for Boots. All's well in Boots's world despite the dramatics and humorous misunderstandings that plague her life, and everything wraps up on a feel-good note. The message seems rather clear: though *Boots and Her Buddies* readers may struggle with the same difficulties of contemporary adulthood, an easygoing nature and sweet sense of humor can help you through anything.

In 1947, just before Boots made her comic book debut, Waugh described her as a sexy, girl-next-door figure with a sweet disposition—often too sweet to survive in the world unprotected: "Boots seems pleasantly helpless. She will do her best to rise to difficult occasions, but she needs some strong fellow to take care of her," argues Waugh. Boots appealed to both men and women because her poise and beauty are located largely in her commonness (Waugh notes, for one, how her speech has a "soft laziness in it, a slur, as in "H'lo").[20] The Boots who debuted in Standard Comics' *Boots and Her Buddies*, though more mature, carries with her the same sweetness and patience for what the world throws at her. While *Boots* did little to challenge the dominant, patriarchal order of the 1940s and 1950s (and even reinforced it in many ways), the evocation of common issues of marriage and parenthood may have offered adult readers an outlet for coping where other stories failed.

Torchy, on the other hand, was closer to pure, pin-up escapism with a side of personal autonomy and independence. *Torchy*, like *Boots*, debuted as a newspaper comic strip in 1944. Unlike *Boots*, however, *Torchy* received much more limited circulation—in United States Army newspapers—around the world, in part because Bill Ward, her creator, was deployed when he created her and also because her more sexualized appearance would not have allowed her to achieve the same kinds of mainstream success that other female title characters enjoyed as the stars of comic strips. Nonetheless, Torchy made the jump to comic books as a backup feature in 1946 and received her own title from Quality Comics in 1949. The solo *Torchy* title lasted for only six issues and was canceled in 1950, but Torchy's impact on the comic book industry is tangible; Ward is widely regarded as a prominent practitioner of Good Girl art, a comic art style notorious for exaggerated depictions of busty women in form-fitting clothing.[21]

While male artists initiated the Good Girl art trend, numerous non-male artists (including Nina Albright, Ruth Atkinson, Ann Brewster, Fran Hopper, Lily Renée, and Marcia Snyder) worked on Good Girl comics in the 1940s, particularly during World War II while their male counterparts were fighting overseas.[22] Not all enjoyed working in the amplified Good Girl mode, however, preferring to draw characters in a more realistic style. Trina Robbins describes how Timely Comics inker Valerie Barclay "never really liked working on the more cartoony comics of the Stan Lee–Martin Goodman teen line, preferring romance comic books for which she could draw beautiful women."[23] Barclay was just one of many artists who found inspiration for their female figures in the pages of fashion magazines. The models found in the pages of *Vogue*, *Harper's Bazaar*, and others served as the basis for many of the female characters found in romance comics, though most with their own title were done in the Good Girl style.[24]

Despite not being drawn as some female artists would have preferred at the time, Torchy is remembered as an icon of sexuality in the Golden Age: most, if not all, issues of *Torchy* feature her wearing lingerie, bent over in a suggestive manner, and being manipulated by the carnal-minded men around her. She was, after all, created as a tantalizing pin-up strip for members of the Army to ogle while deployed. What has been forgotten with time, however, is Torchy's dedication to her independence and personal autonomy. Though she is often unobservant when it comes to the nefarious ways in which men manipulate her into various stages of undress—such as aiming an oversized vacuum at the hem of her dress to rip it off or offering her a skimpy showgirl's costume when she complains of getting warm in front of a stove while cooking—Torchy's naivete doesn't come from a place of stupidity. Torchy is easily manipulated because she is always willing to help others in whatever way she can; that she is a statuesque beauty with "the hair of Helen of Troy, the brow of Mona Lisa, the eyes of Venus, the nose of Diana, [and] the mouth of a rosebud" isn't something she takes into consideration when offering her help.[25] She isn't unaware of her appeal, but she also does not knowingly use it to her advantage. While she *is* able to leverage situations to her advantage with her flirtatious behavior, *Torchy* makes clear that this is simply who Torchy is. She is not purposefully manipulative or deceptive, just naturally beautiful and flirtatious.

Still, Torchy revels in her independence and often turns down the men who chase her in favor of pursuing her own independent wealth and happiness. In the first issue, she participates in a radio game show that tests her knowledge for the chance to win $50,000. Instead of a fair game, a fight breaks out in the radio studio over who gets to spend some (forced) alone time in a small room with Torchy. The game show's sponsor, upon meeting Torchy, gives her the $50,000 in prize money though she did not win, and Torchy promptly returns it when she finds out that the owner has gone bankrupt. Because of this act of kindness, she is given the chance to answer another question: Will she marry the game show's host? Her answer ("Oh, I'm afraid I can't! You see, I'm already married to my dreams of a career!")[26] is, of course, not the one the host is looking for, and she walks away empty-handed. What kind of career Torchy is dreaming of is unclear, but what *is* clear is that Torchy does not want to be kept by any man, especially if the arrangement is not on her own terms.

Just as *Boots and Her Buddies* downplays the seriousness and emotional weight of some of its subject matter with humor, *Torchy* undermines its title character's autonomy by pitting her against other women. Rivaling female characters were a common trope in Golden Age comics, but *Torchy* makes painfully explicit what it thinks of women who weren't as beautiful, sexual, or kind as Torchy. In the second issue of *Torchy*, Torchy takes a job at a taxi company, where she is quickly promoted to president for boosting the company's profile with her beauty. As she drives, she causes fights to break out on the street between men competing to take a ride in her car. Two older women are shown reporting Torchy to the state police for causing a traffic jam and making them late for their "Bachelor Girls' Club."[27] The joke is that these unattractive, unmarried women who are seemingly proud of their independence are actually jealous of Torchy and the male attention she commands. These two unnamed characters who appear for no more than three panels of a single story in a single issue serve as a reminder that much of Torchy's ability to exercise

Torchy #2, 1950, Quality Comics.

her personal autonomy lies with her beauty. If she were not so beautiful, Torchy would likely not have access to the majority of opportunities her world affords her.

Torchy stands as an example of an independent female character whose power is located primarily in her beauty and the privileges that beauty gives her access to. Other unmarried female title characters who worked to earn their living while also juggling boyfriends, social lives, and their own autonomy, such as *Flyin' Jenny*, *Canteen Kate*, and *Starlet O'Hara*, ask us to consider, too, whose stories are told and from whom readers tolerate subversion of cultural norms. They may have been created as eye candy for young men, but the complex and competing issues of autonomy, privilege, and sexuality present in *Torchy* and similar titles raise important questions about who is valuable in both the comic book industry and society at large.

Conclusion

The female title characters who dominated the comic book scene throughout the Golden Age were not always busty, brainless beauties created by clueless men. While it's true that the majority of the writers and illustrators who created and worked on these characters were men whose ideas of femininity and womanhood were often skewed, it is also true that female title characters were a diverse bunch who cannot be reduced to a sentence or two in the larger history of comics.

There are, however, more complex issues at work within many of these comics that warrant further discussion. Female creators were far outnumbered by men during the Golden Age, but there were many notable women artists at work on comic strips. *Mopsy*, created by Gladys Parker, was one such strip. It ran from 1939 through 1965 and spawned the nineteen-issue *Mopsy* comic book series published by St. John Publications from 1949 to 1953.[28] Parker not only drew the *Mopsy* comic strip and comic books, but also worked for several years on *Flyin' Jenny*. *Mopsy* is, like many leading lady comics, about an attractive, unmarried working girl whose life is one humorous, fashionable adventure after another. Parker herself was a well-known socialite beyond her comics career and even designed a successful clothing line that was sold in department stores around the United States.

Parker was not the only female creator with a reputation for style and wit. Jackie Ormes was another successful cartoonist working during the Golden Age, and one of the few female African American comics artists working at this time. Her strips *Torchy Brown* (of no relation to *Torchy*), *Candy*, and *Patty-Jo 'n' Ginger* were all widely read and nationally syndicated in Black newspapers such as *The Pittsburgh Courier* and the *Chicago Defender*, but her work never made the jump from comic strips to comic books. That Parker and Ormes followed similar career paths and were similarly known as fashionable, popular female comics creators but ultimately wound up in very different places in terms of success says much about the state of race relations in the comics industry at the time.

While Ormes's characters were often just as glamorous as their white counterparts—if not more—they were also often much more politically and socially outspoken. Ormes herself was not shy about sharing her feelings on race relations, war, and even the environment, but her characters, Torchy especially, were always fashionably dressed, impeccably coiffed, poised, and ambitious. It's difficult, if not impossible, to find examples of Black female characters in prominent roles within comics at this time. Even Orrin C. Evans's *All-Negro Comics* focuses almost exclusively on male heroes such as Ace Harlem and Lion Man, with the only thing devoted specifically to women being a one-page feature called "Hep Chicks on Parade," which offered four fashion-related gags. Ormes's representations of Black women flew in the face of the racist stereotypes that populated *all* media around the same time. As Nancy Goldstein notes in *Jackie Ormes: The First African American Woman Cartoonist*, Ormes's characters "directly confront racism" in her work. *Patty-Jo 'n' Ginger*, for instance, "boldly critiques American foreign and domestic policy during the cold war years," while her work overall was marked by "political satire, cultural commentary, and protest," writes Goldstein.[29]

More mainstream strips, such as *Dixie Dugan* and *Boots and Her Buddies*, also included characters of color, but never as main characters and never as anything more than a racist caricature; *Dixie Dugan*'s creators seem to have had a particular fascination with offensive stereotypes of Native Americans ("Injuns"), and there is a recurring character named Opal in *Boots and Her Buddies* who is little more than a stereotypical Mammy character. Given *Boots*' tenure as a newspaper strip that made the transition to comic books, something *Torchy Brown* never managed to do, Opal's existence as one of the few Black characters among this particular set of comic strips and books is disappointing. Instead of offering readers an affirming and aspirational representation of Black femininity in the form of Ormes and her characters, *Boots* shows, yet again, a dehumanizing stereotype who adds little to the comic. While *Torchy Brown*'s chances of making the jump from strip to book can't be definitively determined, that a character like Opal could exist where characters like Torchy Brown or Candy could not is indicative of a wider pattern of both racism *and* misogyny that dictated which types of women were acceptable, desirable, and appealing to a mass audience.

Similarly, the need to appeal to a wide array of readers had an impact on how female sexuality was represented in Golden Age titles, too. Robbins pits "dumb blond" titles like *Sunny*, *Meet Corliss Archer*, and *Torchy* against more wholesome offerings like *Patsy Walker* and *Katy Keene*, but there are differences even among the more sexual titles Robbins mentions. The themes and basic subject matter of *Sunny* and *Meet Corliss Archer* are not the same as those of *Torchy*, and titles such as Lily Renée's *Lucy, the Real Gone Gal* further complicate these divisions. While Robbins derides these characters as large-chested, long-legged, empty-headed trash, they *are* distinct characters (for more than just their differing hair colors and lingerie preferences). For all of her mishaps and hijinks, Torchy Todd, protagonist of *Torchy*, is a kindhearted character whose primary motivation is always to help those around her. Often her naive kindness leads to men taking advantage of her, but Torchy is genuinely altruistic. Sunny, on the other hand, has attitude and a great deal of animosity toward anyone who wrongs her or stands in her way; her sweaters and stockings were, undoubtedly, much of her appeal. More importantly, Torchy is a grown woman whose readers included a large percentage of men, and Sunny is a high schooler whose stories would have appealed to teens. Who the intended readers of these titles were is an important part of analyzing and interpreting how these representations work.

Lucy, the Real Gone Gal presents a complex case, as it is a title drawn by a woman *and* one that trafficked in the same kinds of oversexualized imagery that *Torchy* and *Sunny* utilized. And it gets more complicated yet: though Renée's illustrations are in *Lucy*, she originally drew them for the St. John Publications title *Kitty*, which was then reprinted as *Lucy* by St. John with Renée's artist credit removed.[30] The narrative content of most *Lucy* stories, too, is that of the typical teen title, but the covers and the illustrations are a little more racy. Like Sunny, Lucy is not the most pleasant teen to read about, but, based on the cover art, it seems that St. John was not necessarily targeting the discerning comics fan. So while Renée's original *Kitty* illustrations were repurposed—perhaps without her consent or knowledge, based on the lack of an artist's credit—they were still illustrations of an attractive, curvy teen girl drawn by a successful female artist. That women artists were complicit in this system of hypersexualizing young female characters further complicates any conclusions that might be drawn about these sexualized titles.

Taken as a whole, the female title characters of the Golden Age are a complex entity. Like their readers, they are a diverse group of people whose interests, characterizations, appearances, and levels of intelligence cannot be easily typified. Their comic books served different purposes for different audiences: some of the women in these comic books offer examples of female empowerment, while others do little more than reinforce hegemonic notions of traditional femininity. Many of these characters embody pseudo-feminism and patriarchal ideals of femininity. They cannot be categorized easily (though many comics historians have tried), but they *can* be taken seriously and treated with as much gravity as comics led by male characters have, especially given how central books such as *Millie the Model* and *Patsy Walker* were as the comic book industry shifted from the Golden Age into its next era.

CHAPTER 7

SCIENCE FICTION COMICS

The story goes that on a summer evening in 1816, eighteen-year-old Mary Wollstonecraft Shelley, challenged by her husband, Percy Bysshe Shelley, and Lord Byron, sat down to write a ghost story. In doing so, she wrote the very first science fiction novel: *Frankenstein; or, the Modern Prometheus.*[1] Whether one considers Shelley to be the inventor of science fiction or not, it is impossible to ignore that women have played a foundational role in the formation of the genre. This is as true of science fiction on the whole as it is of the sci-fi comics published during the Golden Age of comic books in the 1940s and 1950s.

The prevailing narrative about sci-fi is that it, like the vast majority of popular genres, existed as a boys' club until women forced themselves in, or were brought into the fold by well-meaning men. There is some amount, great or small, of truth here; men have dominated the vast majority of social, cultural, and professional spaces in the United States for as long as America has existed. Efforts have been made in both science fiction and the STEM (science, technology, engineering, and mathematics) fields to address the issue of gender disparity, and while women sci-fi authors and women scientists have become more visible with time, equitable gender representation remains an issue in both areas. In STEM, educators often refer to the underrepresentation of women as a "leaky pipeline" in which girls and women are filtered out of the field at various points in their careers, consistently at a higher rate than men.[2] Female science fiction authors, in turn, have been working to increase the recognition of their contributions for decades, with the first anthology of science fiction written about and by women published in the 1970s.[3] As media scholar Marleen S. Barr notes, "Feminist science fiction presents blueprints for social structures that allow women's words to counter patriarchal myths," which is as true in comic books as it is in literature.[4] The former saw more female characters than creators, but the ways in which powerful women spoke words of consequence within sci-fi comics still allowed for the potential to challenge the status quo of gender normativity.

While sci-fi fans might be aware that Mary Shelley published what is regularly considered the first sci-fi novel,[5] and it is common knowledge that women scientists like Marie Curie have made important scientific contributions, women in sci-fi and science are largely viewed as outliers or exceptions as opposed to icons and innovators. But women were prominent creators of sci-fi stories in the early decades of twentieth-century publishing, writing stories about which feminist scholars such as Jane L. Donawerth and Carol A. Kolmerten note that "gender roles can be more easily revised when the reader is estranged from her ordinary world."[6]

Science fiction has long been considered a forum through which allegorical explorations of social and political issues might thrive, from the effects of technological change to considerations of race and gender.[7] In 1905, Bengali author Begum Rokeya wrote the feminist novel *Sultana's Dream*, and in 1915 Charlotte Perkins Gillman wrote the novella *Herland*. Both works depict utopian spaces in which women control society, allowing for a feminist critique of patriarchal and colonial systems.[8] Pulp magazines, which were vital precursors to comic books, also saw the number of women writing science fiction tales grow steadily between the 1920s and 1960s. Between 1926 and 1960, nearly 1,000 pulp sci-fi stories were written by 203 different women, with successive decades seeing "a doubling, tripling or quadrupling over the prior decade of female science fiction authors and stories by them."[9]

The pulps were also home to short stories, not just prose, in comics form, many starring women in leading roles. Between 1937 and 1938, Harry Donenfeld's *Spicy Mystery Stories* featured the adventures of Olga Mesmer ("The Girl With the X-Ray Eyes"), whose superhuman strength and X-ray vision mark her as both a pioneering figure in the history of sci-fi comics as well as an important precursor to Superman.[10] Mesmer inherited her powers from her mother, Margot, the queen of an underground kingdom on the planet Venus, who married Earth scientist Dr. Hugo Mesmer. Her interplanetary exploits take her to Venus, where she helps her mother reclaim the throne from a villain named Ombo, who had forced Margot to flee her subterranean realm. Like most of the heroines in Donenfeld's pulp comics, Olga Mesmer is scantily clad in many of her appearances. Despite being framed as a sex object, Olga is a powerful heroine—literally—in terms of her fantastic abilities and her rejection of men's sexual advances. Together, Olga and Margot Mesmer rank among the earliest science fiction heroes of comics outside of newspaper strips like *Buck Rogers* and *Flash Gordon.*

Within comic books themselves, some of the most iconic and enduring sci-fi narratives and characters were directly created or shaped by women. Fiction House's *Planet Comics* featured work from several female comics creators, who undoubtedly influenced how women were represented within the title's pages. Considered by many to be the first dedicated science fiction title of the Golden Age, and one of the most popular to come out of the era, *Planet Comics* ran for seventy-three issues over thirteen years, from 1940 to 1953. Lily Renée and Fran Hopper played significant roles in the shaping of the series, with Hopper drawing much of the art for the popular features "Gale Allen and the Girl Squadron" and "Mysta of the Moon," both of which had significantly lengthy runs in the title. Renée drew such features as "Norge Benson" and "The Lost World," and even drew the covers to several issues of *Planet Comics.*

Although Renée, Snyder, Hopper, and Atkinson lack the name recognition of men such as Jack Kirby and Will Eisner, they were vital to the development of science fiction comics. *Planet Comics* has been dismissed by some comics historians, however, as being less important to the genre's evolution in the comics medium than later series like EC Comics' *Weird Science* and *Weird Fantasy.* In *The Comic Book in America*, Mike Benton describes how the latter two series "gave their readers beautifully drawn stories with messages more powerful than ever before found in the comic-book medium." *Planet Comics*, on the other hand, is rebuffed as having "emphasized more adventure and action than any real science," despite what Benton describes as the regular presence of "slobbering aliens" in the series.[11]

The erasure of women's contributions to science fiction isn't restricted to comics, of course. Revisionist work dedicated to re-examining the role of women in the development of science fiction literature began appearing as early as 1974, with the publication of Pamela Sargent's *Women of Wonder: Science Fiction Stories by Women about Women.*[12] Feminist science fiction authors and scholars generally agree that during the peak period of pulp sci-fi literature, between 1938 and 1946, approximately 10 to 15 percent of the authors contributing to popular science fiction publications were women, although it's difficult to know the exact number given the prevalent use of pen names.[13] While similar statistics about the women who made sci-fi comics are not available, the number of stories about women—specifically women who aren't merely sex objects or damsels in distress—found in sci-fi titles across numerous publishers suggests that creators and readers alike understood that the genre wasn't just a male-oriented one in this era.

Sci-Fi Heroines: Alice of the Winged People, Amazona, and the Magician from Mars

The increased representation of active, autonomous female characters in science fiction comics does not indicate an inherently feminist or subversive bent in the genre, however. Throughout the Golden Age, sci-fi comics featuring women were almost entirely interested in depicting young, conventionally attractive white women who were either heroines in their own right or prizes for male heroes to win. On the rare occasion that other types of women—aging, nonwhite, nonhuman—were depicted, they were almost always an enemy. In many cases, even the extraterrestrial queens who kidnapped and attacked the protagonists of several sci-fi stories were depicted as beautiful, humanoid creatures whose evil deeds were motivated by their desire for the barrel-chested heroes of science fiction.

In Joe Simon and Jack Kirby's *Blue Bolt*, for instance, debuting from Novelty Press in 1940, the lightning-powered hero protects "the subterranean land of Deltos" from the mysterious Green Sorceress. "She's certainly a tricky wench, travelling about in that infernal green aura," proclaims Blue Bolt as he discusses a new invention called the cyclotron with Deltos's ruler (a scientist named Dr. Bertoff), which was meant to "unleash countless trillions of volts of pure energy" against the sorceress.[14] Despite knowing that the hero seeks to destroy her, the Green Sorceress cannot bring herself to kill Blue Bolt when given the chance because of how attracted she is to him. Using her "green aura" to teleport herself into Blue Bolt's bedroom while he sleeps, the Green Sorceress declines to use a "magic potion" on her enemy: "No, I cannot administer the potion to one so strong and handsome!" she cries before disappearing.[15] The beautiful green-skinned sorceress regularly finds herself torn between her kingdom and her unrequited love for Blue Bolt. Literally holding him in her hand after Blue Bolt has been injected with a shrinking serum, the Green Sorceress muses, "How ironically droll fate can be! I had never dreamed that I'd hold him in the palm of my hand—this way! . . . Oh why do I love one whom I must destroy that my empire's destiny may be fulfilled!"[16]

Despite her green skin, the sorceress still adheres to a western standard of female beauty—long, flowing (albeit pink) hair, big breasts, a narrow waist, long legs, and high cheekbones. The same physical traits are often seen in the women of *Planet Comics* drawn by Atkinson, Hopper, Renée, and Snyder (along with male artists such as George Appel, Joe Doolin, and George Evans). But while the aesthetic features of the Golden Age's sci-fi tales are important because they were so heavily shaped by women creators, the physical appearances of these characters are also often the *least* compelling aspect of their stories. Science fiction was one genre in comics that made particular room for female characters who, while still young and beautiful, held real power and autonomy at a time when world-saving was so often left to the men. It is these characters who represent both sci-fi's subversive possibilities and its reliance on well-worn tropes and skimpy outfits to attract readers. From the start, powerful women were central to science fiction comics.

The female characters who emerged during the Golden Age acted more often as vigilantes than state-sanctioned superheroines. The more popular and abundant sci-fi stories, however, were those that focused on the exploits of male heroes in the tradition of Buck Rogers and Flash Gordon, like Spurt Hammond, Planet Flyer (*Planet Comics* #2, 1940) and Yank Wilson, Super Spy (*Fantastic Comics* #4, 1940). These male characters were often aligned with government and state institutions, and their intergalactic battles against "evil" were often on behalf of the United States, or at least the futuristic equivalent of it. The line between space-faring vigilantism and state-sponsored heroism isn't a clear demarcation, but it's worth examining how female characters of this era continued or defied the American exceptionalism so often exemplified in Golden Age comics of all genres. Greg Grewell argues that throughout the genre's long history, science fiction narratives have consistently embodied colonialist themes. Drawing on the film scholar Vivian Sobchack's influential book *Screening Space: The American Science Fiction Film*, Grewell writes that sci-fi narratives, instead of exploring the idea of a meaningful unknown, often found "analogues" for familiar Earthly beings and contexts in space: "'Space' is now more often a 'text' than a 'context,' a 'space' more familiar than not, a 'space' that . . . has 'bec[o]me semantically inscribed as inescapably domestic and crowded.' . . . Time and space through the medium of science fiction film have become re-cognizable—no matter the time period, no matter the place in space."[17]

While many male sci-fi characters in this period possessed some form of magic or fantastical power, their actions were often militaristic and imperialistic, and they roamed the universe on behalf of futuristic states and kingdoms. The heroines of science fiction comics, however, were more diverse in their aims. Their stories also revolved around saving the universe (or parts thereof), but the characters appear to be largely unburdened by the expectation that they embody and enact the imperialistic desires of an Americentric/white state. Characters like the Magician from Mars (*Amazing Man Comics*, 1939), Alice of the Winged People (*Fantastic Comics*, 1940), and Amazona the Mighty Woman (*Planet Comics*, 1940), were endowed with more magical, experimental, and truly fantastic capabilities than many of their ray gun–wielding peers. While the Magician from Mars gained her powers in an accident as a child, Alice's strength comes from years of living underground among an ancient race of winged people. Amazona's abilities are attributed simply to her status as a member of an ancient race of superhumans.

Common among this trio, however, is a sense of loneliness or seclusion; all three of these women escape some form of isolation at the beginning of their stories but remain misfits ("I am lonely here, with nothing but snow and ice for company!" says Amazona of her arctic home).[18] They altruistically want to help the worlds they exist in, but they don't rely on armies or state sponsorship to do so. They rely on themselves and the goodness of others, and occasionally the men with whom they are romantically involved. Their stories reinforce that sci-fi narratives centered on women could at once subvert traditional notions of feminine autonomy *and* perpetuate hegemonic and patriarchal ideals. They represent the "galactic suburbia," a science fiction future world that advances ideas of progress and evolution without re-examining existing gender relations.[19] While the sci-fi heroines of the mid- to late 1940s more clearly reflected the changing status of women in the workforce during the war, the Magician, Alice, and Amazona were representative of a society uncertain about where women would belong in both the near and distant future.

The Magician from Mars, Amazona, and Alice of the Winged People represent a spectrum of possibilities for women at this time, and they best exemplify how the conventions of sci-fi could be used to challenge or conform to prevailing notions of gender, morality, and justice. The Magician from Mars—real name Jane-QX3—appeared in five issues of Centaur's *Amazing Man Comics* from November 1939 to April 1940. She was a protector of *all* people and traveled the universe taking the necessary steps to ensure that good prevailed and evil was punished. In her first appearance in issue 7, the half-martian, half-human Magician discovers that she possesses an extraordinary array of powers due to her ability to access 100 percent of her brain power. At sixteen, she is orphaned and taken in by an aunt who attempts to suppress her powers and denies her access to Earth. Despite claiming that Jane is capable of "destroying time

"Magician from Mars," *Amazing Man Comics* #7, 1939, Centaur Publications.

and space," the story maintains that her aunt is the one being whom she is not capable of conquering, and her aunt eventually imprisons her. To that, Jane replies, "Why not have freedom? I have everything else!"[20]

On her escape voyage to Earth, Jane takes advantage of an emergency on the commercial rocket ship she is flying on to steal $3 million in gold, half of which she donates to a pediatrician and half of which she keeps to invest in her new Magician from Mars persona. Earth, she concludes, *needs* her.[21] Her desire to help others is fueled not by a desire to protect any one state; she takes on issues both big and small because she cares about the well-being of humanity as a whole, and she often succeeds where government and army efforts fail. She is the clearest example of a female Golden Age vigilante in the sci-fi genre; though she sometimes participates in military efforts to defeat an enemy, she defies government orders when they don't suit her and ultimately displays that she has her own moral code that doesn't align with those of other sci-fi heroes and heroines. In her second issue, she rescues a suicidal man who wants to kill himself to avoid having his reputation ruined by a greedy politician. In the same story, she deters a would-be bank robber wielding a gun from harming anyone by transforming his gun into a stack of money. She later faces down a giant Eldritch alien attacking villages that an unspecified army has failed to defeat, and finally she faces off against the mysterious Hood, who uses a small army to carry out a personal vendetta against Jane. It is later revealed that the Hood is Jane's scorned aunt, come to punish her for daring to defy the bounds that were placed on her on Mars.

"Magician from Mars" is overtly critical of corrupt politicians and economic institutions in a way that many Golden Age comics were not. While popular characters such as Superman often worked outside of the boundaries of the military or police and sometimes pointed out how these systems could fail citizens, they just as often upheld the ultimate authority of the state by turning criminals and enemies over to the police and parroting nationalistic notions of "justice." And because many of these characters were white and male, whether their actions fell inside or outside of the rule of law seems to be of little importance to creators and readers alike.[22] It was extremely common for heroes and heroines at this time to act as law enforcement officers with superpowers and spandex costumes, which is what makes the Magician from Mars as a vigilante character so important. Gavin Weston notes how superheroes largely

> act as enhanced police officers unbound by legal restrictions (bypassing rules regarding surveillance or the use of force, for example) in ways that police are unable to—but they rarely punish criminals. Superheroes generally use force as part of apprehending the criminals in order to turn them over to the police. In other words, superheroes rely on and reinforce the existing judicial system; they do not attempt to replace it. Vigilantes on the other hand often disagree with aspects of the judicial system and enact punishment (often through killing offenders).[23]

The conventions of the sci-fi genre are different from those of the superhero genre, but there remain echoes of this divide between superheroism and vigilantism in Golden Age sci-fi comics. As a female character who emerged on the cusp of America's involvement in World War II, the Magician's rejection of the patriotism and jingoism evident in so many Golden Age comics, and her defiance of common ideas of morality and justice, makes her a significant outlier who predates the comics industry's turn toward the antihero in later decades. As the Magician from Mars, Jane succeeds at restoring justice to both downtrodden individuals and entire nations; though she possesses more powers than any other female character appearing in early sci-fi comics, she does not have particularly grand aspirations beyond helping any and all people who need it.

Although the robbery in which Jane intervenes during her second tale is a brief moment in her larger adventures, it is the most striking instance of heroics because of the empathy Jane displays in her confrontation with the would-be criminal. Golden Age heroes and heroines often worked alongside law enforcement and military officials, reinforcing that the law and its arbiters are popularly believed to be (and commonly portrayed as) the ultimate moral authority in the United States.[24] Jane, however, frequently shirked the law and social constructions of polite morality by doing what she felt would improve the material conditions of people's *lives*, not what would reinforce the interests of the state. It doesn't occur to her to lasso the shabbily dressed bank robber and hand him over to the police. Instead, she observes that he looks unemployed, hungry, and desperate. She has already decided to help him before he draws his gun, and the possibility of a criminal act does not deter her. In the panel, the man is shown clutching a wad of cash and is described as deeply appreciative and tearful. On the same page, in the following scene, Jane is shown punishing an entitled Washington politician for his rude behavior by washing him away in a tsunami of ink. Jane is, in every way, an ally to the working, the poor, and the oppressed in her stories. She defies direct government orders and constructs her own definition of morality in her attempts to eradicate whatever oppression Earthlings face.

Jane's tireless dedication to improving the lives of Earthlings may appear to perpetuate the myth that women, no matter how strong or independent, must constantly nurture, protect, and care for others. However, "Magician from Mars" and its rejection of common notions of American morality offer critical insight into how science fiction comics could uniquely challenge accepted notions of justice. Jane isn't *just* a caregiver, and she doesn't pursue heroics because she feels obligated to do so. To return to her early exclamation that she might as well have freedom because she already has everything else, Jane's vigilantism is about providing individuals with the same freedom that she enjoys. It is about equity and empathy in a way that other Golden Age comics are not. That it is a female character who provides this lesson is a triumph, not a drawback.

In contrast, "The Golden Knight" (debuting in Fox Features Syndicate's *Fantastic Comics* #1 in 1939) and its protagonists, Richard and

Alice, were purportedly the ultimate champions of the needy. Despite the proclamation at the beginning of every "Golden Knight" tale that Richard, the titular Golden Knight, carries out an "unrelenting crusade against the oppressors of his day" and "punishes the wicked, but gives succor to the needy," both Richard and Alice are ruthless in their attacks on anyone they deem unfamiliar and unworthy of protection. Alice, the daughter of the sorcerer Bawala, appears in issue 4 of *Fantastic Comics*. She is introduced as queen of the winged people, a subterranean species of humanoids who speak in broken English. Alice had assumed the role of Queen of the Winged People as a child when she fell down a well in the small town of Namara, which Bawala cursed in retaliation. A decade later, Richard arrives in Namara, tasked with lifting the curse and rescuing Alice; his first instinct, upon descending into the well, is to immediately slaughter the winged people who approach him with his massive sword. It isn't until he pauses to recognize that they are speaking English to him, telling him that they want to take him directly to the woman he claims they are keeping him from ("You devils are hindering me from finding Alice!"), that he puts his sword away.

In lieu of apologizing for his unprovoked attack, Richard tells the winged people, "Now you're showing some sense. I don't have to kill you all to be left alone." Richard's blind, homicidal behavior is not Alice's fault, but as the series progresses and they take each other as lovers and partners-in-heroics, she participates in and defends his seemingly aimless violence. Issue 11, for instance, features Alice battling a queen who wishes to take Richard as her king because Richard refuses to fight "weak women," and the story ends with the two agreeing that they "must fight against evil until justice prevails." As a concept and a goal, "justice" is entirely devoid of substance. While characters like the Magician from Mars exemplified how sci-fi could craft a world where women prevailed against the inequalities and injustices of a corrupt society, Alice stands as a reminder that "female empowerment" sometimes comes in the form of women assuming the power men have held for centuries and perpetuating the same kinds of harm. Indeed, the word "empowerment" could itself be called into question; Hester Eisenstein argues that in the last fifty years or so, there has been a widespread "de-fanging" of women's liberation that has stripped the movement of its radical aims and reduced it down to a singular goal: empowerment.[25] She writes that as the United States has adopted neoliberalism as its ruling ideology,

> this interpretation of feminism—broad support for individual achievement in business, government, and other areas of society,

Alice of "The Golden Knight," *Fantastic Comics* #19, 1941, Fox Feature Syndicate.

> and a dismissal of the collective goals of the women's movement—has achieved widespread acceptance as part of a broad imperialist agenda of cultural and economic domination in the Unites States and other rich countries. We are told that the key to creating wealth and producing social justice is in fact the "empowering" of individual women. . . . Thus, empowerment actually means the incorporation of women into the structures of capitalist power, whether as entrepreneurs or as low-wage workers.[26]

The use of the word "empowerment" here may be an entirely appropriate analysis of Alice as a character, then. Her role in the "The Golden Knight" is a near-perfect example of how science fiction and fantasy narratives can cloak regressive and harmful ideologies in the images of progress, fantasy, and unreality. Though Alice was a formidable partner to Richard in her earlier appearances in "The Golden Knight," in subsequent issues her character was reduced to little more than a damsel in need of constant rescue. Even when she begged Richard to let her come along on adventures, he was often able to persuade her to stay behind; when she didn't, the danger she found herself in (and saved from, thanks to Richard) was a lesson for her. In issue eighteen of *Fantastic Comics*, one of the final "Golden Knight" tales, Alice promises Richard that she will stay behind, only to commandeer a horse and race off on her own. Only moments later, she finds herself in the path of an oncoming avalanche that Richard only narrowly saves her from. He chides her for being "foolish" in the following panel, but Alice tells him that she feels she always belongs by his side.[27]

Alice, ultimately, may not read as a particularly feminist character, though she *does* embody an "empowerment" that considers only her ability to fight alongside Richard as an equal (in strength, at least, if not in battle) and the individual, personal success she achieves because of this. Just as sci-fi's generic boundaries are often blurred to point of being almost nonexistent, the difference between the words "feminism," "empowerment," and "liberation" as they have been used is difficult to parse. There should, perhaps, be some demarcation between "empowered" characters and "liberated" characters, and a recognition that although strong female characters like Alice may not have presented a necessarily positive image of women, there is a place for Alice and characters like her in comics history that should not be overlooked. Even as "The Golden Knight" fails to imagine a future in which "justice" might mean something beyond strong white men (and women) killing aliens to defend property and power, it reminds contemporary readers that there is a place for empowered but not *liberated* female characters in comics history.

The one-off feature "Amazona the Mighty Woman" from *Planet Comics* #3 in 1940 walks a similarly fine line between establishing its own sense of morality, like "Magician from Mars," and perpetuating existing norms, like "The Golden Knight." Like Jane, Amazona—a member of an arctic super race from eons ago—has her own ideas of morality. And like Alice, Amazona is the female half of a crime-fighting couple that emphasizes the male half's professional power over the female half's physical prowess and tenacity. As the only Amazona story to be published (though more were promised), "Amazona the Mighty Woman" achieves much in a few, short pages. Written by Toni Blum (under the pseudonym Wilson Locke) with art by her father, Alex Blum, the opening narration tells us, "In the vast cold reaches of the far North lives Amazona, woman of surpassing strength and unmatched beauty. She and her people are the last survivors of a super race that perished during the period of the last ice age." Amazona is further described in the story as one of the "descendants of an ancient people" who "know nothing of the outer world!"[28]

Though her amazing powers might also qualify her as a superhero, Amazona's origin story stresses her heritage as part of an ancient, secret civilization as a way of situating her within *Planet Comics*' emphasis on the science fiction genre. When shipwrecked reporter Blake Manners

"Amazona the Mighty Woman," *Planet Comics* #3, 1940, Fiction House. Written by Toni Blum.

discovers Amazona and her people, she offers to assist him in exchange for bringing her back with him to America. Manners reluctantly agrees to "take her back with him to civilization."[29] While impressed with her strength, Manners is concerned that she will not assimilate well into "civilized" society. As they discuss her anxieties in a taxi on the way to a society soiree, the cab driver assures Amazona, "those society guys will go for a sweet gal like you!" In response, Amazona plucks the man from his seat at the steering wheel, hurls him to the ground, and shouts, "Nobody asked you for your opinion—I'll show you how sweet a 'babe' I am!" before overturning his taxi with her bare hands.[30]

Amazona's response here feels entirely appropriate in light of modern campaigns against catcalling and unsolicited sexual advancements, but for readers of the period her response may have seemed extreme, unwarranted, or, depending on personal experiences, perfectly justified. Blum frames this moment, however, as a severe violation of social norms and appropriate behavior; instead of apologizing to Amazona, the cabby promises Blake that he didn't mean any harm, and Blake, in turn, apologizes for what he calls Amazona's "untamed" behavior.[31] Still, Amazona is later shown defeating a group of armed robbers alongside Blake, though she is the one to ultimately take them down—literally: she steers their car off a cliff while inside of it and survives. As the story draws to a close, Blake is promoted from covering society functions to covering homicide cases, and Amazona cheekily asks if "all society parties are that exciting."[32] Blake achieves professional success directly because of Amazona's actions, and had her stories continued, it is reasonable to assume that the two might have become something of a crime-fighting couple.

Blum writes Amazona as a champion of the neoliberal conception of the "empowered" woman, perhaps even more so than Alice; her empowerment relies not only on her ability to protect herself but on her partnership with Blake and the police. That characters like the Magician from Mars, who in many ways enacted the kind of liberation Eisenstein sets as a counterpoint of empowerment, could exist at the same time as characters like Alice and Amazona is evidence of the complexity and richness of female characters of this era. The women of the Golden Age have been most commonly represented as a homogenous mass of doe-eyed sidekicks and sexpots in tight clothing, but, though it is undeniably true that there was a standard look to the vast majority of female characters, the roles they played are far more varied and cannot simply be reduced to sidekicks versus love interests.

Though the sci-fi premise that opens Amazona's adventure soon shifts into superheroics, and "The Golden Knight" blends science fiction with fantasy, the two are noteworthy foils to "Magician from Mars" because they demonstrate how science fiction comics of this era struggled with ideas of social and cultural progress. In the afterword of *Fantasy: The Literature of Subversion*, Rosemary Jackson contends that "merely on a thematic level, fantastic literature is not necessarily subversive. To attempt to defend fantasy as inherently transgressive would be a vast, over-simplifying and mistaken gesture. Those elements which have been designated 'fantastic' . . . have been re-worked, re-written and re-covered to *serve* rather than to *subvert* the dominant ideology."[33]

Jane, Alice, and Amazona all fall under the broad heading of strong female characters in science fiction, but on the individual level they still represented a tepid exploration of where women might belong in the future. "Magician from Mars" divorces Jane from the conventions of the superhero genre and the expectations of the patriarchy; though she is briefly romantically involved with a prince, he dies in her arms in her final story. Few adventure, superhero, or sci-fi comics inflicted actual loss upon their heroes and heroines, but "Magician from Mars" asks its readers to imagine a world where a woman could pursue her passions independently, without relying on the expectations or norms of existing institutions. "The Golden Knight" and "Amazona," however, are more accurate in their depictions of women's roles in the future—at least, as Golden Age sci-fi comics imagined the future. They allow their heroines physical and mental power but ultimately put them in service of the men who are willing to take on the burden of the untamed woman.

Hurtling toward the 1950s: Gale Allen, Sun Girl, Moon Girl, and Venus

The entrance of the United States into World War II in 1941 signaled a shift in the kinds of stories and characters that appeared in the pages of sci-fi comics. The early to mid-1940s saw the arrival of a number of space-faring women who happily battled aliens and invaders alongside—or in place of—men. *Planet Comics* alone had the features "Mysta of the Moon," "Futura," and "Gale Allen and the Girl Squadron," in addition to other features that included numerous women who served as sidekicks and companions to male protagonists. In the wartime era, the comics industry became, like many other forms of entertainment media, another avenue to promote the American war effort, and the sci-fi genre became yet another way to reach (and persuade) the public.

Features such as "Gale Allen of the Women's Space Battalion" (which became "Gale Allen and the Girl Patrol," then finally "Gale Allen and the Girl Squadron") portrayed military service as the ultimate form of empowerment for women.[34] The feature was printed in almost every issue of *Planet Comics* between 1940 and 1946 (and was drawn by Fran Hopper between 1944 and 1945), and then again for a five-issue run between 1951 and 1953. Because "Gale Allen" appeared at numerous points throughout the Golden Age, it's possible to trace the trends and popular attitudes and expectations that shifted and evolved throughout this period. Just as wartime comics from across genres peddled jingoistic tales of battalions facing off against foreign enemies, "Gale Allen" began its run in 1940 primarily as a feature about women succeeding at militaristic endeavors. By the time the immediate postwar years arrived, many comics readers had moved past their desire to see images of war in the publications they turned to for entertainment. It's at this point, in the later "Gale Allen" features, that Gale's stories become more escapist and fantastical.

Like the superhero/heroine stories that emerged in 1938 through the early 1940s, science fiction narratives were preoccupied with stories that championed vaguely defined and overtly Americentric notions of freedom and justice. Sci-fi comics dealt with the changing shapes of American society by transforming the unfamiliar and cold depths of space into something knowable for American audiences: a frontier to be explored, defended, and even won by force. In her discussion of the methods used by comics to communicate propaganda to women, Mia Sostaric writes,

> Women were told to become strong by earning their own living through the armed services and to fight for their country. Wonder

"Gale Allen and Her Girl Squadron," *Planet Comics* #33, 1944, Fiction House. Art by Fran Hopper.

Woman reminded readers that the better they fought, the less work they would have to do. By earning a living and empowering themselves, women could become independent from men. In this case, women were told to empower themselves through the use of the armed services and by fulfilling their public political obligation to contribute to the war effort.[35]

From her very first appearance, Gale Allen was a champion of, and a testament to, the empowerment that serving in the armed forces could offer women. In that first story, Gale meets Jack North, the man who would go on to become her will-they-won't-they best friend and companion, who is horrified to discover that an all-women's squadron has been sent to support him in his fight against space pirates. In the end, Jack's men are repeatedly rescued by Gale's women, and Gale does not let Jack forget his bigotry. When Jack is captured by the pirates, Gale sneers, "Letting them take him, without even putting up a fight! That's he-man stuff, eh?" And when Jack's men are rescued (for the second time in the same story) by Gale's battalion, Gale tells Jack that he'll find his "fine, male squad" safe and sound on Saturn, then remarks, "Now, who's a sissy?" In the following issue, Gale's battalion is captured, and Jack uses this as evidence that women should "stay in the home where they belong."[36]

This is the rhythm of the first several "Gale Allen" stories: Jack expresses doubt in Gale and her team of incredibly talented female fighters, and Gale proves him wrong; Gale needs minor assistance, Jack makes another misogynistic comment, and Gale saves his skin. She is, much like the Magician from Mars, incredibly independent-minded and unfailing in her abilities. Even when facing down the likes of extraterrestrial ogres, Gale bravely leads her women into battle brandishing her ray gun and a shield, all while wearing a costume that amounts to little more than a bikini. "Gale Allen" was empowering but far, far from perfect, and as the mid-1940s approached, it drifted away from portraying Gale as rescuer and toward turning her into the *rescued*. Her stories also became less focused on semi-realistic war stories and became almost pure escapism, much like fellow *Planet Comics* features "Mysta of the Moon" and "Futura." The growing focus on cheesecake illustrations of heroines in teeny outfits battling inhuman opponents foreshadowed the decline of superhero comics in the years following the end of World War II. Because the science fiction and superhero genres were often heavily entangled (given the extraterrestrial origins of heroes like Superman and the incredible powers of ancient society members like Amazona), sci-fi was able to transition away from stories that focused so heavily on war and strife without sacrificing its popularity.

Part of that transition included moving away from tales of squadrons of strong women battling their foes and toward stories about individual protagonists. Just as they did in the prewar years, the women-centric science fiction comics of the late 1940s focused more on the lives and happenings of singular characters who often acted alone or sometimes with a sidekick. For example, the 1947 EC Comics character Moon Girl and Timely Comics' 1948 offerings Venus and Sun Girl were sci-fi heroines who, instead of appearing in anthologies, carried their own titles. Earlier heroines of the Golden Age, like Amazona and the Magician from Mars, appeared only as features in larger anthology comic books, but by 1947, EC and Timely apparently felt confident enough in their female characters to give them their own titles.

Sun Girl #1, 1948, Timely Comics.

Ultimately, their success—and tenure—varied wildly. Moon Girl was granted her own title, *Moon Girl and the Prince*, by EC in 1947. A year later, Timely published *Sun Girl* and *Venus* in August of 1948. *Sun Girl* was the shortest-lived of the three titles, the character appearing for only three issues before she joined the Human Torch in *his* titular comic book in September 1948. She then appeared in *Captain America Comics* #69 and *Sub-Mariner Comics* #29 in November, after which she joined *Marvel Mystery Comics* for a handful of issues between 1948 and 1949. While her appearances in *The Human Torch*, *Captain America*, and *Sub-Mariner* were all alongside their male title heroes, she was given solo features in *Marvel Mystery Comics*. Moon Girl appeared under a number of titles and appeared in a total of eight issues. The first title, *Moon Girl and the Prince*, was abandoned after a single issue. For the ensuing five issues, the title was shortened to *Moon Girl*, then became *Moon Girl Fights Crime!*, and finally *A Moon, a Girl . . . a Romance* (though Moon Girl only appears in one issue of this particular incarnation of the title). *Venus*, however, ran for nineteen issues before being canceled in 1952.

Despite their similarities—beauty and brawn—Venus's and Moon Girl's successes as solo title characters and Sun Girl's relative failure in this particular arena could, perhaps, be attributed to the different kinds of stories they told. While the three issues of *Sun Girl* published in 1948 featured tales of giant monsters, bank robbers and crooked cops, and otherworldly science experiments—the same kinds of stories readers had seen time and again in earlier superhero and sci-fi stories led by both women and men—both Moon Girl and Venus proved to be more adaptable characters. In *Moon Girl and the Prince*, Moon Girl is established as a descendant of a long line of undefeated female warriors and vows that she will never marry a man who cannot defeat her in battle.[37] Though in this first issue she protests that no man could ever surpass her strength and abilities, the various incarnations of the *Moon Girl* title dipped into the romance, crime, action, and even horror genres over the course of its limited run.

Likewise, for much of its run, *Venus* told stories that focused more often on romance than on outer space adventures. By 1948, the newly minted romance genre had already gained significant ground in the comics marketplace, largely because it catered to more mature readers. *Moon Girl* and *Venus* exemplify the ways in which science fiction comics adapted the core content of their stories to fit whatever fads had taken over the industry at the time without losing their sci-fi slant; *Sun Girl*, however, shows how titles that failed to update based on the demands and expectations of the industry were, often, lost to time.

Where Sun Girl faltered and Venus thrived, Moon Girl offered something of a middle ground. She, like Venus, adapted to comic book consumers' changing tastes by shifting away from strict superheroics, and, like Venus, her quest for romance played a significant role in driving her stories forward. The first five issues of *Moon Girl*, however, were much

Cover of *Moon Girl* #6, 1949, EC Comics.

more focused on her strength than on her love life. On the first page of the very first issue, she is described as "a woman of sensational strength, superhuman speed and endurance . . . surpassing loveliness."[38] Her powers come from an ancient moonstone, passed down to her by her ancestors in the Uzbekistani city of Samarkand. Tradition plays an important role in *Moon Girl*, though the title fails to acknowledge her Arabic ancestry in any significant way. Although she is drawn in a vague and ambiguously "foreign" way, with dark hair and dark features, the backdrop of Samarkand is used to lend an air of mystic and ancient power to Moon Girl and her adventures; however, the title quickly drops Samarkand as its backdrop. Aside from featuring technically the only non-white heroine with her own title during this time, there is little about *Moon Girl* (and its various incarnations) that stands out from other sci-fi-tinged superheroine tales. In fact, Moon Girl blends in so smoothly with other superheroines that she is widely regarded as a blatant Wonder Woman knock-off.[39]

In an interview with the comics artist Sheldon Moldoff, the former Marvel editor in chief Roy Thomas states that "EC changed the title to

Moon Girl Fights Crime, and then dropped *Moon Girl* totally and turned it into a love comic called *A Moon . . . a Girl . . . Romance* for four issues. I guess she just never caught on in that time when super-heroes weren't the big thing anymore."[40] Although, as noted by Moldoff, the *Moon Girl* title also played with the horror genre, its combination of sci-fi, horror, and romance elements were not enough, ultimately, to keep the title afloat as readers' interests shifted. *Venus*, however, continued to evolve to meet the needs of the industry and its readership even as the popularity of romance and horror comics dwindled. For the first half of its run, *Venus* primarily focuses on its title character (as in Venus, the goddess of love, a.k.a. Aphrodite) and her pursuit of a "normal" existence on Earth as well as a romance with a mortal man. Having grown bored of the endless adoration she receives on her home planet, Venus wishes her way into a life on Earth. Though her powers are never clearly stated, she seems to be able to bend others to her will simply by wishing for something to happen or by persuading them using her great beauty.

While *all* (yes, all) Golden Age superheroines were beautiful—their beauty often emphasized and leveraged in their narratives—other superheroines used their feminine wiles to leverage their *other* powers; Venus, however, only possessed the ability to charm others through beauty and to travel between worlds. Almost all of her adventures center on her ability to fail upward in her career while also helping others with their interpersonal relationship issues. In the very first issue, Venus finds herself on Earth after wishing to be "normal," and she is promptly given a job as an editor at Beauty Magazine simply because she is beautiful. Nearly all of her professional and personal success comes from her ability to charm others with her beauty. Her own romance with the owner of Beauty Magazine, Whitney Hammond, is also of great concern for her. For the first half of her title run, Venus's greatest adversary is Hammond's secretary, Della, who is fueled by jealousy, attempting to sabotage both Venus's career and her relationship nearly every issue, but she somehow dodges all of them. There isn't much here that is identifiably "science fiction" save for her occasional journeys back to space. However, by 1950, halfway through its nineteen-issue run, *Venus* had become more of a science fiction and horror title than a romance title. Once again, the title survived by pivoting to stories that appealed to current industry trends; it did not, however, manage to survive the burgeoning moral panic about comics and juvenile delinquency spearheaded by Fredric Wertham.

Although *Venus* was canceled in 1952, two years before the publication of *Seduction of the Innocent*, it exemplifies both how the industry broadened its appeal to female and adult readers *and* how the science fiction

Venus #1, 1948, Timely Comics.

genre almost singularly managed to survive the ever-evolving trends in the comics industry and popular culture at large. Because the science fiction comics of the Golden Age drew from a number of neighboring genres without losing site of their unifying themes and motifs—space travel, alien beings, futuristic gadgets, and so forth—it, almost singularly, managed to retain its popularity into the Silver Age. The blurriness of sci-fi as a genre is, arguably, one of its defining characteristics. Where most genres folded under the pressure of negative public opinion and formal regulation, sci-fi managed to adapt by creating and consistently utilizing characters who could both do battle with alien queens and pursue tender romantic relationships. Rosemary Jackson argues that fantasy literature creates the potential for subversion because it is thought to be unchained from the constraints of "reality." She writes,

> A characteristic most frequently associated with literary fantasy has been its obdurate refusal of prevailing definitions of the "real" or "possible," a refusal amounting at times to violent opposition. . . . Such violation of dominant assumptions threatens to subvert (overturn, upset, undermine) rules and conventions taken to be normative. This is not in itself a socially subversive activity: it would be naïve to equate fantasy with either anarchic or revolutionary politics. It does, however, disturb "rules" or artistic representation and literature's reproduction of the "real."[41]

The science fiction comics and characters that emerged during the Golden Age are representative of the malleability of fantasy that Jackson is describing here. All at once, these comics presented readers with unknown worlds and the empowered (or liberated) female characters who occupied them; they both reinforced and challenged prevailing notions of morality and justice, but, more than anything, science fiction allowed complicated and difficult female characters to step to the forefront. Characters as varied as the Magician from Mars, Amazona, and Venus appeared in the same genre at the same time, but, with time, they have been largely forgotten or written out of comics history.

Science fiction comics thrived well into the late 1950s and 1960s as the industry transitioned into the Silver Age, with titles such as *Mystery in Space* (DC Comics, 1951–1966) continuing to feature female characters, like Alanna Strange (née Lewis), who weren't just sex objects, sidekicks, or love interests. Between the female artists who shaped *Planet Comics* and the numerous female characters who exemplified all the difficult, sometimes problematic, but often empowering roles women could occupy in society, the sci-fi genre would not have survived without women.

CHAPTER 8

ROMANCE COMICS

As new genre trends arose within the comic book marketplace by the late 1940s, readers were increasingly happy to try new types of stories. Crime, horror, and western titles grew steadily, while superheroes began to fall out of favor. While most genres offered up thrilling adventures starring brave heroes who battled dastardly villains, a new kind of comic book emerged in the decade's final years that provided fans with tales of passion instead of powerful do-gooders, flirtation in lieu of fist-fights, and courtship rather than combat. Romance comics thrived by capturing the attention of a wide range of women and girls, appealing to teenage and adult fans alike thanks to the work of both male and female creators including Joe Simon, Jack Kirby, Ray Herman, and Ruth Roche.

Romance titles didn't invent the use of melodrama in comics, but they capitalized on its popularity by using tropes such as the love triangle, pathos, and histrionic emotional displays in stories about everyday people rather than powerful figures. Other genres frequently embraced romantic elements throughout the 1940s: jungle queens Sheena and Camilla had respective love interests named Bob Reynolds and Ben Austin, the Green Sorceress steadily pined for sci-fi hero Blue Bolt, Clark Kent and Lois Lane flirted with each other for years ("Can it be that Lois is finally breaking down and recognizing my charm at last?" says Clark after Lois agrees to take what he hopes will be a romantic drive with him in *Action Comics* #29),[1] and Steve Trevor regularly asked Wonder Woman to marry him well before full-fledged romance comics came along. While the lovelorn figures found in titles such as *First Love Illustrated*, *Flaming Love*, *Romantic Stories of True Love*, *Secret Hearts*, *Sweethearts*, and *Teen-Age*

Cover of *My Date* #4, 1948, Hillman Periodicals Inc.

Romances came to specialize in tales of infatuation, courtship, and unrequited love, such narrative elements were also commonly found in smaller doses in a range of other genres in this era.

Many newspaper strips found success in the 1930s and 1940s through their regular use of such themes of love, courtship, and heartbreak, including Allen Saunders and Dale Connor's *Mary Worth* (1938–present)[2] and Dal Curtis's *Rex Morgan, M.D.* (1948–2013).[3] In 1950, Jackie Ormes's strip *Torchy in Heartbeats* brought back the African American protagonist of her earlier effort *Torchy Brown in Dixie to Harlem* (1937–1938), adding melodrama and romantic entanglements in the pages of *The Pittsburgh Courier*.[4] Other literary forms served as precursors as well. In *Reading the Romance*, Janice A. Radway analyzes how romance novels became a steady part of the American publishing landscape once the rise of "mass produce[d] cheap paperback books" began in the late 1930s.[5] Similarly, the comics historian Michelle Nolan describes how early romance titles were part of a pattern of lurid romantic fiction in this era, which also included "true confession magazines, pulp fiction, [and] paperbacks," with comics as just one of many forums for women to read about love and lust.[6] Given that the romance genre was an increasingly popular part of other publishing formats in this era, romance comics were not an unusual direction for the industry but rather a natural one.

As a highly successful genre that largely targeted women and girls, romance comics *should* be celebrated for the fact that publishers finally recognized that titles could be tailored to demographics other than white, heterosexual boys and men, much like how feminist media and cultural scholars such as Radway and Charlotte Brunsdon have analyzed the ways in which popular literature, soap operas, and other formats have served as forums for the exploration of non-male identities.[7] Romance comics should also be praised for their ability to find favor with both men and women despite centering around stories that have historically been considered largely feminine. Further, while romance comics did promote heterosexual monogamy—and, often, housewifedom as the end goal for the couples found in their pages—they didn't always confine their female characters to the domestic realm. Women were free to explore life outside of the home—a sentiment echoed in popular nonfiction magazines at the time—so long as they eventually found their way back.

Young Romance

While some comics genres, such as horror and science fiction, developed relatively slowly before they established a strong hold in the marketplace, for romance comics it was a case of love at first sight for readers. Although teen humor comics like *Archie* and *Patsy Walker* were successful precursors to the more serious romantic tales to come, Joe Simon and Jack Kirby launched the first romance title in 1947 with Crestwood Publications' *Young Romance*, replacing a comedic approach to love with melodrama. The two had tested their format earlier that year with the teen title *My Date* for Hillman Periodicals; many comic book fans have often described *My Date* as "the first romance comic," but Michelle Nolan notes in *Love on the Racks: A History of American Romance Comics* that the series is more properly categorized as a teen humor title with romantic subplots involving comically named characters such as Swifty Chase, Sunny Daye, and Ultra Violet.[8]

Simon came up with the idea of creating a serious romance title while serving in the United States Coast Guard during World War II. He says, "There were so many adults, the officers and men, the people in the town, reading kid comic books. I felt sure there should be an adult comic book."[9] Simon recalls, "I'm looking around, I see the girls are reading that stuff and I'm thinking, 'There's really nothing for the girls in these comic books.' I thought, 'Let's get something really different that sells to girls." Men, he realized, might also be counted on for buying romantic tales. "I remembered my Dad and brother used to read these true romance books, and at one time they had a contest to send in a story. . . . My parents, who had no writing skills whatsoever—they were sitting down, writing the story of their romance. I thought, 'Gee, this would make a good comic book.'"[10]

After four issues of *My Date*, Simon and Kirby were confident that there was an audience for *Young Romance*, shifting the focus from comedy to what the artist Richard Howell describes as stories that were "comparatively faithful" in representing the hormonal and emotional shifts involved in adolescence through young adulthood, especially when it came to "romantic experiences and aspirations."[11] Simon realized that teen titles like *Archie* appealed to boys and girls equally, noting that "there wasn't anything specifically for teenage girls and even older" on the market.[12] Non-male readers were indeed an untapped market: a whopping 81 percent of teenage girls read comics regularly in the mid-1940s, as did 28 percent of adult women age thirty and under.[13] In turn, *Young Romance* was an instant hit that lasted over two decades. Published by Crestwood until 1963, the series then ran until 1975 after DC Comics took it over.[14]

Simon credits *Young Romance* and its follow-up, *Young Love*, with being "by far the most profitable ventures" of his career.[15] The first printing of *Young Romance* #1 had a sales rate of 92 percent, with Simon and Kirby's contract earning them half of all profits.[16] "For over ten years, they sold two million copies a month, and with high percentage figures," says Simon, noting that their success quickly led to imitators. "Of course, everyone was copying them, but there's something about the *first* titles. If they're pretty good, they'll outlast all the others, and nobody seemed to approach them in sales," he notes. His romance comics even outsold popular non-comics magazines on many newsstands: "Young Romance and Young Love were the leading magazines in sales in Hawaii, for instance, leading Life magazine and everything else!"[17]

Part of the appeal of romance comics was their narrative strategies, which borrowed the method of directly addressing readers from the title character comics described in chapter 6. Many romance titles also used first-person narration as a way of engaging readers more directly and connecting with them on a personal level. The first tale from *Young Romance* #1 sets the trend of having a character address readers directly, as a young woman named Toni cautions us to heed her tragic words: "I'm Toni

Cover of *Young Romance* #1, 1947, Feature Publications Inc.

Benson, and this is *my true story*—let it be a warning to *you*, if you should ever face temptation as I did," she says while facing the reader, hands on her hips.[18] Benson narrates the story in first-person captions throughout; taken along with her dialogue and thoughts in various speech balloons and thought bubbles, this means that there are only a few panels in which Toni's voice isn't represented. As a genre, romance comics were committed to telling women's stories and regularly attempting to do so from a non-male perspective (even if many creators were men themselves).

The genre branded itself as a more realistic alternative to the fantastical events featured in science-fiction, horror, superhero, jungle, and western titles, offering readers stories about everyday people with identifiable hopes and fears about life and love. Simon and Kirby positioned the characters in these romantic tales as being somehow more than just fictional characters—as instead akin to readers' friends and neighbors who shared the same hopes, fears, and desires as them. A story from issue 11 of *Young Romance* called "The Town and Toni Benson" brings back the title character from its first issue, with the opening editorial narration setting up

Young Romance #1, 1947, Feature Publications Inc.

Toni's tale as more than mere fiction: "Just one year ago, this magazine published the story of Toni Benson, the girl they called 'Pick Up.' Our readers recognized Toni to be a living, heart-warming personality" the narration proclaims, emphasizing Benson's vitality and lifelike nature. The editorial goes on to position Benson as an apparently real person whom Simon and Kirby consulted for her follow-up story:

> For since the publication of her story, Young Romance has been flooded with numerous requests—asking one question—Did Toni and her ex-gambler husband eventually find happiness in the two that didn't want them? We decided to get the answer from Toni herself. . . . *For we knew that, unlike fictional characters, Toni's problems did not end with her marriage to the man she loved—there was still—The Town and Toni Benson!*[19]

Part of Simon and Kirby's strategy to make the series seem realistic involved recruiting fans to provide the creators with their own true-to-life tales of love and loss. The second issue of *Young Romance* announced a contest in which readers could submit story ideas (whether based on their own experiences or just their fantasies):

> Win Cash Prizes!
> For Your True Romance
> The editors of Young Romance Comics will pay $50.00 in cash for the most interesting and unusual true romance stories.
> First Prize $25.00
> Second Prize $15.00
> Third Prize ...... $ 10.00
> Anyone can win. You do not have to be a writer. Just tell your story simply and the editors of Young Romance will do the rest.[20]

This emphasis on "true romance" and real-world concerns extended to the rhetoric found on the front covers of many romance titles. *Young Romance* #1 emphasizes a true-to-life focus with such taglines as "52 Pages of Real Life Stories" and "All True Love Stories." The first issue's cover also sets the series apart from other comics by underscoring how its contents are meant for more mature readers: "Designed For The More *Adult* Readers Of *Comics*" boasts a large banner.[21] The designation of the book as an "adult" comic served a dual purpose, not only signaling to older readers that the book was not just another teen-oriented humor title, but also telling younger readers who were eager to experience tales of love beyond their years that *Young Romance* offered a vicarious peek at adult life. In turn, the artwork in *Young Romance* is much different than that found in *Archie* and *Patsy Walker*, eschewing the rounder faces and less detailed outfits for a relatively more realistic approach to how the human face and body are rendered. The less animated art style and more robust narration found in most romance comics lends an air of legitimacy to the melodrama in their pages.

Negro Romance

While the reality that romance titles promised readers was typically one grounded in the white, middle-class experience, the genre was one of the few to attempt any kind of sincere cultural diversity in the audiences it targeted. As previously discussed, while some superhero comics in this era featured non-white characters in supporting roles, few were anything more than harmful stereotypes. Other genres offered the adventures of women of color like Señorita Rio and Starlight, but they largely starred in backup features rather than their own series. While several nonfiction series oriented toward Black readers arose in the late 1940s, such as *Negro Heroes* from Parents Magazine Industries and books about sports legends Joe Louis and Jackie Robinson from Fawcett Publications, the arrival of Fawcett's *Negro Romance* in 1950 marked the start of genre-oriented comics from a major publisher aimed at a non-white audience.

The comics industry largely avoided titles for Black readers in this era because most publishers feared the economic risks involved (be it in targeting the new, narrower demographic of Black customers or in facing backlash from white readers, distributors, or retailers). Given how the historical experiences of Black women were shaped by institutional structures of dominance, the gatekeepers who control how media industries disseminate content have long offered up content that abuses and effaces them. In its own small way, *Negro Romance* sought to counter this erasure, but it ultimately lasted for only three issues. While it wasn't uncommon during this era for titles to disappear just as swiftly as they had arrived, *Negro Romance*'s failure to make an impact on the market is especially disappointing when compared to Jackie Ormes's successful romance strip, *Torchy in Heartbeats*, which debuted in the Black-owned, widely circulated *Pittsburgh Courier* the same year *Negro Romance* arrived, and which lasted for four years. While *Torchy in Heartbeats* dealt with similar issues as *Negro Romance*—economic stability, respectability, and so forth—the strip managed to speak to its readers in a more sustained way than *Negro Romance* was able to.

Few comics of this era featured Black women in any kind of role, let alone as the protagonist of their own stories. The Black women characters found in the pages of Golden Age comics, when you could find them at all, often fell into the category of "domestic help" and tended to embody the "Mammy" stereotype.[22] Young, attractive, cosmopolitan Black women were all but nonexistent in comics, but more than a few publications featured happily subservient Black caretakers who offered sage advice to white heroines or, more commonly, acted as comic relief.

Cover of *Negro Romance* #1, 1950, Fawcett Publications Inc.

For instance, the humor feature "Superkatt," from ACG's *Giggle Comics*, and Standard Comics' *Boots and Her Buddies* both featured Black women, respectively named Petunia and Opal, who served as domestic employees and fulfilled the Mammy role. They both were shown speaking in stereotypical, offensive dialects and were played for laughs.

With *Negro Romance* regularly presenting Black women as strong characters within a genre geared toward older readers, young women of color could finally find comics in the early 1950s that valued their identities. The comics historian Naomi Scott points out that Black characters "were excluded from 'white' romance comics" in the 1950s, and that rather than create a wider range of stories for readers of color in the 1960s it was common practice for companies to instead take certain characters that had been drawn in the background and give them darker skin tones during the coloring stage of the book's production as a way of adding the appearance of integration to the story.[23]

Even a comic specifically created for Black readers like 1947's *All-Negro*

Comics contained few female characters. *All-Negro Comics* offered readers a young, mermaid-like girl; one page of fashion-inspired gags called "Hep Chicks on Parade"; and a big-bosomed farmer's daughter with the unfortunately sexist name Ample-Mae, who serves as the object of lust for two visiting male hobos.[24] Given the ways that titles including *Katy Keene*, *Patsy Walker*, and *Millie the Model* incorporated fashion, "Hep Chicks on Parade" had the potential to be expanded into a regular feature or even its own series. Jackie Ormes regularly incorporated fashion elements into her strips *Patty-Jo 'n' Ginger* and *Torchy in Heartbeats*, from the range of different dresses worn by the characters to the paper-doll cutouts that readers could dress Torchy in.[25] Ormes had an early stronghold on comic strips featuring independent, young Black women. *Torchy in Heartbeats* saw the eponymous Torchy navigate a number of romantic endeavors over the course of its four-year run. The strip ended, as many romance stories at the time did, with a happily-ever-after, but not before putting Torchy through the same kinds of trials and tribulations that the women in more mainstream romance comic publications experienced. In her analysis of Ormes's representations of romance, Nancy Goldstein argues,

> Independence was standard fare in romance stories but this convention had added meaning for young, urban African American female readers who could identify with Torchy looking for employment beyond the want-ad listings for "domestic help" and yearning to step beyond the bounds of patriarchal control.
>
> [She] personified the very desire for economic freedom, self-improvement, and emotional happiness that would resonate with Ormes's readers. Along the way, and in contrast to the often sexually scandalous stories in women's magazines, Torchy provided a model for virtuous behavior.[26]

The characters and stories found in *Negro Romance* function similarly but perhaps not as successfully. The opening story of *Negro Romance* #1 focuses on the dual love lives of a young woman named Marjorie and her Aunt Louise, beginning much like any other Golden Age romance story by establishing middle-class values and societal gender roles: "[I was at] the McLaughlin's to play bridge," says Aunt Louise. "They found a very charming partner for me, his name is Jim Taylor, and he brought me home. So you see, I was in perfectly good hands," she explains to her concerned niece.[27] Similarly, the settings in *Negro Romance* are largely interchangeable with those of other romance titles. Many stories take place in what appear to be the same suburban neighborhoods surrounded by

"My Heart's Dilemma," *Negro Romance* #1, 1950, Fawcett Publications Inc.

white-picket fences as those found in titles with white faces, reinforcing the normalization of whiteness. While Andrew Wise describes in *Places of Their Own: African American Suburbanization in the Twentieth Century* that suburbs with a significant African American presence did exist in this period,[28] we rarely see Black neighbors or passers-by in *Negro Romance*'s suburban moments. It is only when the series' characters are placed in public settings that we are reminded of how these tales take place in Black communities rather than white ones, such as when Black diners surround the protagonists at nearby tables or work behind the counter.

Even if some Black readers didn't see themselves reflected in the largely middle-class experiences portrayed in *Negro Romance*, the series is remarkable for how it made room within the marketplace for non-white faces and voices. For white readers who may have bought or browsed through an issue at the newsstand, it presented a vision of equality rarely seen in mainstream media at the time, showing Black characters with the same hopes and concerns as white characters in other romance titles. Nevertheless, while these narratives were a far cry from the (stereo)typical representations of Blackness in most comics and are ostensibly less "damaging," it is important to note that *Negro Romance*'s 1950 publication occurred well before the 1954 *Brown v. Board of Education* decision that nominally abolished "separate but equal" segregation practices in the United States. The need for representative comic books is far less dire than the need for accessible and equitable educational, medical, professional, and public facilities, but the depiction of a Black suburbia in these romance titles was at best misleading and at worst a tacit reinforcement of the white myth that desegregation was unnecessary because Black Americans were separate but equal.

But considering the wider availability of *Negro Romance* and the potential platform Black comics offered to creators and readers of color to tell their own stories, the possibility that these comics created inroads for non-white comics readership and creation cannot be discounted. Since Hollywood made so few films with Black protagonists in this era—and the lower-budget independent films with Black stars, known as "race films," mostly played in segregated theaters far from white neighborhoods[29]—*Negro Romance* was unique in how it reached a mass audience on a monthly basis during its brief run, thanks to Fawcett's access to a wider distribution network.

Negro Romance #2 is especially notable for its work by the Black artist Alvin Hollingsworth, who drew two of its three stories. Born in Harlem, Hollingsworth began his comics career at the young age of twelve, drawing tales of terror for the horror series *Eerie* and *Beware*, jungle goddesses in *Rulah* and *Tiger Girl*, and hardened criminals in *Crimes by Women* and *Police Trap*, along with romance titles featuring white characters, such as *Youthful Romances*. By the late 1950s, he had left comics to pursue other artistic opportunities, including the African American art collective Spiral in 1963 and becoming an art professor at Hostos Community College in New York in the 1970s.

"Possessed," *Negro Romance* #2, 1950, Fawcett Publications Inc.

While the stories by the white author and editor Roy Ald typically match the tone and substance of romance comics intended for white readers, Hollingsworth's artwork for *Negro Romance* #2 opens new opportunities for interpretation. The issue's first story, for instance, opens with a character named Gloria Conan being chastised by her future sister-in-law: "I told my brother everything! How you regulated our lives and dominated our every thought and desire!" We then watch as Gloria collects a pink slip from her employer, causing her to slip into hopelessness: "And when I walked dejectedly along Corlane Park, opposite the office building, I suppressed resentful tears. It was so miserably hard to dig a root of permanency, to feel sure and settled," she laments in her narration.[30] While most romance comics trade in feelings of loneliness and uncertainty, the way the rhetoric here emphasizes "regulation," "domination," and "resentment" held distinct connotations for Black readers in the years leading up to the adoption of the Civil Rights Act in 1964. The presence of Hollingsworth's hand in the book's creation, along with the ability to decode the material through a sociopolitical lens, allow us to read the stories in *Negro Romance* as much more than just a mere carbon copy of white romance comics.

Unfortunately, because the comic book industry was almost entirely white-dominated, resonant and firsthand representations of Black romance, like those found in *Torchy in Heartbeats*, failed to break through into the mainstream in any meaningful way. The short-lived nature of *Negro Romance* could point to an unwillingness on the publisher's part to commit to the publication, or it could point to a failure to sell among the targeted market. A small-scale study of comics readership among Black adolescents in Chicago published in 1945 found that Black boys and girls read comics at a higher rate than their white counterparts.[31] Although the study surveyed only 207 students in grades four through six, its findings suggest that there was no lack of Black readership, even (or especially) among titles not specifically geared toward Black audiences.

Likely, *Negro Romance*'s abrupt cancellation can be attributed to disinterest from both publisher and audience, although distribution and retailing practices in this era may have prevented readers in some areas from accessing the title, much like how *All-Negro Comics* went unshelved on newsstands in many cities.[32] Though the language used in some of its stories points to an understanding of the systemic oppression under which Black communities have long suffered in the United States, the reception of *Negro Romance* versus that of *Torchy in Heartbeats* exemplifies that some disconnect existed. It stands to reason, then, that stories of Black love written by white men did not have authenticity or understanding of the complex, codified nature of moving through the world as a Black person in the mid-twentieth century. Even though certain stories, like the one about Gloria found in issue 2, utilize the language of "domination" to nod at the United States' history of exploiting and enslaving its Black citizens, the image of "respectable" middle-class Blackness presented in *Negro Romance* perhaps failed to reach its intended audience because lessons of respectability and acceptable expressions of sexual desire and love rang hollow—oppressive, perhaps—when coming from a white publisher.

Audiences and Creators

Between 1949 and 1950, romance comics accounted for one out of every four titles published, a testament to the power of female readers in this era. Nolan describes how in the first half of 1949, 42 issues of comics devoted to love and romance were published, followed by 256 issues from July to December that same year. The first half of 1950 saw that number increase to 332.[33] Love was big business at local newsstands: a 1950 issue of *Newsdealer* showed that more young women age seventeen to twenty-five were reading comics that year than men of that age.[34] The St. John Publications editor Irwin Stein notes that its romance titles sold "about 300,000 [copies] on most of them."[35] Stein attributed this success to how St. John's romance books featured characters who were slightly older than its average readers: "The theory was that the kids liked to read about people who were just a few years older. So since your readership generally stopped about 13, 14 for these things . . . then you wrote about high school aged girls."[36]

Many titles had non-male writers and editors at the helm, making romance comics a genre in which women had strong creative control. Artist Ann Brewster worked on such titles as *All Love*, *All Romances*, *Glamorous Romances*, *Love at First Sight*, *Love Experiences*, *Popular Romances*, *Real Love*, *Real Secrets*, *Revealing Romances*, and *Western Love Trails* for Ace Magazines between 1949 and 1954, as well as working for the Simon and Kirby studio.[37] DC Comics saw a steady succession of women editing romance comics—first Zena Friedland and then Ruth Brant. Phyllis Reed began as a romance comics writer before serving as editor on such titles as *Falling in Love*, *Girl's Love Stories*, and *Heart Throbs*. Reed remained at DC until 1966, while Barbara Friedlander also worked as a romance editor for the publisher between 1964 and 1970.

At the Roche & Iger Studio, co-owner Ruth Roche edited such titles as *All True Romance*, *Bride's Secrets*, *Lonely Heart*, *Secret Love*, and *Today's Brides*. Ace Magazines' line of romance titles (including *All Love*, *All Romance*, *Complete Love Magazine*, *Glamorous Romances*, *Love at First Sight*, *Love Experiences*, *Real Love*, *Revealing Romances*, and *Ten-Story Love*) often featured the work of editor Rose Wyn, writer Isabel Mangum, and artists Valerie Barclay, Ann Brewster, and Alice Kirkpatrick. Wyn was also the co-owner of Ace Magazines, whose output between 1940 and 1956 also included a range of crime, horror, and science fiction titles, many of which were written by Mangum.[38]

Like Roche and Wyn, Ray Herman was also the owner and publisher of her own comics company, Orbit Publications. Born Ruth Rae Herman, she co-formed Orbit in 1946 with Marjorie May, making it the only all-female-owned comics company of the Golden Age (Wyn co-owned Ace with her husband Aaron, while Roche partnered with Jerry Iger). Herman had worked at Holyoke Publishing in the early 1940s and was listed as co-owner of the company along with Frank Z. Temerson and his wife, Esther, but both women served in the role in name only for tax purposes. At Orbit, Herman wrote and edited their two romance series, *Love Diary* and *Love Journal*, also penning advice columns (which were usually written by men using female pen names).

While she often used the male pseudonym Ray Mann for her scripts, Herman joined Ruth Roche as a powerful triple threat in the comics industry: publisher, writer, and editor. But Herman could boast one more talent, as she penciled and inked several crime comics for D. S. Publishing in 1948. Orbit folded in 1955, the victim of the overall market downturn that ended so many other publishers in the wake of the rise of both television and the Comics Code Authority (CCA). Herman was actually a founder of the Association of Comic Magazine Publishers (ACMP) in 1947 along with other publishers such as Lev Gleason and EC Comics' Bill Gaines. The group sought to be an early version of the CCA to stave off rising cultural criticisms of the comic book medium, drafting a code of conduct and seeking to review publishers' material for approval. They only convinced fourteen out of thirty-five publishers to join.[39] The ACMP was over by 1948, and, like Gaines and Gleason's companies, Orbit Publications also only lasted into the mid-1950s.

While romance comics proved profitable for many publishers, there was still the need to create a distinctive product as newsstands filled with an increasing number of torrid love titles. As the genre developed, the influence of the first-person narrative style of Simon and Kirby's early romance work could be seen in the numerous titles from Fox Feature Syndicate that took a subjective slant in the hopes of connecting with readers: *My Great Love*, *My Love Affair*, *My Love Life*, *My Love Memoirs*, *My Love Secret*, *My Past Thrilling Confessions*, *My Secret*, *My Secret Life*, *My Secret Stories*, and *My True Love Thrilling Confession Stories*. Publishers also realized the need to offer titles about the various stages of romantic life, so that once teenagers graduated from simple feelings of puppy love, there were more stories about more thorny types of romantic relationships available to them. Comics about courtship were later joined by books about brides, including Harvey Comics' *Teen-Age Brides*, *True Bride-to-Be-Romances*, and *True Brides* as well as Prize Comics' *Young Brides*.

Comics about married life followed, such as Charlton's *Just Married* and *Secrets of Love and Marriage* plus St. Johns' *Romantic Marriage*. For each stage of a woman's life, comics publishers had a title ready for them from the late 1940s through the 1960s, from high school puppy love to courtship to engagement to marriage. By evolving alongside its readers as they grew up, the genre endured longer than others in this era. As the 1960s saw youth culture affected by new social and political changes, romance comics tried to keep pace by offering readers their take on modern love: a 1968 issue of Charlton's *Teen Confessions*, for instance, featured the story "Flower Love," in which a high school girl named Elena joins a hippie commune in Greenwich Village. The opening splash page shows Elena appealing to the commune leader Lama to let her stay and "go on studying universal love" when her friend Greg arrives to take her back home. But the story ends with her sober realization, "I . . . I don't want to be a hippie anymore. I've been a fool," as she and Greg kiss passionately.[40]

But despite offering stories about the fresh appeals of free love, romance comics were hampered by the self-enforced morality of the Comics Code. "Flower Love" ends with Elena choosing monogamy over the polyamorous life of a hippie commune, in keeping with the code's emphasis on traditional family values. "The treatment of love romance stories shall emphasize the value of the home and the sanctity of marriage," the code states, along with "Sex perversion or any inference to same is strictly forbidden,"[41] which explains why Elena chooses Greg over being one of Lama's many lovers.

As divorce rates escalated in America through the 1960s, the Comics Code also hampered romance creators' ability to show how not all love stories end happily ever after: "Divorce shall not be treated humorously nor represented as desirable," it said, a tenet that was kept verbatim when the code's language was updated in 1971. Publishers were so wary of having stories rejected by the CCA that few attempts were made. Mostly, divorce was hinted at within stories that ended happily ever after, such as 1952's "Married to His Work" from Ziff-Davis Publishing's *Romantic Marriage* #13. When a workaholic named Harry neglects his wife, Ruth, in favor of his career, she laments how "miserable" her life is. "Sometimes I wish I'd never come here with Harry. Maybe our marriage was a mistake!" she thinks to herself while decrying how "business seemed to take more of Harry's time than ever." Ruth packs her things and moves back in with her parents, but she is ultimately convinced to give her husband another chance after her mother offers up a strong defense of patriarchal gender roles: "What do you think marriage is, if it isn't being a help-mate to your husband? It's a wife's job to make the kind of home a husband needs and wants!"[42]

By 1970, after two decades of romance tales that sidestepped the reality of broken marriages, Jack Kirby felt the time was finally right to create a new series for DC Comics centered around unhappy endings, called *True-Life Divorce*. But when he delivered the first issue to his editors, "the material was deemed unworthy of publication" and never saw print.[43] While creators tried to keep up with the times in their romance stories, the industry still sought to uphold the morals and values of the Comics Code that were forged in 1954 and sustained for decades to come.

By the 1960s it was clear that the postwar patterns surrounding women's roles in society described by Betty Friedan in 1963's *The Feminine Mystique* had been deeply entrenched in the romance genre. In an era when women faced limited opportunities, what Friedan calls the "vision of the happy modern housewife" was touted as an ideal that women should readily embrace.[44] Throughout the 1950s, housewives were popularly depicted across a wide range of films, television shows, and other media as cheerful and acquiescent, with romance comics continuing the trope in the majority of their stories. But romance comics also pushed the idea that women could be more than "just happy homemakers."

In one tale about a young artist, the narrator, Nina, describes how falling in love helped her learn that one needs the "best of both worlds" in order to live a fulfilling life. "The Plumber and Me," from Prize Comics Group's *Young Love* #1, sees Nina, an aspiring painter, move to New York City to live among a group of bohemian intellectuals. Though Nina cavorts with an arty crew that often mocks the outside world's preoccupation with money and aesthetics, she agrees to go on several dates with Pete Jackson, a plumber who frequently talks about the good money he earns and derides Nina and her friends' snobbishness. For much of the story, Nina insists that her relationship with Pete is based on wanting to see how "the other side" lives; however, after Pete confesses that he planned to propose to her (a proposal he nixed upon overhearing Nina mocking him to her friends), Nina realizes that she truly loves Pete for the simplicity and stability he brought to her life. In true romantic fashion, Pete and Nina's love story ends with a marriage—both a literal marriage and, Nina tells the audience in direct address, a marriage of lifestyles. In the final panel of the story, Nina is shown painting in her home with Pete and their son. With her eyes on her child and husband, Nina tells the audience, "My life is complete. I have my home, and my baby and my husband. My art is just a hobby. . . . But I would have gone on all my life, in an empty, brittle, cynical circle if my Pete hadn't come along."[45]

Nina's story (and others) may run counter to the image of the aproned housewife chained to the stove that Friedan popularized in *The Feminine Mystique*; however, it wasn't uncommon for popular press publications such as *Ladies' Home Journal* and *Ebony* to regularly feature nonfiction articles about working women who also happened to be wives and mothers.[46] In her analysis of several popular press magazines aimed at women, Joanne Meyerowitz found that "domestic ideals coexisted in ongoing tension with an ethos of individual achievement that celebrated nondomestic activity, individual striving, public service, and public access" and directly grappled with issues of gender, domesticity, and relationships.[47] What

Nina's story—"The Plumber and Me"—shows is that romance comics permitted their female heroines to explore life outside the domestic realm but never allowed them to stray so far that they might discover that not every woman is destined for maternal, wedded bliss.

"That Strange Girl": Genre, Sexuality, and Queerness

Indeed, maternal, wedded bliss is presented as both a problem and solution for certain characters in the romance genre. Much like *Negro Romance* addressed the systemic oppression of Black Americans using codified language, the romance genre sometimes addressed alternative expressions of sexuality and gender. Just as Black readers could decode a series like *Negro Romance* differently than white readers, queer theory allows for alternative readings of how romance comics encoded sexuality. While the Comics Code prevented publishers from discussing homosexuality directly, some creators got around the restriction with varying degrees of subtlety in their romance series. Several tales about men who are controlled by their mothers question the masculinity of their characters, such as "I Married a Mama's Boy" from Quality's *Heart Throbs* #25: "I wouldn't have married you if I'd known you were such a weakling!" screams newlywed Marilyn at her husband, Keith.[48] Similarly, in "I Was Engaged to a Puppet!" from Atlas's *My Love* #4 in 1950, when a young woman named Edith begins to realize just how much influence her fiancé Arnold's mother has over him, she turns for comfort to his brother, Allen. "Ever since I was born, my mother has dominated my life . . . has told me what to wear . . . when I could do something and when I couldn't! I have just enough manhood in me to object to this!" says Allen, implicitly questioning his brother's gender identity in the process.[49]

In confronting Arnold before they leave to start a new life together, Allen calls his brother a "spineless milksop" while Edith tells him, "I want to marry a man . . . not a timid, cringing puppet!"[50] Along with questioning the masculinity of these "mama's boys," such stories often question their characters' interest in women altogether. In 1958's "Mama's Boy!" from the fifth issue of Charlton's *Just Married*, a coworker warns a woman named Lila about getting too interested in her new neighbor: "I saw you with John Venel, Lila! You're wasting your time! He never dates girls." Lila's family also cautions her against getting involved with John: "I warned you, Lila—I told you he had no time for girls!" her father scolds.[51]

Quality's *Love Scandal* recounts a similar tale of a child dominated by

"I Married a Mama's Boy," *Heart Throbs* #25, 1953, Quality Comics.

a parent, but reverses the genders. The 1950 publication describes the life of Matty Comstock, the beautiful young heiress of a shipping line who "longed for the freedom of a man's life!"[52] In the story, titled "I Hated Being a Woman," Matty describes how her father raised her to be the son he had wished for, how "as best he could, he tried to act as if he had a son!"[53] Throughout the story, Matty fights to become the captain of one of her father's ships but is continually put down and reminded that women cannot occupy such roles. The story uses the language of feminism to characterize Matty's nonnormative femininity; when she kisses an acquaintance, she rebukes further advances by excoriating the entire concept of heterosexual monogamy:

> That kiss meant nothing to me! But to you it would be the beginning of a lifetime of domination over me! [. . .] You men all think all you have to say is "I love you" and a girl will fall all over herself to make you her lord and master! Why should I marry you? I don't need a protector, I can do anything you can do and better![54]

Although Matty's story, like most (if not all) Golden Age romance tales, ends with a wedding, the strength and clarity of Matty's language here should not be discounted. Such a strong reproach of patriarchal attitudes would not have been common during the era, especially not from a character whose beauty and capability are repeatedly emphasized.

As the romance genre entered its final years, a story called "That Strange Girl" from *Young Romance* was more blatant in how it framed its protagonist's sexuality. "What was there about me that made me *different?*" asks a sixteen-year-old girl named Liz Baker as the story begins. "What set me apart from the *normal* girls? It pains me to tell this story, but if it can help ease the hurt in one girl who, like me, is torn by doubts and mixed emotions, it will be worth all the shame and torment I lived through when I was known as . . . *That Strange Girl*," she says.[55]

While Liz's queerness is never directly addressed, the front cover strongly implies as much. "Strange Girl! The Story They Dared Us to Print!" reads a tagline below an image of her on a ladder painting a house while two of her classmates pass by. "Don't waste your time, Fred. . . . Liz isn't interested in boys . . . you know what I mean!" says one. Multiple characters also make the suggestion within the story itself: "There's Liz Baker. . . . I wonder how she'd look in a dress?" a boy named Fred asks a friend, who responds with a variation of the same line of dialogue from the cover: "You're wasting your time, Fred. Liz isn't interested in *boys*! You know what I mean?" Her mother also shames Liz when the subject of dresses comes up: "A lot of girls wear pants to school . . . some just don't like dresses!" Liz says, to which her mother shoots back, "and some girls don't like *boys*, Liz!" In turn, her family, friends, and peers regularly call her "strange" ("That Liz, she's a strange one!").[56]

In *A Genealogy of Queer Theory*, William B. Turner explains, "The goal of queer theory is to investigate the historical circumstances by which

"I Hated Being a Woman," *Love Scandals* #5, 1950, Quality Comics.

'sexuality'—especially the charge of 'homosexuality'—can automatically render subjects the somewhat pitiable victims of a determinism that 'heterosexual' subjects supposedly remain free from."[57] This "determinism" is on full display in "That Strange Girl," starting with the opening narration's emphasis on "difference" and "normalcy." But while the ending

"That Strange Girl," *Young Romance* #197, 1974, DC Comics.

upholds traditional norms of gender and sexuality, the story provides numerous areas for alternative readings: when Liz first kisses Fred, she feels "frightened . . . and ashamed." As she runs home crying, Liz tells us with first-person narration, "I was all mixed up inside" and of how she hated both her peers and herself. When her mother asks what's wrong,

Liz replies, "Nothing, mother! Everything!" These lines connote how the heavy-handed plot isn't being faithful to Liz's true identity.

The nonnormative expressions of gender and sexuality that the romance genre infrequently engaged with point toward a not-so-secret understanding between creators and readers that the union of man and woman could not, would not solve all of life's problems. For some readers, representations of adolescents who defied normative gender representation could have been affirming, but the generic necessity that all stories end with a passionate kiss between a man and woman all but negated any positive result that may have come out of these representations. Identities outside of strict heterosexuality that were explored or acknowledged in the romance comics of the Golden Age were often framed as obstacles the men and women in relationships needed to overcome in order to find happiness.

Generously, these nonnormative representations could be read as a kind of normalization, an integration of the "abnormal" into the "normal" in order to police or redeem. In the sociological sense, "normalization" refers to the process of identifying behavior and lifestyles that are the norm in an effort to discipline or pressure behaviors or lifestyles that fall outside of that norm (the abnormal) into behaving in accordance with it.[58] All of these nonnormative characters—mama's boys and strange girls alike—are either cast aside in favor of romantic partners who fulfill traditional gender roles more adequately *or* made "normal" through romance. As the "mama's boys" stories exemplify, the romance genre cast a harsher light on male characters who failed to embody traditionally masculine traits than on female characters who strayed from normative femininity. This is not necessarily a victory for feminism, however; while men who weren't perfectly masculine were viewed, perhaps, as irredeemable, they were allowed (presumably) to find fulfillment elsewhere in these romance titles whenever they were cast aside by a woman. Characters like Matty and Liz, who initially shirked the expectations of traditional femininity, were reformed through marriage and motherhood. Romance comics may have judged them to be "fixable," but what this ultimately meant was that expressions of alternative forms of womanhood and gender by women were judged to be doubly illegitimate.

Conclusion

The romance genre was one of the few genres that offered non-male creators a regular voice. While traditional nuclear family values dominated their stories, romance titles occasionally showed off the genre's potential to offer challenging representations of racial and sexual identity. More often than not, however, alternatives to the white, heterosexual, middle-class lifestyle presented in these publications appeared as problems to be solved. Instead of looking at alternative expressions of gender and romance as viable pathways through life, the romance genre made cautionary tales of them. This is, in large part, due to the restrictive nature of Comics Code Authority. The CCA hindered the ability for publishers to authentically respond to the massive social, cultural, and political shifts of the 1960s.

By the mid-1970s, even flagship titles like *Young Romance* and *Young Love* were canceled. As Michael Barson notes in *Agonizing Love: The Golden Age of Romance Comics*, the industry's attempts to update its formula fell flat: "No matter how many headbands and tie-dyed T-shirts appeared on the characters . . . readers must have been able to sense that something inauthentic was afoot back at the storyboard."[59] As the second wave of feminism grew stronger, romance comics seemed more and more the product of an outdated vision of who women were.

Still, the image of the subservient housewife presented in *The Feminine Mystique* does not paint the entire picture of who women were at the time. Popular magazines often celebrated women who had it all—accomplishments outside of the home, a gaggle of children, a satisfied husband, and, yes, an immaculately maintained domestic life. Women were expected, whether they had pursuits outside of the home or not, to work hard "without complaint."[60]

While some of the more fantastic genres—sci-fi, horror, and superhero—were able to deal with social and cultural issues using metaphor and symbolism, the romance genre dealt with some of the stickier social issues in euphemistic but still obvious ways. In many ways, romance was the only genre that could have dealt with alternative expressions of sex and gender meaningfully, but both the Comics Code and the generic expectations of readers limited how these stories could end.

CONCLUSION

The roles played by the women who work on and star in comics have changed drastically since the 1930s. As the comics marketplace has expanded to include new genres (such as the memoir and coming-of-age tales), audiences (such as tweens and LGBTQ+ readers), and formats (such as graphic novels and webcomics), new opportunities have emerged for stories by and about women. While creators like Toni Blum, Barbara Hall, June Tarpé Mills, Lily Renée, Ruth Roche, and others made inroads with their work on such characters as Miss Fury, Sally O'Neil, Señorita Rio, and the Black Cat, there are more women making comics now, and more comics about women, than ever before.

In *Why Comics? From Underground to Everywhere*, Hilary Chute explains, "In the graphic novel world, girls are the new superheroes. They are the action stars, the focal point, the figures whose backstories, ideas, inclinations, struggles, and triumphs are presented with detailed attention in autobiography and fiction alike."[1] Graphic novels, which typically contain full-length tales and achieve wider distribution in bookstores than serialized monthly comics, have become a prominent venue in recent years for stories about women, especially younger ones, in the work of Svetlana Chmakova, Jillian Tamaki, Raina Telgemeier, and others.

It's easy to take for granted just how many changes have taken place since the Golden Age surrounding how, and for whom, comics are made. In 1999, Ramona Fradon and Marie Severin sat down to discuss their careers and what it was like working at a time when so few women were part of the comic book industry. Both women began working in comics around the same time, with Severin starting at EC Comics in 1949 and Fradon at DC in 1950. Because they were so vastly outnumbered by men at each company, Fradon and Severin often felt like they weren't being taken seriously by their male peers:

> FRADON: It just seemed like we were a couple of weirdos in this business.
>
> SEVERIN: We were oddities, because we were working in a field that . . . no other women were there, and probably people were wondering why, and we were just paying the bills, and I enjoyed the work . . .[2]

When asked about the workplace sexual harassment that was so common at the time, Fradon told Severin about the unwanted advances she regularly faced:

> FRADON: I was talking about this one production guy who, every time I came up to deliver work, he would come up, sneak behind me, and start kissing me on the back of the neck, and I could not stop him from doing it. I always had this feeling that if I went into the bullpen, there would be some kind of a disaster or something . . .
>
> SEVERIN: These lechers running up to you with their pants falling off!
>
> FRADON: Yeah! That's what it felt like! There were a couple of men who behaved that way, and they really . . . it scared me, you know? I felt really vulnerable.
>
> SEVERIN: You know, it's funny, because with the smaller group at EC, the guys were all gentlemen, no one would dare do something like that! But in a big group like that, where they're the majority, it's the bullpen, and here comes a little calf in there making cover sketches! Wow.
>
> FRADON: That's it exactly.
>
> SEVERIN: I would be intimidated. I'd be scared stiff with that.
>
> FRADON: I really was. They were deranged in there. They were in this dark room with no windows, they're in there working all day, looking at these nutty pictures, and around 3 o'clock they'd all get a little weird, and that's when I'd come in. So it was scary . . .[3]

Self-portrait by Ramona Fradon, 2019.

Fradon drew for DC from 1950 to 1965, working on such titles as *Gang Busters*, *Star Spangled War Stories*, and *World's Finest Comics*. Best known for drawing Aquaman in *Adventure Comics* in this era, Fradon cocreated a new character in 1965 called Metamorpho the Element Man. Debuting in the pages of *The Brave and the Bold* in 1965 before quickly gaining his own solo series, Metamorpho could alter his body in any combination of chemical forms. The character was so unique that an animation producer tried to develop a series by adding limited motion to her original artwork to make the character talk. While the show never emerged because DC discouraged its development,[4] Marvel found success using a similar approach with its 1966 series *The Marvel Super Heroes* from Grantray-Lawrence Animation, using artwork from Steve Ditko, Don Heck, Jack Kirby, and other male artists. While the latter television program remains a fan favorite and helped launch the early stages of Marvel's modern multimedia empire, the failed Metamorpho series remains one of many paths not taken for female artists in comics' earlier decades—a path that would have offered a prominent spotlight to one of the few female artists from the Golden Age still working in comics by the 1960s.

After drawing the early adventures of Metamorpho, Fradon left the business in 1965 to focus on raising her daughter, a common reason why women left comics in this era. She resumed her career in 1973, drawing *Fantastic Four* for Marvel—but not before drawing pages for a soon-to-be-canceled series called *The Cat* starring the titular female hero. Written by Linda Fite with art by Marie Severin, the first issue debuted in 1972 but was only followed by three more installments before its abrupt cancellation saw Fradon's art go unused.[5] *The Cat* was part of a brief effort by Marvel in the early 1970s to add new series starring women, alongside *Night Nurse* and *Shanna the She-Devil.* All three series debuted in 1972, and all three were canceled the next year after just four or five issues. Fradon recalls, "Because of the Women's Movement, they were looking for a woman to draw" *The Cat.*[6] But a sustained attempt at a series inspired by second-wave feminism had to wait until 1977 with *Ms. Marvel* from writer Gerry Conway and artist John Buscema, by which point Marvel seemed less committed to using female talent to tell stories about female heroes.

The 1970s and 1980s also saw a major shift in how readers bought comics, with newsstand sales overtaken by the rise of stores dedicated specifically to selling comics (known as the direct market within the industry). While more women, such as June Brigman, Nancy A. Collins, Colleen Doran, Mary Jo Duffy, Jan Duursema, Barbara Kesel, Ann Nocenti, and Jill Thompson, wrote and drew comics throughout the 1980s and 1990s, the direct market also proved unwelcoming to many women who might have become new comics readers. In a 1989 interview, the DC writer and editor Mike Gold lamented the need to reach women through traditional bookstores rather than specialty comic book stores because the latter was rarely welcoming to non-male customers: "I don't think we can reach women in traditional comic books because we can't get them into the comic-book stores and almost no comics are sold outside of comic-book stores. Comic-book shops are very *male* places, and many women who go into comic-book stores feel creepy." Gold's wife, the freelance writer and cofounder of Chicago Comicon Ann Elizabeth DeLarye-Gold, adds that when you walk in to an average comic book shop, "there are cheesecake posters and posters of guys with half their teeth knocked out and blood flowing down their face. This is not a place I relax in."[7]

The "cheesecake" imagery that DeLarye-Gold describes was different than the Good Girl art of decades past. By the 1990s, scantily-clad, buxom superheroes and supernatural vixens were commonplace in such series as *Lady Death* and the annual *Marvel Swimsuit Special.* Starting in 1996, DC teamed up its popular characters Black Canary and Barbara Gordon/Oracle (formerly Batgirl) in several *Birds of Prey* series, but its early installments often demeaned its female heroes with artwork that fetishized Black Canary's revealing costume when not placing her in a skimpy bikini. Writer Gail Simone began writing *Birds of Prey* in 2003 after starting the Women in Refrigerators website in 1999 as a way of tracking misogynist tropes in comics. Named after an incident from an issue of *Green Lantern* in which a villain kills the hero's girlfriend and hides her body in a refrigerator, the website chronicles the ways in which comics regularly use violence against women as a central plot point, often to advance the story arc of a male hero. As Simone describes it, "It occurred to me that it was really unhealthy to be a female in a superhero comic, as most of the best female characters were getting depowered or stuck in a wood chipper."[8]

Echoing DeLarye-Gold's feelings about the industry well before the #Comicsgate movement arose, Simone saw comics as a frequently unwelcome space for non-male readers. She told Shannon E. Riley in 2012,

> All these guys were wondering online all the time, "Why don't women read comics?" And the sheer immensity of the violent and often sexualized portrayals really weighed down on me as a reader—I quit reading for a good while. Male heroes sometimes died, but not in the same manner. . . .
>
> The girls were being killed just to make the hero's quest for vengeance more justified. It got hugely boring on *top* of being nasty as a gender issue.[9]

Simone became part of a new generation of women who began making comics in the early 2000s. Today, comics companies employ male, female, and nonbinary creators in a wide range of roles: colorists, writers, artists, editors, letterers, and executives alike. But the comics scholar (and Image Comics editor) Jennifer M. Smith reminds us that while comics "are a collaborative medium," most roles go largely unnoticed and unappreciated by readers: "Other than the few women who are working in writing and drawing comics, the women tend to be largely invisible because they're in roles like editorial and coloring that is not as well recognized and visible in the public eye," she says. Editorial work, Smith notes, involves "a lot of emotional labor. You're managing personalities, you're encouraging people . . . or nagging." With pioneering editors such as Gwen Hansen, Ray Herman, Ruth Roche, Roberta Ross, Kay Woods, and Dorothy Woolfolk paving the way for those of later decades, including Sana Amanat, Karin Berger, Bobbie Chase, Mary Jo Duffy, Jenette Kahn, Janice Race, Diana Schutz, and Louise Simonson, the fact that editorial work was one of the "only places in comics where women have always made such significant inroads in the history of comics says something about the ways in which this labor is particularly gendered," says Smith.[10]

Comics studies, too, has been a highly gendered endeavor for much of its existence. Little scholarly work was done until recently about female creators, readers, or characters. Anna Peppard notes, for instance, that "the scholarly neglect of female superheroes goes hand in hand with scholarly neglect that comics can and do have female readers. This neglect is inexcusable."[11] In her introduction to a special issue of *Feminist Media Histories* on comics and history in 2018, Kathleen McClancy describes how "the standard history of American comics leaves out" the contributions of "women, queers and people of color in the medium."[12] These exclusions have only recently begun to be questioned with any frequency within the field, leading to a need to reclaim racial, sexual, gender, and other identities from a relatively small but already entrenched canon of literature about the history of comics that has centered voices that are primarily white, male, and cisgender.

While representation is the key focus of scholars and artists working to reclaim space in the comics industry and the field of comics studies, representation alone is not enough to "solve" the issues women face here. Suzanne Scott and Ellen Kirkpatrick acknowledge this in their discussion of the female Thor introduced in 2014 by Marvel, writing that "though Marvel has decided that a woman is 'worthy' of Thor's mantle . . . until systemic changes are made to reflect a commitment to female creators and fans, their 'worthiness' will remain a source of debate within comics culture and comics studies."[13] Still, equitable representation is a necessary starting point in the fight against the devaluation of women's labor within the industry and fandom in the marketplace.

At its core, the issue is less about how female characters of the Golden Age can be reframed as "empowered" or "feminist" and more about what it means for many of the female characters of the Golden Age to be simultaneously empowered and deeply flawed. No representation of any kind of character is ever going to be entirely accurate, truthful, or realistic, but the question of what good came out of these representations is an especially sticky one. The overwhelming majority of the Golden Age's female characters were created, written, and drawn by men. All but a handful of these characters are white, thin, conventionally beautiful, and, in the case of certain genres, explicitly involved with imperialist/colonialist narratives. The question is not "Is this character empowered or empowering?" but "Who does this character empower?"

To an even greater degree, we must also ask who is harmed by certain representations. Hester Eisenstein's argument about how neoliberalism has coopted feminism and molded it to its agenda rings especially true here. She writes, "We are told that the key to creating wealth and producing social justice is in fact the 'empowering' of individual women. . . . Thus, empowerment actually means the incorporation of women into the structures of capitalist power, whether as entrepreneurs or as low-wage workers."[14] Under this definition, the majority of the characters examined in this analysis fall under the umbrella of neoliberal empowerment, but to end there would be disingenuous. Many of these characters are also racists and colonizers; the empowerment written into them is intertwined with the latent racism, classism, and misogyny that is omnipresent in American culture and that cannot be ignored.

This doesn't detract from the fact that these characters also offered readers a glimpse of female characters who could be smart, autonomous, and resilient. The positive attributes remain and should be celebrated, but not at the expense of acknowledging the characters' less savory attributes. To resituate women characters and creators in their rightful place in comics history alongside their male counterparts does not require that every female character be reframed as a universally empowering or feminist representation. Instead, it requires that we not only acknowledge the good, but carefully examine and critique where women characters and creators have perpetuated harmful cultural, social, and political norms.

Smith reminds us that it's important "to be careful when assigning terms like *progress*" to the study of marginalized identities. She notes that since she started working in the industry almost a decade ago, there has "definitely has been a marked increase" in the amount of comics both made by and featuring women: "The number of titles starring female characters [has grown] by leaps and bounds[;] the number of female writers has definitely increased. I could count them on two fingers at one point less than ten years ago, and now I could probably start listing off the number of female writers who are working and still miss a couple." But while she considers it a small victory, Smith urges us to consider how any considerations of "progress" must be contextualized against the industry's overall gender gap:

> I'm still grading on a curve because the number of male writers still vastly outnumbers. And in terms of other roles, the number of male pencillers still vastly outnumbers. There are almost no female letterers, no female inkers that I can think of (unless they work in partnership like Rachel Dodson). There are a lot of female colorists . . . but the fact that colorists and editors are probably the highest percentage of women working in comics says something about the

> history of women's labor. Women being associated with coloring goes back to the days of early Disney animation—the "color girls" who were the ones painting all of the cels by hand. So this is a role that has been traditionally coded "female" and so in that way it's not surprising. . . . I think it's one of the only roles in comics that comes close to parity.[15]

Even if comic book publishers such as Marvel and DC fail to achieve gender parity in the years ahead, the expansion of the graphic novel market and the popularity of creators like Raina Telgemeier among young women shows us how the overall marketplace for comics in a variety of forms has shifted in recent years. In their 1989 interview, Mike Gold and Ann Elizabeth DeLarye-Gold speculated about just such a shift. Gold saw the facts that Jenette Kahn was publisher at DC and that Karen Berger was one of their leading editors as a sign that "the doors are open, the role models are beginning to be there, the accessibility is beginning to be there." When DeLarye-Gold asked her husband whether this means that "as a result, there will be an evolution of the product as well," he replied, "That will be more accessible to women, yes I hope so."[16]

While these changes came slowly at DC and Marvel, titles such as *Batgirl*, *Batwoman*, *Birds of Prey*, *Black Widow*, *Captain Marvel*, *Harley Quinn*, *Ms. Marvel*, *Moon Girl and Devil Dinosaur*, *Patsy Walker, A.K.A. Hellcat*, *She-Hulk*, *Storm*, and *The Unbeatable Squirrel Girl* were commonplace by the 2010s. Women of color have grown more prominent as writers and artists at many top publishers in recent years, including Vita Ayala, Eve Ewing, Yonah Harvey, Nilah Magruder, Nnedi Okorafor, and Mariko Tamaki at Marvel. While some genres, like jungle comics, have seen little in the way of feminist revision by modern creators, others have seen new takes by non-male creators seeking to update the way women are represented. Joelle Jones's *Lady Killer* reinvented the crime genre with its portrayal of an assassin/wife/mother, while horror comics have found new voices in Emil Ferris's *My Favorite Thing Is Monsters* and Emily Carroll's *Through the Woods* and *When I Arrived at the Castle*. Romance comics have embraced a wealth of new identities in books such as Mariko Tamaki's *Laura Dean Keeps Breaking Up with Me*, Tillie Walden's *I Love This Part*, and Tee Franklin's *Bingo Love*. Kelly Sue DeConnick has offered new takes on both the western in *Pretty Deadly* and science fiction in *Bitch Planet*, while sci-fi has been taken in new directions with Sloane Leong's *Prism Stalker*, Magdalene Visaggio's *Kim and Kim* and *Vagrant Queen*, and Tillie Walden's *On a Sunbeam*.

Though women who are interested in comics and their creation may still have to grade representations of women on a curve, comics and comics studies are by no means unique in their marginalization of female creators, characters, and consumers. The struggle to identify equitable representations and creative involvement of women in media extends far beyond the boundaries of comics or the Golden Age. The goal of this analysis is to connect the rift that exists in the relationship between comics and women to larger issues of marginalization in the United States, to identify where women have been denied or granted the ability to see and share their own stories, to challenge popularly accepted notions of "empowerment," and to highlight the power that women occasionally *did* have during the Golden Age. Comics from this era have been rightly criticized for peddling harmful representations of women and people of color, but these ideologies did not originate with comics, nor did they end with the self-censorship and suppression that overtook the industry in the 1950s. The exclusion or misrepresentation of women creators, characters, and consumers resulted from larger patterns of misogyny and patriarchy that have been embedded in the United States for as long as the country has existed. The fight for an equitable place in the comics industry is a fight against larger patterns of marginalization in our society, but this does not clear comics of all culpability. If anything, the structural nature of this marginalization highlights the importance of identifying where, when, and how it appears throughout the medium's history. The roots of this struggle are far older than much of the literature about comics' history would have readers believe, but the struggle is not futile; if change is going to be made in the industry, then the characters and creators who have made inroads for that change need to be recognized for their complicated—sometimes messy, often problematic—place in this fight.

ACKNOWLEDGMENTS

Many thanks to Trina Robbins for her foreword to our book. Her pioneering work has been an inspiration to our scholarship, and her opening words here are equally inspiring. We are also enormously grateful to Ramona Fradon and June Brigman for their original artwork. We would also like to thank Qiana Whitted and Kate Polak for their generous comments about the manuscript and for pointing us in many useful directions along the way. DePaul University provided much-needed funding for this project through a University Research Council grant. At the University of Texas Press, Jim Burr, Sarah McGavick, and Lynne Ferguson provided tremendous editorial support, and Sarah Hudgens provided stellar copyediting.

Peyton thanks:

First and foremost, I am eternally grateful for Bella Jorgensen, the Veronica to my Betty, without whom I would have never made it through grad school—or my early twenties. Her hard work, insight, and late-night phone calls were invaluable to the development of this project.

My gratitude to Daniel Bashara and Paul Booth at DePaul University, who patiently listened to all of my frustrations and anxieties before, after, and sometimes during class; their encouragement kept me going when 7-Eleven coffee couldn't.

Thanks to my parents, for buying me comics on our weekly trips to the neighborhood coffee shop. And finally, thanks to my sisters, Paige and Perrin, and best friends, Pat Ramos, Caroline Pejcinovic, and Marisa Clogher, for being more complicated, powerful, and loving than any comic book character could ever hope to be.

Blair thanks:

Erin, Audrey, and Ewan for everything, every day.

NOTES

Introduction

1. Margaret Galvan and Leah Misemer, "Introduction: The Counterpublics of Underground Comics," *Inks* 3, no. 1 (Spring 2019): 1.

2. The temporal designations of Golden Age, Silver Age, and the like have been challenged by some comics scholars as being too narrowly conceived—tied, for instance, to nostalgia (Benjamin Woo, "An Age-Old Problem: Problematics of Comic Book Historiography," *International Journal of Comic Art* 10, no. 1 [2008]: 268–279) and the developmental patterns of the superhero genre (Marc Singer, *Breaking the Frames: Populism and Prestige in Comics Studies* [Austin: University of Texas Press, 2018], 61–62). But as much as these labels might need to be rethought, that is not our fight at this moment. We use the term "Golden Age" regularly throughout this book as a way of more fully integrating women into the public discourses that surround the history of comics, because that history is in dire need of correction.

3. *Batman*, no. 1 (New York: Detective Comics, Spring 1940), 39.

4. Jennifer M. Smith, personal interview, March 17, 2018.

5. Maurice Horn, ed. *The World Encyclopedia of Comics* (New York: Avon, 1976).

6. bell hooks, *Feminism Is for Everybody: Passionate Politics* (New York: Routledge, 2015), 20.

7. Nicky Wheeler-Nicholson, *DC Comics before Superman: Major Malcolm Wheeler-Nicholson's Pulp Comics* (Neshannock, PA: Hermes Press, 2018), 34.

8. Will Murray, "Introduction," *Golden Age Marvel Comics Omnibus* (New York: Marvel, 2009), 12–13.

9. Jack Elmy, "In Search of Lloyd Jacquet," *Alter Ego*, vol. 3, no. 22, March 2003, 24.

10. Elmy, "In Search of Lloyd Jacquet," 27.

11. Joan Schenkar, *The Talented Miss Highsmith: The Secret Life and Serious Art of Patricia Highsmith* (New York: St. Martin's Press, 2009), 127, 170. While Schenkar describes Highsmith as working on a character called "Betty the Nurse," no such character exists in comics. Given that Schenkar places Highsmith at Timely in 1949, it is reasonable to assume that she meant Nellie the Nurse.

12. Schenkar, *Talented Miss Highsmith*, 161.

13. Schenkar, *Talented Miss Highsmith*, 162.

14. Joan Schenkar, "Patricia Highsmith and the Golden Age of American Comics," *Alter Ego*, vol. 3, no. 90, December 2009, 36.

15. Jim Amash, "'When You Do a Lot of Super-Heroes, All You're Drawing Is Men in Long Underwear,'" *Alter Ego*, vol. 3, no. 65, February 2007, 8.

16. Jim Amash, "'Maybe I'm in the Wrong End of This Business!,'" *Alter Ego*, vol. 3, no. 79, July 2008, 50.

17. Jim Amash, "'Simon Says!,'" *Alter Ego*, vol. 3, no. 76, March 2008, 43. Simon goes on to say of Ann Brewster in his interview with Amash: "I never knew much about her. . . . She was the only woman who ever worked for me

that I can remember, even though you've said there were others." In other words, the only woman whom Simon recalls working for him is remembered for her body type and little else.

18. Jim Amash, "'I Always Felt That Storytelling Was as Important as the Artwork,'" *Alter Ego*, vol. 3, no. 48, May 2005, 20.

19. David Laurence Wilson, "A Timely Pair," *Jack Kirby Collector*, no. 69, Fall 2016, 32–33.

20. David N. Rapp, "Dell Comics," in *Icons of the American Comic Book*, ed. Randy Duncan and Matthew J. Smith (Santa Barbara, CA: Greenwood, 2013), 200. Despite being a marketplace leader, Meyer has been the target of misogynist vitriol by some who worked in the Golden Age of comics. Artist Lou Cameron tells of how Dell "was presided over by an ogress named Mrs. [Helen] Meyer, and she was an infamous person. She practically ran Dell into the ground, and she was an arbitrary old bitch. A lot of people just wouldn't work for Dell after a while." Amash, "'Maybe I'm in the Wrong End,'" 54.

21. In addition to her role as editor at Funnies Inc., Roberta Ross was also a short-lived publisher: together with artists Leonard Starr and Warren King, Ross put out a single issue of *Hi-Lite Comics* in 1945, with stories from a range of genres. Starr recalls that "the returns were terrific" on the issue, but the trio couldn't publish a second issue because of war-era paper shortages. Jim Amash, "'I Think I Worked for Every [Comics] House in the City,'" *Alter Ego*, vol. 3, no. 110, June 2012, 7–8.

22. Jim Amash, "'I Was Contemptuous, Basically of the Comics,'" *Alter Ego*, vol. 3, no. 99, January 2011, 38.

23. *Bomber Comics*, no. 1 (New York: Elliot Publishing Co., March 1944), 51–52.

24. Martha H. Kennedy, *Drawn to Purpose: American Women Illustrators and Cartoonists* (Jackson: University Press of Mississippi, 2018) 4.

25. Kennedy, *Drawn to Purpose*, 17–18.

26. Kennedy, *Drawn to Purpose*, 20; 167n68.

27. Alice Sheppard, *Cartooning for Suffrage* (Albuquerque: University of New Mexico Press, 1994), 120.

28. Trina Robbins, *Pretty in Ink: North American Women Cartoonists, 1896–2013* (Seattle: Fantagraphics Books, 2013), 17–18; Kennedy, *Drawn to Purpose*, 31–33, 39–40.

29. Kennedy, *Drawn to Purpose*, 28–29. See also William Cole and Florett Robinson, eds., *Women Are Wonderful* (Boston: Houghton Mifflin, 1956), a collection of cartoons by and about women from the 1800s through the early to mid-twentieth century.

30. Kennedy, *Drawn to Purpose*, 29.

31. See Tim Jackson, *Pioneering Cartoonists of Color* (Jackson: University Press of Mississippi, 2016), 43, 64, 71.

32. King Features Syndicate began distributing *Mary Worth* in 1987.

33. Rebecca Wanzo, *The Content of Our Caricature: African American Comic Art and Political Belonging* (New York: New York University Press, 2020), 5.

34. See Blair Davis, "*All-Negro Comics* and the Birth of Lion Man, the First African-American Superhero," *Inks* 3, no. 3 (Winter 2019): 273–297.

35. Leonard Rifas, "Race and Comix," in *Multicultural Comics: From Zap to*

Blue Beetle, ed. Frederick Luis Aldama (Austin: University of Texas Press, 2010), 28.

36. Deborah Elizabeth Whaley, *Black Women in Sequence: Re-inking Comics, Graphic Novels, and Anime* (Seattle: University of Washington Press), 8.

37. Judith Butler, "Performative Acts and Gender Constitution: An Essay in Phenomenology and Feminist Theory," *Theatre Journal* 40, no. 4 (1988): 519–531.

38. Butler, "Performative Acts and Gender Constitution," 522.

39. Hillary Chute, *Graphic Women: Life Narrative and Contemporary Comics* (New York: Columbia University Press, 2010), 26.

40. Ana Merino, "Women in Comics: A Space for Recognizing Other Voices," trans. Derek Peterey, *Comics Journal*, no. 237, September 2001, 45.

Chapter 1. Superhero Comics

1. Noah Berlatsky describes how "Wonder Woman remains popularly considered the first female superhero." Berlatsky, *Wonder Woman: Bondage and Feminism in the Marston/Peter Comics, 1941–1948* (New Brunswick, NJ: Rutgers University Press, 2017).

2. Carolyn Cocca, *Superwomen: Gender, Power, Representation* (New York: Bloomsbury, 2016), 25.

3. Gerard Jones, *Men of Tomorrow: Geeks, Gangsters, and the Birth of the Comic Book* (New York: Basic Books, 2004), 93, 120.

4. Comic books, newspaper strips, and the pulps were often an interconnected realm, particularly in the 1930s and 1940s (with many of the creators who made comic books aspiring to do newspaper strips and many comic books publishers also producing pulp magazines). While much of the early work in comics studies was focused on comic strips—such as Ian Gordon's *Comic Strips and Consumer Culture, 1890–1945* (Washington, D.C.: Smithsonian Institution Scholarly Press, 1998) and Robert C. Harvey's *The Art of the Funnies: An Aesthetic History* (Jackson: University Press of Mississippi, 1994)—more scholarly work needs to be done on the connections between comic strips and comic books. The same is true about the links between comics and pulp magazines, an area that has seen minimal focus to date and that might serve as a way of tracing a longer history of popular literary forms back even further historically.

5. Michael Schumacher, *Will Eisner: A Dreamer's Life In Comics* (New York: Bloomsbury, 2010), 48.

6. Jones, *Men of Tomorrow*, 162.

7. Jones, *Men of Tomorrow*, 192.

8. Jim Amash, "'I'm Trying to Prod People to Think,'" *Alter Ego*, vol. 3, no. 92, March 2010, 42.

9. Adrian Quinlan, "A Real Life Comic-Book Superhero," *Newsweek*, July 20, 2010, https://www.newsweek.com/real-life-comic-book-superhero-74267.

10. Jim Amash, "'I'm Not Typical for Doing Comics, You Know!': The Life and Times of Golden Age Artist Lily Renée," *Alter Ego*, vol. 3, no. 85, May 2009, 8.

11. Mark Seifart, "Meeting Golden Age Art Goddess, Lily Renée," Bleeding Cool, November 9, 2011, https://www.bleedingcool.com/2011/11/09/meeting-golden-age-art-goddess-lily-renee/.

12. Quinlan, "Real Life Comic-Book Superhero."

13. Amash, "'I'm Not Typical,'" 16.

14. Jim Amash, "'Sales Don't Tell You Everything!,'" *Alter Ego*, vol. 3, no. 94, June 2010, 44.

15. Jim Amash, "'It Was a Daily Identity Crisis,'" *Alter Ego*, vol. 3, no. 69, June 2007, 38.

16. Schumacher, *Will Eisner*, 49.

17. Will Eisner, *Will Eisner: Conversations*, ed. M. Thomas Inge (Jackson: University Press of Mississippi, 2011), 53.

18. Richard Burton, "Interview: Chris Claremont," *Comic Reader*, no. 164, January 1979, 8.

19. Alastair Mabbott, "Graphic Mogul: Stan Lee," in *Stan Lee: Conversations*, ed. Jeff McLaughlin (Jackson: University Press of Mississippi, 2007), 123.

20. Mark Salisbury, *Writers on Comics Scriptwriting* (London: Titan Books, 1999), 9.

21. Mabbott, "Graphic Mogul," 123.

22. Amash, "'I Was Contemptuous,'" 39.

23. Amash, "'I Always Felt That Storytelling,'" 20. Bossert confirms that Eisner "may have given [Blum] special assignments where he wanted a whole script," likely for artists such as Lou Fine who needed them. Amash, "'I Was Contemptuous,'" 44.

24. Jim Amash, "'I Graduated from Plato and Aristotle to Superman and Batman,'" *Alter Ego*, vol. 3, no. 93, May 2010, 42.

25. Amash, "'I'm Trying to Prod People,'" 43.

26. Jim Amash, "'I Let People Do Their Jobs!,'" *Alter Ego*, vol. 3, no. 11, November 2001, 13.

27. Amash, "'I Was Contemptuous,'" 39.

28. Amash, "'I Was Doomed to Be an Artist,'" *Alter Ego*, vol. 3, no. 48, May 2005, 44.

29. David Hadju, *The Ten-Cent Plague: The Great Comic-Book Scare and How It Changed America* (New York: Picador, 2008), 26.

30. Robert C. Harvey, *The Art of the Comic Book: An Aesthetic History* (Jackson: University Press of Mississippi, 1996), 74.

31. Ken Quattro, "Eisner-Blum Addendum," *Alter Ego*, vol. 3, no. 127, August 2014, 28.

32. Peter Depree, "Night of the Paper Noir," in *Will Eisner: Conversations*, edited by M. Thomas Inge, 131–175 (Jackson: University Press of Mississippi, 2011).

33. Quoted in Bob Andelman, *Will Eisner: A Spirited Life* (Raleigh, NC: TwoMorrows Publishing, 2015), 56.

34. M. Keith Booker, ed., *Comics through Time: A History of Icons, Idols, and Ideals* (Santa Barbara, CA: ABC-Clio, 2014), 260.

35. Trina Robbins, "Miss Fury and the Very Personal Universe of Tarpé Mills," in Tarpé Mills, *Miss Fury: Sensational Sundays, 1944–1949*, edited by Trina Robbins (San Diego: IDW Publishing, 2011), 8.

36. Trina Robbins, *Pretty in Ink: North American Women Cartoonists, 1896–2013* (Seattle: Fantagraphics, 2013), 69.

37. Male creators occasionally adopted a female pen name, such as artist

Munson Paddock. Starting in the 1930s, he used the pseudonyms Cecelia Munson and Cecilia Munson for his work.

38. Charles Hatfield, Jeet Heer, and Kent Worcester, eds., *The Superhero Reader* (Jackson: University Press of Mississippi, 2013), 6.

39. Hatfield, Heer, and Worcester, *Superhero Reader*, 5.

40. *Planet Comics*, no. 3 (New York: Fiction House, March 1940), 14.

41. *Famous Funnies*, no. 82, (New York: Famous Funnies Inc., May 1941), 6.

42. Robbins, *Pretty in Ink*, 66. See also Trina Robbins, *The Great Women Super Heroes* (Northampton, MA: Kitchen Sink Press, 1996), 18–23.

43. Jim Amash, "'I Come from a Very Primitive Background,'" *Alter Ego*, vol. 3, no. 103, July 2011, 38.

44. *All-American Comics*, no. 20 (New York: All-American Comics Inc., November 1940), 13.

45. *All-American Comics*, no. 20, 15.

46. *All-American Comics*, no. 21 (New York: All-American Comics Inc., December 1940), 11.

47. *All-American Comics*, no. 21, 13–14.

48. *All-American Comics*, no. 22 (New York: All-American Comics Inc., January 1941), 12. Hunkel was not the only costumed character who challenged gender norms in the early 1940s. Quality's *Crack Comics* saw male stock market mogul Richard Stanton fight crime as Madame Fatal by disguising himself as an elderly woman. Infiltrating the criminal underworld in this seemingly innocent guise, the character proved to be little more than a gimmick—using a cane as a weapon, for instance—who lacked the layers of social commentary embedded in Hunkel's appearances as Red Tornado.

49. In their essay "Postgenderism: Beyond the Gender Binary," George Dvorsky and James Hughes describe how "technology is eroding the biological, psychological and social role of gender" and how the subsequent "erosion of binary gender will be liberatory," building off the work of Donna Haraway and Judith Butler. Dvorsky and Hughes, *Postgenderism: Beyond the Gender Binary* (Hartford, CT: Institute for Ethics and Emerging Technologies, 2008), 44–57.

50. *Jungle Comics*, no. 2 (New York: Fiction House, February 1940), 58.

51. *Jungle Comics*, no. 3 (New York: Fiction House, March 1940), 58, 60.

52. See Paul Karasik, ed., *Turn Loose Our Death Rays and Kill Them All!: The Complete Works of Fletcher Hanks* (Seattle: Fantagraphics Books, 2016) for an overview of his career.

53. *Jungle Comics*, no. 27 (New York: Fiction House, March 1942), 21, 25.

54. Hatfield, Heer, and Worcester, "Introduction," *Superhero Reader*, xii.

55. In *Our Gods Wear Spandex: The Secret History of Superhero Comics*, Chris Knowles describes the Phantom as embodying "the visual model of the superhero in his form-fitting bodysuit, nifty skull logo and eye mask" but goes on to offer a dismissive assessment of the hero as being little more than "essentially a circus-costumed version of Tarzan." He ultimately aligns the Phantom with the jungle genre even as he sees the character as a predecessor of later superheroes. Knowles, *Our Gods Wear Spandex: The Secret History of Superhero Comics* (San Francisco: Wieser Books, 2007), 107. In contrast, Kevin Patrick has no qualms about labeling the character as the first superhero in his

book *The Phantom Unmasked: America's First Superhero* (Iowa City: University of Iowa Press, 2017).

56. Richard Reynolds, *Superheroes: A Modern Mythology* (Jackson: University Press of Mississippi, 1994), 7.

57. Peter Coogan, "The Hero Defines the Genre, the Genre Defines the Hero," in *What Is a Superhero?*, ed. Robin S. Rosenberg and Peter Coogan (New York: Oxford University Press, 2013), 3–4.

58. Coogan, "Hero Defines the Genre," 4.

59. *Jumbo Comics*, no. 2 (New York: Fiction House, October 1938), 30.

60. Maurice Horn, *The World Encyclopedia of Comics* (New York: Avon Books, 1976), 611.

61. Chris Murray, "*Pop*aganda: Superhero Comics and Propaganda in World War II," in *Comics & Culture: Analytical and Theoretical Approaches to Comics*, ed. Anne Magnussen and Hans-Christian Christiansen (Copenhagen: Museum Tusculanum Press, 2000), 143.

62. Robbins, *Great Women Super Heroes*, 72.

63. Clive Smith, "The Great Canadian Comic Books," *Alter Ego*, vol. 3, no. 71, August 2007, 14.

64. Adrian Dingle, *Nelvana of the Northern Lights*, ed. Hope Nicholson (Winnipeg: Bedside Press, 2017) 274–275.

65. *Daring Mystery Comics*, no. 7 (New York: Timely Comics, April 1941), 34.

66. Christina M. Knopf, "'Hey Soldier!—Your Slip Is Showing!': Militarism vs. Femininity in World War II Comic Pages and Books," in *The Ten Cent War: Comic Books, Propaganda, and World War II*, ed. Trischa Goodnow and James M. Kimble (Jackson: University Press of Mississippi, 2016), 26.

67. *Pocket Comics*, no. 3 (New York: Harvey Comics, November 1941), 53.

68. Kurt Mitchell and Roy Thomas, *American Comic Book Chronicles: 1940–1944* (Raleigh, NC: TwoMorrows Publishing, 2019), 101.

69. Maren Williams, "She Changed Comics: Pre-Code and Golden Age," Comic Book Legal Defense Fund, March 4, 2016, http://cbldf.org/2016/03/she-changed-comics-pre-code-golden-age/.

70. Trina Robbins, *Babes in Arms: Women in Comics during the Second World War* (New Castle, PA: Hermes Press, 2017), 8.

71. Robbins, *Great Women Super Heroes*, 44.

72. Amash, "'I'm Trying to Prod People,'" 38.

73. Knopf, "'Hey Soldier!,'" 27.

74. *Feature Comics*, no. 42 (Stamford, CT: Quality Comics, March 1941), 17.

75. *Captain Aero Comics*, vol. 3, no. 11 (New York: Et-Es-Go Magazines Inc., January 1944), 16, 18.

76. *Star Studded Comics*, no. 1 (New York: Cambridge House, May 1946), 20.

77. Les Daniels, *Marvel: Five Fabulous Decades of the World's Greatest Comics* (New York: Harry N. Abrams, 1991), 54; Amash, "'I Let People Do Their Jobs!,'" 9, 15.

78. *Captain America Comics*, no. 66 (New York: Timely Comics, April 1948), 6.

79. *Captain America Comics*, no. 66, 7. In 2020, President Donald Trump implied that washing dishes was women's work when he described how he'd rather have Secretary of State Mike Pompeo "on the phone with some world leader than have him wash dishes because maybe his wife isn't there." Jill Filipovic, "Trump's Stone-Age Views on 'Women's Work,'" CNN, May 19, 2020, https://www.cnn.com/2020/05/19/opinions/trump-pompeo-remarks-misogyny-filipovic/index.html.

80. *Captain America Comics*, no. 66, 12.

81. Quoted in Jones, *Men of Tomorrow*, 207.

82. William Moulton Marston, "Why 100,000 Americans Read Comics," *The American Scholar* 13, no. 1 (Winter 1943): 35–44.

83. Johnny E. Miles, *Superheroes and Their Ancient Jewish Parallels: A Comparative Study* (Jefferson, NC: McFarland, 2018), 140.

84. Richard J. Arndt, "The First Amazon," *Alter Ego*, vol. 3, no. 157, March 2019, 9.

85. Les Daniels, *Wonder Woman: The Complete History* (San Francisco: Chronicle Books, 2003), 76.

86. Arndt, "First Amazon," 23.

87. Jill Lepore, *The Secret History of Wonder Woman* (New York: Knopf Doubleday, 2014), 254.

88. *Wonder Woman*, no. 12 (New York: All American Publications, March 1945), 1.

89. See Maureen Honey, *Creating Rosie the Riveter: Class, Gender, and Propaganda During World War II* (Amherst: University of Massachusetts Press, 1984).

90. Arndt, "First Amazon," 9–10.

91. Arndt, "First Amazon," 9.

92. Fredric Wertham, *Seduction of the Innocent (*New York: Rinehart & Company, 1954), 34.

93. See Tim Hanley, *Wonder Woman Unbound: The Curious History of the World's Most Famous Heroine* (Chicago: Chicago Review Press, 2014), 210–214.

94. Fredric Wertham and Frank Santana, *The Circle of Guilt* (New York: Rinehart & Company, 1956). See also Bart Beaty, *Fredric Wertham and the Critique of Mass Culture* (Jackson: University Press of Mississippi, 2005), 91–92.

95. Wertham, *Seduction of the Innocent*, 2.

Chapter 2. Jungle Comics

1. See, for instance, John McBratney, *Imperial Subjects, Imperial Space: Rudyard Kipling's Fiction of the Native-Born* (Columbus: Ohio State University Press, 2002); and Chinua Achebe, "An Image of Africa: Racism in Conrad's *Heart of Darkness*," in *Heart of Darkness: An Authoritative Text, Backgrounds and Source Criticism*, 3rd ed., ed. Robert Kimbaugh (New York: Norton, 1988), 251–262.

2. For critical rereadings of the jungle genre in literature through the lens of postcolonial theory, see Leslie Wylie, *Colonial Tropes and Postcolonial Tricks: Rewriting the Tropics in the Novela de la Selva* (Liverpool, UK: Liverpool Uni-

versity Press, 2009); and Elahe Haschemi Yekani, *The Privilege of Crisis: Narratives of Masculinities in Colonial and Postcolonial Literature, Photography and Film* (Frankfurt, Germany: Campus Verlag, 2011).

3. Jeremy Agnew, *The Age of Dimes and Pulps: A History of Sensationalist Literature, 1830–1960* (Jefferson, NC: McFarland, 2018), 106.

4. See David Lemmo, *Tarzan, Jungle King of Popular Culture* (Jefferson, NC: McFarland, 2017).

5. Joseph Conrad, *Heart of Darkness* (Cambridge: Cambridge University Press, 2018), 8.

6. *Daring Mystery Comics*, no. 5 (New York: Timely Comics, June 1940), 7; *Daring Mystery Comics*, no. 3 (New York: Timely Comics, April 1940), 34.

7. *Daring Mystery Comics*, no. 4 (New York: Timely Comics, May 1940), 54.

8. *Fight Comics*, no. 36 (New York: Fiction House, February 1945), 13.

9. *Jumbo Comics*, no. 2 (New York: Fiction House, October 1938), 30.

10. See Kenneth M. Cameron, *Africa on Film: Beyond Black and White* (New York: Continuum, 1994).

11. Rhona J. Berenstein, "White Heroines and Hearts of Darkness: Race, Gender, and Disguise in 1930s Jungle Films," *Film History* 6, no. 3 (1994): 318.

12. Berenstein, "White Heroines and Hearts of Darkness," 318.

13. Berenstein, "White Heroines and Hearts of Darkness," 320.

14. *Jungle Comics*, no. 1 (New York: Fiction House, June 1940), 26.

15. Alex Jay, "Comics: Marcia Snyder, Artist," *Tenth Letter of the Alphabet* (blog), January 18, 2018, http://alphabettenthletter.blogspot.com/2018/01/comics-marcia-snyder-artist.html.

16. Amash, "'I Let People Do Their Jobs!,'" 12.

17. Amash, "'I'm Not Typical,'" 13.

18. In her "U.S. Rangers" story for *Rangers Comics* #20 (December 1944), for instance, Snyder's name appears as if scratched into a bamboo pole at the bottom of the page among the bombed-ruins of a Chinese village.

19. Paul Lopes, "Culture and Stigma: Popular Culture and the Case of Comic Books," *Sociological Forum* 21, no. 3 (2006), 387–414; Erving Goffman, *Stigma: Notes on the Management of Spoiled Identity* (New York: Touchstone, 1963).

20. Wertham, *Seduction of the Innocent*, 25.

21. Wertham, *Seduction of the Innocent*, 23.

22. Lopes, "Culture and Stigma," 404.

23. *Jungle Comics*, no. 56 (New York: Fiction House, November 1944), 19.

24. *Marvel Masterworks: Atlas Era Jungle Adventure*, vol. 2 (New York: Marvel Comics, 2011), 90.

25. *Jungle Comics*, no. 56, 34.

26. bell hooks, *Talking Back: Thinking Feminist, Thinking Black* (Cambridge, MA: South End Press, 1989), 6.

27. Maria Miller Stewart, "Religion and the Pure Principles of Morality, the Sure Foundation on Which We Must Build," in *Words of Fire: An Anthology of African-American Feminist Thought*, ed. Beverly Guy-Sheftall (New York: The New Press, 1995), 25, 29.

28. *Fight Comics*, no. 34 (New York: Fiction House, October 1944), 12–13.

29. See "Afterword: The 'Unseen' of Culture," in Rosemary Jackson, *Fantasy: The Literature of Subversion* (New York: Routledge, 1981), 173–174.

30. Frantz Fanon, *Black Skin, White Masks (*London: Pluto Press, 2008), 112.

31. Fanon, *Black Skin, White Masks*, 112–114.

32. *Slave Girl Comics*, no. 2 (New York: Avon Periodicals Inc., 1949), 11, 29.

33. *Cave Girl*, no. 11 (New York: Magazine Enterprises, 1953), front cover.

34. Tarpé Mills, *Miss Fury: Sensational Sundays 1941–1944*, ed. Trina Robbins (San Diego: IDW Publishing, 2013), 84.

35. *Prize Comics*, no. 1 (New York: Feature Publications, March 1940), 36.

36. *Prize Comics*, no. 2 (New York: Feature Publications, April 1940), 35.

37. See Jake Austen and Yuval Taylor, *Darkest Africa: Black Minstrelsy from Slavery to Hip-Hop* (New York: Norton, 2012), for an overview of these racist tropes. This trend continued in many jungle comics well into the 1950s, including Jay Scott Pike's artwork for "Jann of the Jungle" in 1955's *Jungle Tales* #4 from Timely/Atlas.

38. Mills, *Miss Fury*, 95.

39. Mills, *Miss Fury*, 164.

40. Robbins, "Miss Fury and the Very Personal Universe," 84.

41. Trina Robbins, "Albino Jo, the Man with the Tigre Eyes," in Tarpé Mills, *Miss Fury: Sensational Sundays 1941–1944*, ed. Trina Robbins (San Diego: IDW Publishing, 2011), 215.

42. Robbins, "Albino Jo," 225.

43. Amash, "'I'm Not Typical,'" 13.

44. See Mitch Maglio, *Fiction House: From Pulps to Panels, from Jungles to Space* (San Diego: IDW Publishing, 2017), 27–28, for Renée's full biography.

45. Amash, "'I'm Not Typical,'" 6, 8.

46. Amash, "'I'm Not Typical,'" 10.

47. Arlen Schumer, "Superhero Comics of the Twenty-First Century: Origins," in *The Education of a Comics Artist: Visual Narrative in Cartoons, Graphic Novels, and Beyond*, ed. Michael Dooley and Steven Heller (New York: Allworth Press, 2005).

48. For examples of this approach, see in particular Renée's work on *Fight Comics* #34 and #38, *Planet Comics* #37 and #39, and *Rangers Comics* #20, #23, and #24. This "scratchy" linework, although not always as extreme as that of later artists, can be seen not only in her drawings of brutish men and supernatural creatures, but also in certain renderings of clothing, architecture, and landscapes, making her work an important precursor to later trends.

49. See, for instance, Byrne's work on *Fantastic Four* #244, in which the character Juliette D'Angelo is drawn with the same wide eyes and long jaw as many of Renée's women, a pattern seen in how he drew many female characters. The same pattern is often found in McFarlane's initial work for DC Comics, such as *All-Star Squadron* #47, as well in his renderings of Mary Jane Watson for Marvel's *Amazing Spider-Man*.

50. Amash, "'I'm Not Typical,'" 17.

51. Jim Amash, "'An Artist for All Seasons,'" *Alter Ego*, vol. 3, no. 99, January 2011, 13.

52. Maglio, *Fiction House*, 23.

53. Amash, "'I'm Not Typical,'" 9.

54. Robbins, *Great Women Super Heroes*, 86.

55. Berenstein, "White Heroines and Hearts of Darkness," 316.

Chapter 3. Crime Comics

1. For readings of the femme fatale's role in popular culture, see Helen Hanson and Catherine O'Rawe, eds., *The Femme Fatale: Images, Histories, Contexts* (New York: Palgrave, 2010); and Katherine Farrimond, *The Contemporary Femme Fatale: Gender, Genre and American Cinema* (New York: Routledge, 2017).

2. See John L. Rowett, ed., *Genre Theory and Historical Change: Theoretical Essays of Ralph Cohen* (Charlottesville: University of Virginia Press, 2017), for an overview of Cohen's work on genre and historical revisionism. Also see David Hyman, *Revision and the Superhero Genre* (Cham, Switzerland: Palgrave Pivot, 2017), for a detailed look at how genre revisionism can be applied within comics studies.

3. *Crime Does Not Pay*, no. 22 (New York: Comic House Inc., July 1942), cover, inside front cover.

4. Mike Benton, *The Comic Book in America: An Illustrated History* (Dallas: Taylor Publishing, 1989), 155.

5. *New Fun* #1 had "an on-sale date of January 11, 1935," and was published in an oversized "tabloid" format that was larger than other comic books. Nicky Wheeler-Nicholson, *DC Comics before Superman: Major Malcolm Wheeler-Nicholson's Pulp Comics* (Neshannock, PA: Hermes Press, 2018), 29.

6. Wheeler-Nicholson, *DC Comics before Superman*, 29.

7. *More Fun Comics*, no. 7 (St. Louis: More Fun Magazines Inc., January 1936), 1.

8. Tim Hanley, "Introduction," in Adolphe Barreaux, *Sally the Sleuth* (Winnipeg: Bedside Press, 2018), 9.

9. Hope Nicholson, *The Spectacular Sisterhood of Superwomen: Awesome Female Characters from Comic Book History* (Philadelphia: Quirk Books, 2017), 19.

10. Alan Cowsill and Daniel Wallace, *DC Comics Year by Year: A Visual Chronicle* (London: DK Publishing, 2010), 16–17.

11. Claire S. Moe signed much of her work with her full name regardless of the genre, be it crime tales or otherwise. As Trina Robbins notes that Moe "drew a series of children's adventure strips with circus-related themes" for Centaur starting in 1938, including "*The Circus and Sue*, *Circus Days*, and *Little Mary of the Circus*." Robbins, *A Century of Women Cartoonists* (Northhampton, MA: Kitchen Sink Press, 1993), 92–93.

12. *Wonderworld Comics*, no. 3 (New York: Fox Feature Syndicate, July 1939), 28.

13. *Champion Comics*, no. 4 (New York: Harvey Comics, February 1940), 22.

14. *National Comics*, no. 1 (New York: Quality Comics, July 1940), 16.

15. Mitchel P. Roth, *Crime and Punishment: A History of the Criminal Justice System* (Boston: Cengage, 2010), 210.

16. *National Comics*, no. 1, 19.

17. *National Comics*, no. 8 (New York: Quality Comics, February 1941), 10.

18. *National Comics*, no. 8, 11.

19. *National Comics*, no. 8, 11.

20. *National Comics*, no. 8, 14–15.

21. Maurice Horn, *The World Encyclopedia of Comics* (New York: Avon Books, 1976), 115.

22. N. C. Christopher Couch, *Jerry Robinson: Ambassador of Comics* (New York: Abrams ComicArts, 2010), 95.

23. *Crime Does Not Pay*, no. 22, 1.

24. Dale Jacobs, *Graphic Encounters: Comics and the Sponsorship of Multimodal Literacy* (New York: Bloomsbury, 2013), 103.

25. *Crime Does Not Pay*, no. 22, inside front cover.

26. Despite the fact that early issues of *Crime Does Not Pay* rarely centered around women, the series saw the participation of at least one other woman in addition to Hubbell Bloch: Frances Biro, wife of writer/editor Charles Biro. Frances regularly aided Charles in his writing duties throughout the early 1940s. Their daughter Denise notes, "When they used to work late at night coming up with the stories, my mother would do the typing, and she would come up with a lot of the storylines along with my father." Their other daughter, Penny, adds, "It was like any collaborative relationship. She would say, 'What about this?' or 'I've got an idea for that.'" Jim Amash, "'He Always Wanted Immortality for His Work,'" *Alter Ego*, vol. 3, no. 73, October 2007, 40.

27. *Crime Does Not Pay*, no. 39 (New York: Comic House Inc., May 1945), 18.

28. *Crime Does Not Pay*, no. 39, 25.

29. David Hadju, *The Ten-Cent Plague: The Great Comic Book Scare and How It Changed America* (New York: Picador, 2008), 87.

30. Hadju, *Ten-Cent Plague*, 67.

31. Art Spiegelman and Chip Kidd, *Jack Cole and Plastic Man* (San Francisco: Chronicle Books, 2001), 91.

32. *True Crime Comics*, no. 2 (New York: Magazine Village Inc., May 1947), 7.

33. See, for instance, Martin Barker, "Fredric Wertham: The Sad Case of the Unhappy Humanist," in *Pulp Demons: International Dimensions of the Postwar Anti-Comics Campaign*, ed. John A. Lent (Madison, NJ: Fairleigh Dickinson University Press and Associated University Presses, 1999), 215–233; and Christopher Pizzino, "Comics History and the Question of Delinquency: The Case of *Criminal*," in *Comics Memory: Archives and Styles*, ed. Maaheen Ahmed and Benoît Crucifix, 165–185 (London: Springer International Publishing, 2018).

34. *True Crime Comics*, no. 2, 19.

35. Spiegelman and Kidd, *Jack Cole and Plastic Man*, 91.

36. *Justice Traps the Guilty*, no. 4 (New York: Prize Comics, May–June 1948), 8.

37. *Crimes by Women*, no. 1 (New York: Fox Feature Syndicate, June 1948), 1.

38. *Crimes by Women*, no. 1, 5.

39. See Jeff Guinn, *Go Down Together: The True Untold Story of Bonnie and Clyde* (New York: Simon and Schuster, 2012).

40. *Crimes by Women*, no. 2 (New York: Fox Feature Syndicate, August 1948), 2.

41. Betty Friedan, *The Feminine Mystique* (New York: Norton, 1963), 1.

42. Friedan, *Feminine Mystique*, 2, 4.

43. Julie Grossman, *Rethinking the Femme Fatale in Film Noir: Ready for Her Close-Up* (New York: Palgrave Macmillan, 2009), 1.

44. See Dwain Carlton Pruitt, "It Rhymes with Lust? Matt Baker and the Ironic Politics of Race, Sex and Gender in the Golden Age," *Journal of Graphic Novels and Comics* 7, no. 2 (2016): 197–209; and Stephen Weiner, "The Development of the American Graphic Novel," in *The Cambridge Companion to the Graphic Novel*, ed. Stephen E. Tabachnick (Cambridge: Cambridge University Press, 2017), 41.

45. *It Rhymes with Lust* (New York: St. John Publications, 1950), 1.

46. *It Rhymes with Lust*, 9.

47. Ken Quattro, "The Gospel According to Archer St. John," *Alter Ego*, vol. 3, no. 77, May 2008, 27.

48. *It Rhymes with Lust*, 11.

49. *It Rhymes with Lust*, 119.

50. *It Rhymes with Lust*, 124.

51. *Boy Comics*, no. 9 (New York: Comic House Inc., April 1943), 4.

52. *Boy Comics*, no. 9, 9. Rachele Kanigel notes how "he-she" has historically been used as a derogatory term for transgender people, meant to "dehumanize" them. Kanigel, *The Diversity Style Guide* (Hoboken: John Wiley & Sons, 2019), 185.

53. *It Rhymes with Lust*, 44.

54. Qiana Whitted, *EC Comics: Race, Shock, and Social Protest* (New Brunswick, NJ: Rutgers University Press, 2019), 12. As Whitted notes, EC Comics was 100,000 dollars in debt when Bill Gaines took over as publisher from his father. While Max Gaines had tried to use comics as an educational platform, Bill saw that other publishers were finding success with crime comics and developed a new approach "aimed at promoting popular genre comics for reading enjoyment and sales. This meant that as the direction of the company changed, the name needed to change too" (12).

55. "Interview: Johnny Craig," in *The Comics Journal Library*, vol. 8, *The EC Artists Part 1* (Seattle: Fantagraphics Books, 2013), 104.

56. "Interview: Al Feldstein," in *The Comics Journal Library*, vol. 10, *The EC Artists Part 2* (Seattle: Fantagraphics Books, 2016), 67. Henry Miller's sexually explicit 1934 novel *Tropic of Cancer* was banned in the United States until 1961.

57. "Interview: Marie Severin," in *The Comics Journal Library*, vol. 10, *The EC Artists Part 2* (Seattle: Fantagraphics Books, 2016), 86.

58. "Spotlight on Marie Severin," in Colleen Coover, Trina Robbins, and G. Willow Wilson, *Girl Comics* (New York: Marvel, 2010).

59. *Crime SuspenStories*, no. 1 (New York: EC Comics, October–November 1950), 9.

60. *Crime SuspenStories*, no. 1, 15.

61. Terrence Wandtke, *The Dark Night Returns: The Contemporary Resurgence of Crime Comics* (Rochester, NY: RIT Press, 2015), 15.

62. See James B. Gilbert, *A Cycle of Outrage: America's Reaction to the Juvenile Delinquent in the 1950s* (Oxford: Oxford University Press, 1988).

63. Carol Tilley, "A Regressive Formula of Perversity: Wertham and the Women of Comics," *Journal of Lesbian Studies* 22, no. 4 (2018): 356.

64. Judith Crist, "Horror in the Nursery," *Collier's Magazine*, March 27, 1948, 22.

65. Crist, "Horror in the Nursery," 23.

66. Fredric M. Thrasher, "The Comics and Delinquency: Cause or Scapegoat," *Journal of Educational Sociology* 23, no. 4 (December 1949): 195.

67. Thrasher, "Comics and Delinquency," 200.

68. Beaty, *Fredric Wertham and the Critique*, 159.

69. Amy Kiste Nyberg, *Seal of Approval: The History of the Comics Code* (Jackson: University Press of Mississippi, 1998), 111.

70. Richard J. Arndt, "Tales from the Code: The Sequel," *Alter Ego*, vol. 3, no. 113, October 2012, 43.

71. "Interview: William M. Gaines," in *The Comics Journal Library*, vol. 8, *The EC Artists Part 1* (Seattle: Fantagraphics Books, 2013), 64.

72. Quoted in Nyberg, *Seal of Approval*, 167–168.

Chapter 4. Horror Comics

1. See chapter 1 of Terrence R. Wandtke, *The Comics Scare Returns: The Contemporary Resurgence of Horror Comics* (Rochester, NY: RIT Press, 2018), for an overview of how horror comics were predated by pulp literature.

2. See chapter 4 of Nicholas Labarre, *Understanding Genres in Comics* (Cham, Switzerland: Palgrave Pivot, 2020), for an overview of the theoretical conditions surrounding the horror genre's origins in comics.

3. Matt Hills analyzes the range of pleasures found within the horror genre for different audience members in *The Pleasures of Horror* (London: Continuum, 2005), while Isabel Cristina Pinedo examines gender implications of horror film spectatorship in *Recreational Terror: Women and the Pleasures of Horror Film Spectatorship* (Albany: SUNY Press, 1997).

4. *Amazing Mystery Funnies*, vol. 2, no. 2 (New York: Centaur Publications Inc., February 1939).

5. Maurice Linde, "Truth Is Held in Disrepute: O. Henry and the Dismantling of Paradigms," *Miscelanea: A Journal of English and American Studies*, no. 38 (2008): 11–27.

6. *Amazing Man Comics*, no. 6 (New York: Centaur Publications, October 1939), 50–51.

7. *Amazing Man Comics*, no. 6, 56–57.

8. Amash, "'I'm Not Typical,'" 18–19. Renée states that she usually sent drawings to the soldiers who asked for them: "I wanted to be nice because they were fighting the Nazis."

9. Amash, "'I'm Not Typical,'" 8, 11.

10. Barbara Creed, *The Monstrous-Feminine: Film, Feminism, and Psychoanalysis* (New York: Routledge, 1993), 3.

11. Barry Keith Grant, ed., *The Dread of Difference: Gender and the Horror Film*, 2nd ed. (Austin: University of Texas Press, 2015), 11.

12. Grant, *Dread of Difference*, 8–9.

13. Christopher S. Mackay, *The Hammer of Witches: A Complete Translation of the Malleus Maleficarum* (Cambridge: Cambridge University Press, 2009), 162.

14. Marilyn Mercer's first installment of "The Secret Files of Dr. Drew" appeared in Fiction House's *Rangers Comics* #47 in 1949 and lasted until #60 in 1951. *Ghost Comics* #11 reprints Mercer's story "The Witch's Doll," while

Monster #1 reprints "The Philosopher's Stone." Also notable is how Fiction House's leading title, *Jumbo Comics*, shifted to the horror genre in 1952, starting with #161. The cover and main story spotlighted tales of horror, while other stories were from a range of genres, including those with Sheena, Queen of the Jungle. The shift to horror was short-lived, ending in 1953 with #167, at which point the series was canceled.

15. *Adventures into the Unknown*, no. 6 (New York: American Comics Group, August–September 1949), 1.

16. *Adventures into the Unknown*, no. 6, 10.

17. *Adventures into the Unknown*, no. 9 (New York: American Comics Group, February–March 1950), 2.

18. *Adventures into the Unknown*, no. 9, 6.

19. *Adventures into the Unknown*, no. 9, 7.

20. Mackay, *Hammer of Witches*, 163.

21. Laura Mulvey, "Visual Pleasure and Narrative Cinema," in *Film Theory and Criticism: Introductory Readings*, ed. Leo Braudy and Marshall Cohen (New York: Oxford University Press, 1999), 833.

22. Mulvey, "Visual Pleasure and Narrative Cinema," 840.

23. Creed, *Monstrous-Feminine*, 55.

24. *The Haunt of Fear*, no. 14 (New York: EC Comics, July–August 1952). An early precursor of the Old Witch can be found in the final three issues of M. L. J.'s *Blue Ribbon Comics* in 1942. Debuting in issue 20, "Tales from the Witch's Cauldron" saw what the narrator describes as a "hideous old hag" show a "pretty picture story" to a young couple via her magic crystal ball. *Blue Ribbon Comics*, no. 20 (New York: M. L. J. Magazines, January 1942), 43–44. The witch's role in these *Blue Ribbon* stories was much like that of EC's later horror hosts, setting up tales of terror about other characters.

25. *This Magazine Is Haunted*, vol. 1, no. 18 (Derby, CT: Charlton Comics, July 1954), 13.

26. *The Vault of Horror*, no. 31 (New York: EC Comics, June–July 1953).

27. Stephanie Coontz, "The Way We Weren't," *National Forum* 75, no. 3 (1995): 11.

28. *Tales from the Crypt*, no. 32 (New York: EC Comics, October–November 1952).

29. Whitted, *EC Comics*, 136.

30. "Interview: Johnny Craig," 108.

31. Dewey Cassell, *Marie Severin: The Mirthful Mistress of Comics* (Raleigh, NC: TwoMorrows Publishing, 2012), 35–36.

32. Wertham, *Seduction of the Innocent*, 46. See also Martin Barker, *A Haunt of Fears: The Strange Case of the British Horror Comics Campaign* (Jackson: University Press of Mississippi, 1984).

33. Carol L. Tilley, "Seducing the Innocent: Fredric Wertham and the Falsifications that Helped Condemn Comics," *Information & Culture* 47, no. 4 (2012): 386, 393.

34. Wertham, *Seduction of the Innocent*, 109.

35. "Interview: Al Feldstein," 79.

36. Michael Walton, *The Horror Comic Never Dies: A Grisly History* (Jefferson, NC: McFarland, 2019), 146.

37. Nyberg, *Seal of Approval*, 124–125.

Chapter 5. Western Comics

1. Maurice Horn, *Comics of the American West* (New York: Winchester Press, 1977), 84.

2. See, for a start, Barry Keith Grant, *Shadows of Doubt: Negotiations of Masculinity in American Genre Films* (Detroit, MI: Wayne State University Press, 2010); Roderick McGillis, *He Was Some Kind of a Man: Masculinities in the B-Western* (Waterloo, ON: Wilfrid Laurier University Press, 2011); and Wendy Chapman Peek, "The Romance of Competence: Rethinking Masculinity in the Western," *Journal of Popular Film and Television* 30, no. 4 (2003): 206–219.

3. Jesús Ángel González, "New Frontiers for Post-Western Cinema: *Frozen River*, *Sin Nombre*, *Winter's Bone*," *Western American Literature* 50, no. 1 (2015): 69.

4. Victoria Lamont, *Westerns: A Women's History* (Lincoln: University of Nebraska Press, 2016). Lamont notes how the rise of so-called quality novels outside of the pulp tradition was a forum for authors of all genders, and that "the first known cowboy novel outside of the dime tradition was written by a woman, the Colorado suffragist Emma Ghent Curtis" in 1889.

5. See also Sue Matheson, *Women in the Western* (Edinburgh, UK: Edinburgh University Press, 2020); and Dee Garceau-Hagen, ed., *Portraits of Women in the American West* (New York: Routledge, 2005), for recent work in feminist revisions of the western genre across various media forms.

6. Horn, *Comics of the American West*, 67. Notably, a young Jack Kirby drew the adventures of both Wilton of the West and Lightnin' and the Lone Rider.

7. *Star Ranger*, no. 2 (St. Louis: Centaur Publications, April 1937), 7.

8. *Cow Puncher Comics*, no. 1 (New York: Avon Comics, January 1947), 33.

9. *Cow Puncher Comics*, no. 1, 34.

10. *Cow Puncher Comics*, no. 2 (New York: Avon Comics, February 1947), 15–17.

11. Peter Stanfield, *Horse Opera: The Strange Case of the 1930s Singing Cowboy* (Urbana: University of Illinois Press, 2002), 98.

12. *Dale Evans Comics*, no. 23 (New York: National Comics Publications Inc., May–June 1952), 5; *Dale Evans Comics*, no. 19 (New York: National Comics Publications Inc., September–October 1951), 6–10.

13. *Dale Evans Comics*, no. 4 (New York: National Comics Publications Inc., March–April 1949), 35–36.

14. *Dale Evans Comics*, no. 18 (New York: National Comics Publications Inc., July–August 1951), 35–36.

15. See chapter 4 of Blair Davis, *Movie Comics: Page to Screen / Screen to Page* (New Brunswick, NJ: Rutgers University Press, 2017), for further analysis of how film stars used comic books to extend their brand in the 1940s.

16. Robert W. Phillips, *Roy Rogers: A Biography, Radio History, Television Career Chronicle, Discography, Filmography, Comicography, Merchandising and Advertising History, Collectibles Description, Bibliography, and Index* (Jefferson, NC: McFarland, 1995), 182.

17. Michael Barrier, *Funnybooks: The Improbable Glories of the Best American Comic Books* (Berkeley: University of California Press, 2015), 313–314.

18. Elizabeth Jameson, "Bringing It All Back Home: Rethinking the History of Women and the Nineteenth-Century West," in *A Companion to the Ameri-*

can West, ed. William Deverell, 186–187 (Malden, MA: Blackwell Publishing, 2004). See also Sarah Carter, ed., *Montana Women Homesteaders: A Field of One's Own* (Helena, MT: Farcountry Press, 2009); and Deborah Fink, *Agrarian Women: Wives and Mothers in Rural Nebraska, 1880–1940* (Chapel Hill: University of North Carolina Press, 1992).

19. *Western Crime Busters*, no. 3 (New York: Trojan Magazines, February, 1951), 1.

20. *Cow Puncher Comics*, no. 2, 28.

21. *Cow Puncher Comics*, no. 2, 32.

22. *Cow Puncher Comics*, no. 2, 32.

23. See, for instance, the 1952 episode "Guns along the Border" of *Hopalong Cassidy* and the 1954 episode "Battle Axe" of *The Gene Autry Show*.

24. *Western Adventures*, no. 1 (New York: Ace Magazines, October 1948), 43.

25. *Western Adventures*, no. 1, 44.

26. *Western Adventures*, no. 1, 48–50.

27. *Western Adventures*, no. 2 (New York: Ace Magazines, December 1948), 43.

28. *Western Adventures*, no. 5 (New York: Ace Magazines, June 1949), 9–10.

29. *Crack Western*, no. 63 (New York: Quality Comics, November 1949), 10–11.

30. Jameson, "Bringing It All Back Home," 184.

31. *Crack Western*, no. 64 (New York: Quality Comics, January 1950), 15.

32. *Western True Crime*, no. 15 (Wilkes-Barre, PA: Fox Feature Syndicate, August 1948), 25.

33. *Tim Holt*, no. 25 (New York: Magazine Enterprises, August–September 1951), 2.

34. See Hope Nicholson, *The Spectacular Sisterhood of Superwomen* (Philadelphia: Quirk Books, 2017), 52–53, for a detailed analysis of the Black Phantom.

35. Sarah Barringer Gordon, "Law and the Contact of Cultures," in *A Companion to the American West*, ed. William Deverell (Malden, MA: Blackwell Publishing, 2004), 193.

36. William J. Devlin, "No Country for Old Men: The Decline of Ethics and the West(ern)," in *The Philosophy of the Western*, ed. Jennifer L. McMahon and B. Steve Csaki (Lexington: University of Kentucky Press, 2010), 228.

37. Wertham, *Seduction of the Innocent*, 157.

38. *Women Outlaws*, no. 1 (Wilkes-Barre, PA: Fox Feature Syndicate, July 1948), 1.

39. Lori Van Pelt, "Cattle Kate, Homesteader or Cattle Thief?" in *Wild Women of the Old West*, ed. Glenda Riley and Richard W. Etulain (Golden, CO: Fulcrum Publishing, 2003), 156.

40. See George W. Hufsmith, *The Wyoming Lynching of Cattle Kate, 1889* (Glendo, WY: High Plains Press, 1993), for a thorough account of Watson's life and death.

41. *Dell Four Color*, no. 438 (New York: Dell Publishing, 1952).

42. *Western True Crime*, no. 15 (Wilkes-Barre, PA: Fox Feature Syndicate, August 1948), 22.

43. Jameson, "Bringing It All Back Home," 193.

44. Jameson, "Bringing It All Back Home," 194.

45. *Firehair Comics*, no. 1 (New York: Fiction House, Winter 1948), 13.

46. *Firehair Comics*, no. 1, 14.

47. The trope of a white hero serving as a commanding force for various native groups was popular in the first half of the twentieth century across popular culture, with such heroes as Tarzan, Jungle Jim, and Ramar of the Jungle seen in movies, comic strips, comic books, and television series.

48. *Indians*, no. 2 (New York: Fiction House, 1948), 22. An earlier character named Starlight appeared in Garrett Price's 1933 comic strip *White Boy*. Maurice Horn describes her as an "Indian maiden" who is "dark-tressed" and "sensitive." Horn, *Women in the Comics*, vol. 1 (Philadelphia: Chelsea House Publishers, 2001), 105.

49. Nicholson, *Spectacular Sisterhood of Superwomen*, 67.

50. *Indians*, no. 2, 23.

51. John P. McWilliams, *Against the Wind: Courageous Apache Women* (Staten Island, NY: Page Publishing, 2015), 10.

52. *Indians*, no. 1 (New York: Fiction House, 1948), 18.

53. *Indians*, no. 1, 21.

54. *The Chief*, no. 2 (New York: Dell Publishing, April 1951), 43.

55. *The Chief*, no. 2, 48.

56. *Indian Chief*, no. 3 (New York: Dell Publishing, July 1951), 9–11.

57. *Indian Chief*, no. 3, 16.

58. Kimberly Moore Buchanan, *Apache Women Warriors*, Southwestern Studies 79 (El Paso: Texas Western Press, 1986).

59. Jerry Bail's website Who's Who of American Comic Books lists Loth as a penciller and inker of unnamed western titles in 1950 (accessed April 2, 2021, http://www.bailsprojects.com/bio.aspx?Name=LOTH%2c+PAULINE), as does the Lambiek Comiclopedia (last updated February 26, 2017, https://www.lambiek.net/artists/l/loth_pauline.htm).

60. Maglio, *Fiction House*, 24–25.

61. *Cow Puncher Comics*, no. 3 (New York: Avon Comics Inc., 1947), 24.

62. *Cow Puncher Comics*, no. 4, (New York: Avon Comics Inc., 1948), 24.

63. *Firehair Comics*, no. 7 (New York: Fiction House, Spring 1951), inside back cover, back cover.

Chapter 6. Title Characters

1. Sean Howe, *Marvel Comics: The Untold Story* (New York: Harper, 2012), 32.

2. *Patsy Walker* ended in 1965, while its spin-off series *Patsy and Hedy* remained on newsstands until 1967. *Millie the Model* ran until 1973.

3. Harvey Zorbaugh, "The Comics—There They Stand!," *Journal of Educational Sociology* 18, no. 4 (December 1944): 197–198.

4. See, for instance, Paul Lewis, *Comic Effects: Interdisciplinary Approaches to Humor in Literature* (Albany: SUNY Press, 1989), for a theoretical overview of the humor genre in literary history.

5. Trina Robbins, *From Girls to Grrrlz: A History of Women's Comics from Teens to Zines* (San Francisco: Chronicle Books, 1999), 14.

6. Coulton Waugh, *The Comics* (Jackson: University Press of Mississippi, 1991), 135.

7. Robbins, *From Girls to Grrrlz*, 30.

8. Booker, *Comics through Time*, 427.

9. Robbins, *Century of Women Cartoonists*, 104.

10. Robbins, *From Girls to Grrrlz*, 9.

11. Kelly Schrum, *Some Wore Bobby Sox: The Emergence of Teenage Girls' Culture, 1920–1945* (New York: Palgrave Macmillan, 2004), 3.

12. Waugh, *Comics*, 350–351.

13. Waugh, *Comics*, 351.

14. Robbins, *From Girls to Grrrlz*, 26.

15. *Miss America Magazine*, vol. 5, no. 3 (New York: Timely Comics, January 1947), 53; *Miss America Magazine*, vol. 4, no. 6 (New York: Timely Comics, October 1946), 25.

16. Jim Amash, "'It Was a Fun Time!,'" *Alter Ego*, vol. 3, no. 35, April 2004, 16.

17. *Patsy Walker*, no. 103 (New York: Marvel Comics, October 1962).

18. Mary Celeste Kearney, "Recycling Judy and Corliss: Transmedia Exploitation and the First Teen-Girl Production Trend," *Feminist Media Studies* 4, no. 3 (2004): 265–295.

19. Zorbaugh, "Comics—There They Stand!," 197–198.

20. Waugh, *Comics*, 173–175.

21. See Ron Goulart, *Good Girl Art* (New Castle, PA: Hermes, 2007).

22. Jean-Paul Gabilliet, *Of Comics and Men: A Cultural History of American Comic Books*, trans. Bart Beaty and Nick Nguyen (Jackson: University Press of Mississippi, 2010), 134.

23. Robbins, *Pretty in Ink*, 105.

24. Robbins, *Pretty in Ink*, 105. See also John Benson, *Confessions, Romances, Secrets, and Temptations: Archer St. John and the St. John Romance Comics* (Seattle: Fantagraphics, 2007), 55–56.

25. *Torchy*, no. 2 (New York: Quality Comics, December 1949).

26. *Torchy*, no. 1 (New York: Quality Comics, January 1950).

27. *Torchy*, no. 2.

28. See Trina Robbins, *Gladys Parker: A Life in Comics, a Passion for Fashion* (New Castle, PA: Hermes Press, 2019).

29. Nancy Goldstein, *Jackie Ormes: The First African American Woman Cartoonist* (Ann Arbor: University of Michigan Press, 2008), 5.

30. Robbins, *Pretty in Ink*, 100.

Chapter 7. Science Fiction Comics

1. See, for instance, Naomi Hetherington, "Creator and Created in Mary Shelley's Frankenstein," *The Keats-Shelley Review* 11, no. 1 (1997): 1–39; and Mary Poovey, "My Hideous Progeny: Mary Shelley and the Feminization of Romanticism," *Publications of the Modern Language Association of America* 95, no. 3 (1980): 332–347.

2. See Clark Blickenstaff, "Women and Science Careers: Leaky Pipeline or Gender Filter?," *Gender and Education* 17, no. 4 (2005): 369–386; and Gulnar Sarseke, "Under-Representation of Women in Science: From Educational, Feminist and Scientific Views," *NASPA Journal about Women in Higher Education* 11, no. 1 (2018): 89–101, for more thorough analyses of why this occurs.

3. Pamela Sargent, *Women of Wonder: Science Fiction Stories Written by Women about Women* (New York: Vintage Books, 1974).

4. Marleen S. Barr, *Lost in Space: Probing Feminist Science Fiction and Beyond* (Chapel Hill: University of North Carolina Press, 1993).

5. In his essay "European Science Fiction in the Nineteenth Century," Terry

Harpold notes that the sci-fi author Brian Aldiss called Shelley's novel "the first work of true SF." In *The Cambridge History of Science Fiction*, ed. Gerry Canavan and Eric Carl Link (Cambridge: Cambridge University Press, 2018).

6. See the introduction to Jane L. Donawerth and Carol A. Kolmerten, *Utopian and Science Fiction by Women: Worlds of Difference* (Syracuse, NY: Syracuse University Press, 1994), 1–2.

7. Marc Bould and Sherry Vint describe, for instance, how early sci-fi authors were "concerned with the social and cultural consequences of technological change, as well as with race, eugenics and the rise of fascism." Bould and Vint, *The Routledge Concise History of Science Fiction* (New York: Routledge, 2011), 54.

8. See, for instance, Desirina Boskovich, *Lost Transmissions: The Secret History of Science Fiction and Fantasy* (New York: Abrams, 2019), 13–17.

9. Eric Leif Davin, *Partners in Wonder: Women and the Birth of Science Fiction, 1926–1965* (Lanham, MD: Lexington Books, 2005), 5.

10. Some debate has arisen about comparisons between Olga Mesmer and Superman. Comics writer and journalist Will Murray sees Mesmer achieving the mantle of superhero before Superman, arguing that the Man of Steel "was not the first superhero." Instead, Murray maintains that "Olga Mesmer was an original. The first superhero to see print . . . definitely the first superheroic in comics history!" Will Murray, "The Roots of Superman," *Comic Book Marketplace*, no. 63, October 1998, 19–21. The superhero scholar Pete Coogan disputes Murray's claims, however, seeing Mesmer as a strictly sci-fi character: "Olga Mesmer has been long forgotten and was probably forgotten by the November 1938 issue of *Spicy Mystery*. Unlikely to have influenced either [Jerry] Siegel or [Joe] Shuster" in their creation of Superman, says Coogan, "Olga Mesmer merely demonstrates the same point that the other comics precursors to Superman demonstrate, that, like the pulps before them, comic books and comic strips contained all the elements of the superhero—the powers, the mission, the identity—but it took Siegel and Shuster to put them all together into Superman." Coogan, "Comics Predecessors," *The Superhero Reader*, ed. Charles Hatfield, Jeet Heer, and Kent Worcester (Jackson: University Press of Mississippi, 2013), 13.

11. Benton, *Comic Book in America*, 172–173.

12. Sargent, *Women of Wonder*.

13. Sargent, *Women of Wonder*, 11; "Lisa Yaszek Interview," *Geek's Guide to the Galaxy* (podcast). February 2, 2019, https://geeksguideshow.com/2019/01/24/ggg346-lisa-yaszek/.

14. *Blue Bolt*, no. 2 (Philadelphia: Novelty Press, July 1940), 1.

15. *Blue Bolt*, no. 2, 3.

16. *Blue Bolt*, no. 4 (Philadelphia: Novelty Press, September 1940), 7.

17. Greg Grewell, "Colonizing the Universe: Science Fictions Then, Now, and in the (Imagined) Future," *Rocky Mountain Review of Language and Literature* 55, no. 2 (2001): 35–36.

18. *Planet Comics*, no. 3 (New York: Fiction House, March 1940), 16.

19. Joanna Russ, *The Image of Women in Science Fiction* (Andover, MA: Warner Modular Publications, 1973).

20. *Amazing Man Comics*, no. 7 (New York: Centaur Publications, November 1939), 30.

21. *Amazing Man*, no. 8 (New York: Centaur Publications, December 1939), 36.

22. See Hal Blythe and Charlie Sweet, "Superhero: The Six Step Progression," in *The Hero in Transition*, ed. Ray B. Browne and Marshall W. Fishwick (Bowling Green, OH: Popular Press, 1983), 184–185, for further explanation.

23. Gavin Weston, "Superheroes and Comic-Book Vigilantes versus Real-Life Vigilantes: An Anthropological Answer to the Kick-Ass Paradox," *Journal of Graphic Novels and Comics*, no. 2 (2013): 225.

24. Scott Vollum and Cary D. Atkinson, "The Portrayal of Crime and Justice in the Comic Book Superhero Mythos," *Journal of Criminal Justice and Popular Culture* 10, no. 2 (2003): 102–105.

25. Hester Eisenstein, "Hegemonic Feminism, Neoliberalism, and Womenomics: 'Empowerment' Instead of Liberation?," *New Formations*, no. 91 (2017): 43.

26. Eisenstein, "Hegemonic Feminism," 37, 45.

27. *Fantastic Comics*, no. 18 (New York: Fox Publications, May 1941), 43.

28. *Planet Comics*, no. 3, 14–16.

29. *Planet Comics*, no. 3, 16.

30. *Planet Comics*, no. 3, 19.

31. *Planet Comics*, no. 3, 19.

32. *Planet Comics*, no. 3, 25.

33. Jackson, *Fantasy*, 175.

34. See Robbins, *Babes in Arms*.

35. Mia Sostaric, "The American Wartime Propaganda during World II: How Comic Books Sold the War," *Australasian Journal of American Studies* 38, no. 1 (2019): 33.

36. *Planet Comics*, no. 4 (New York: Fiction House, April 1940), 56–58.

37. *Moon Girl and the Prince*, no. 1 (New York: EC Comics, 1947), 5.

38. *Moon Girl and the Prince*, no. 1, 3.

39. Roy Thomas, "A Moon . . . A Bat . . . A Hawk: A Candid Conversation with Sheldon Moldoff," *Alter Ego*, vol. 3, no. 4, Spring 2000, 4–14.

40. Thomas, "A Moon . . . A Bat."

41. Jackson, *Fantasy*, 14.

Chapter 8. Romance Comics

1. *Action Comics*, no. 29 (New York: Detective Comics Inc., October 1940), 2.

2. Describing the series generic qualities, Robert C. Harvey describes Mary Worth as offering readers "soap opera continuity . . . that trades in domestic travail or psychological trauma." Harvey, *Art of the Funnies*, 11. M. Thomas Inge also sees it as a "soap opera" strip but notes that such melodramatic efforts also "belong in the adventure category" because of "their use of mystery and suspense" in creating ongoing conflict. Inge, *Comics as Culture* (Jackson: University Press of Mississippi, 1990), 10.

3. Dal Curtis was the pseudonym of psychiatrist Dr. Nicholas Peter Dallis, who wrote the strip until the year before he died in 1991. In 1952, he created the strip *Judge Parker* under the alias Paul Nichols, followed by *Apartment 3-G* in 1961. All three of his strips incorporated melodrama and romantic subplots.

4. See Sheena C. Howard, *Encyclopedia of Black Comics* (Golden, CO: Ful-

crum, 2017), 163–164.

5. Janice A. Radway, *Reading the Romance: Women, Patriarchy, and Popular Literature* (Chapel Hill: University of North Carolina Press, 1984), 25–26.

6. Michelle Nolan, "Introduction," in Joe Simon and Jack Kirby, *Young Romance: The Best of Simon and Kirby's Romance Comics* (Seattle: Fantagraphics Books, 2012), 6.

7. See, for instance, Charlotte Brunsdon, *Screen Tastes: Soap Opera to Satellite Dishes* (London: Routledge, 1997).

8. Michelle Nolan, *Love on the Racks: A History of American Romance Comics* (Jefferson, NC: McFarland Press, 2015), 27–28.

9. Ron Goulart, *Great American Comic Books* (Lincolnwood, IL: Publications International, 2001), 161, 169–172.

10. Amash, "'Simon Says!,'" 25.

11. Richard Howell, "Introduction," in Joe Simon and Jack Kirby, *Real Love—The Best of the Simon and Kirby Romance Comics, 1940s–1950s* (Forestville, CA: Eclipse Books, 2008).

12. Joe Simon, *My Life in Comics* (London: Titan Books, 2011), 163–164.

13. Zorbaugh, "Comics—There They Stand!," 197–198.

14. Nolan, *Love on the Racks*, 29.

15. "Power Lunch—1974," *Alter Ego*, vol. 3, no. 13, March 2002, 6.

16. Michel Gagné, "Simon and Kirby's Romance Comics: A Historical View," in Joe Simon and Jack Kirby, *Young Romance: The Best of Simon & Kirby's Romance Comics*, 198–201 (Seattle: Fantagraphics Books, 2012) 198.

17. "Power Lunch—1974," 6.

18. *Young Romance*, no. 1 (New York: Feature Publications Inc., September–October 1947), 1.

19. *Young Romance*, no. 11, (New York: Feature Publications Inc., May–June 1949), 1.

20. *Young Romance*, no. 2, (New York: Feature Publications Inc., November–December 1947), 14.

21. *Young Romance*, no. 1, front cover.

22. See Donald Bogle, *Toms, Coons, Mulattoes, Mammies, and Bucks: An Interpretive History of Blacks in American Film* (New York: Bloomsbury, 2001), for an overview of how this trend played out in popular culture of this era.

23. Naomi Scott, ed., *Heart Throbs: The Best of DC Romance Comics* (New York: Fireside, 1979), 146.

24. For more on *All-Negro Comics* and its creator, Orrin C. Evans, see Howard, *Encyclopedia of Black Comics*, 71–74; and Tim Jackson, *Pioneering Cartoonists of Color* (Jackson: University Press of Mississippi, 2016), 80–81.

25. See Goldstein, *Jackie Ormes.*

26. Nancy Goldstein, "The Trouble with Romance in Jackie Ormes's Comics," in *Black Comics: Politics of Race and Representation,* ed. Sheena C. Howard and Ronald L. Jackson (New York: Bloomsbury Academic, 2013), 34–35.

27. *Negro Romance*, no. 1 (Greenwich, CT: Fawcett Comics, June 1950), 1.

28. Andrew Wise, *Places of Their Own: African American Suburbanization in the Twentieth Century* (Chicago: University of Chicago Press, 2009).

29. See Barbara Lupack, ed., *Early Race Filmmaking in America* (New York: Routledge, 2016).

30. *Negro Romance*, no. 2, (Greenwich, CT: Fawcett Comics, August 1950), 1.

31. Dorothy Moore and Paul Witty, "Interest in Reading the Comics among Negro Children," *Journal of Educational Psychology* 5, no. 36, 303–304.

32. See Davis, "*All-Negro Comics*," 273–297.

33. Nolan, *Love on the Racks*, 63.

34. John Lustig, "The Terrible, Tragic (>Sob!<) Death of Romance Comics," *Back Issue*, no. 13, December 2005, 16.

35. See "An Interview with Irwin Stein," in Benson, *Confessions, Romances, Secrets, and Temptations*, 10–11.

36. "An Interview with Irwin Stein," 16.

37. Simon, *My Life in Comics*, 167.

38. See Mark Carlson-Ghost, "Coming up Aces!," *Alter Ego*, vol. 3, no. 144, January 2017, 3–34, for a history of Ace Periodicals and Mangum's work therein.

39. See Hadju, *Ten-Cent Plague*, 127–131.

40. *Teen Confessions*, no. 52 (Derby, CT: Charlton Comics Group, November 1968).

41. Quoted in Nyberg, *Seal of Approval*, 168.

42. *Romantic Marriage*, no. 13 (New York: Ziff-Davis Publishing, May 1952), 26, 28.

43. Mark Evanier, "An Introduction," in *Jack Kirby's Dingbat Love*, ed. John Morrow (Raleigh, NC: TwoMorrows Publishing, 2019), 7.

44. Friedan, *Feminine Mystique*, 333.

45. *Young Love*, no. 1 (New York City: Prize Comics Group, February 1949), 12.

46. Joanne Meyerowitz, "Beyond the Feminine Mystique: A Reassessment of Postwar Mass Culture, 1946–1958," *Journal of American History* 79, no. 4 (1993): 1455–1482.

47. Meyerowitz, "Beyond the Feminine Mystique," 1458.

48. *Heart Throbs*, no. 25 (Buffalo: Quality, December 1953), 10.

49. *My Love*, no. 4 (New York: Timely/Atlas, April 1950), reprinted in Michael Barson, *Agonizing Love: The Golden Era of Romance Comics* (New York: Harper Design, 2011), 119.

50. Barson, *Agonizing Love*, 123.

51. *Just Married*, no. 5 (Derby, CT: Charlton Comics Group, October 1958), 8, 10.

52. *Love Scandals*, no. 5 (New York City: Quality Comics, October 1950), 1.

53. *Love Scandals*, no. 5, 2.

54. *Love Scandals*, no. 5, 3.

55. *Young Romance*, no. 197 (New York: DC Comics, January–February 1974).

56. *Young Romance*, no. 197.

57. William B. Turner, *A Genealogy of Queer Theory* (Philadelphia: Temple University Press, 2000), 38.

58. Michel Foucault, *Security, Territory, Population* (Basingstoke, UK: Palgrave Macmillan, 2007), 58.

59. Barson, *Agonizing Love*, 13.

60. Meyerowitz, "Beyond the Feminine Mystique," 1461.

Conclusion

1. Hilary Chute, *Why Comics? From Underground to Everywhere* (New York: Harper, 2017), 276.

2. "CBA Roundtable: The Great Women Cartoonists' Slumber Party of 1999," *Comic Book Artist*, no. 10, October 2000, 40.

3. "CBA Roundtable," 40.

4. Jim Amash, "'It's Important That We Don't Get Forgotten,'" *Alter Ego*, vol. 3, no. 97, October 2010, 54. When asked how far the development of the Metamorpho series got, DC writer/editor George Kashdan, who also worked for the animation company Filmation, explained,

> It never went into cartoons. Some producer up in Canada wanted to do it, but DC didn't encourage him. When he went down to DC, he wanted to see what we had. He fell in love with Ramona Fradon's artwork on Metamorpho, and what he had worked out was . . . he had a little gimmick. He took a comic page, and reproduced it on a screen and ran the story so that whenever a character spoke, with the help of a big balloon, they moved his mouth and had him blinking his eye. But the artificial nature of it came across (54).

5. Howard Chaykin, *The Art of Ramona Fradon* (Mt. Laurel, NJ: Dynamite Entertainment, 2013), 71–74.

6. Chaykin, *Art of Ramona Fradon*, 71.

7. "Interview: Mike Gold," *Comics Interview*, no. 68, 1989, 61.

8. Gail Simone, *You'll All Be Sorry!* (Thousand Oaks, CA: About Comics, 2008), 6.

9. Shannon E. Riley, "Women in Comics Roundtable with Barbara Randall Kesel, Gail Simone, and Jill Thompson," *Back Issue*, vol. 1, no. 54, February 2012, 38.

10. Jennifer M. Smith, personal interview, March 17, 2018.

11. Anna F. Peppard, "'This Female Fights Back!' A Feminist History of Marvel Comics," in *Make Ours Marvel: Media Convergence and a Comics Universe*, ed. Matt Yockey (Austin: University of Texas Press, 2017), 108.

12. Kathleen McClancy, "Editor's Introduction: Comics and History," *Feminist Media Histories* 4, no. 3 (Summer 2018): 4.

13. Ellen Kirkpatrick and Suzanne Scott, "Representation and Diversity in Comics Studies," *Cinema Journal* 55, no. 1 (2015): 123.

14. Eisenstein, "Hegemonic Feminism," 43.

15. Jennifer M. Smith, personal interview, March 17, 2018.

16. "Interview: Mike Gold," 61.

BIBLIOGRAPHY

Abate, Michelle Ann. *Funny Girls: Guffaws, Guts, and Gender in Classic American Comics*. Jackson: University Press of Mississippi, 2018.

Achebe, Chinua. "An Image of Africa: Racism in Conrad's *Heart of Darkness*." In *Heart of Darkness: An Authoritative Text, Backgrounds and Source Criticism*, 3rd ed., edited by Robert Kimbaugh, 251–262. New York: Norton, 1988.

Agnew, Jeremy. *The Age of Dimes and Pulps: A History of Sensationalist Literature, 1830–1960*. Jefferson, NC: McFarland, 2018.

Amash, Jim. "'An Artist for All Seasons.'" *Alter Ego* 3, no. 99 (January 2011): 3–36.

——. "'He Always Wanted Immortality for His Work.'" *Alter Ego*, vol. 3, no. 73, October 2007, 30–48.

——. "'I Always Felt That Storytelling Was as Important as the Artwork.'" *Alter Ego*, vol. 3, no. 48, May 2005, 7–26.

——. "'I Come from a Very Primitive Background.'" *Alter Ego*, vol. 3, no. 103, July 2011, 29–47.

——. "'I Graduated from Plato and Aristotle to Superman and Batman.'" *Alter Ego*, vol. 3, no. 93, May 2010, 40–60.

——. "'I Let People Do Their Jobs!'" *Alter Ego*, vol. 3, no. 11, November 2001, 8–29.

——. "'I'm Not Typical for Doing Comics, You Know!': The Life and Times of Golden Age Artist Lily Renée." *Alter Ego*, vol. 3, no. 85, May 2009, 3–23.

——. "'I'm Trying to Prod People to Think.'" *Alter Ego*, vol. 3, no. 92, March 2010, 37–58.

——. "'I Think I Worked for Every [Comics] House in the City.'" *Alter Ego*, vol. 3, no. 110, June 2012, 3–22.

——. "'It's Important That We Don't Get Forgotten.'" *Alter Ego*, vol. 3, no. 97, October 2010, 42–58.

——. "'It Was a Daily Identity Crisis.'" *Alter Ego*, vol. 3, no. 69, June 2007, 32–54.

——. "'It Was a Fun Time!'" *Alter Ego*, vol. 3, no. 35, April 2004, 2–37.

——. "'I Was Contemptuous, Basically of the Comics.'" *Alter Ego*, vol. 3, no. 99, January 2011, 37–52.

——. "'I Was Doomed to Be an Artist.'" *Alter Ego*, vol. 3, no. 48, May 2005, 40–46.

——. "'Maybe I'm in the Wrong End of This Business!'" *Alter Ego*, vol. 3, no. 79, July 2008, 35–54.

——. "'Sales Don't Tell You Everything!'" *Alter Ego*, vol. 3, no. 94, June 2010, 42–62.

——. "'Simon Says!'" *Alter Ego*, vol. 3, no. 76, March 2008, 5–53.

——. "'When You Do a Lot of Super-Heroes, All You're Drawing Is Men in Long Underwear.'" *Alter Ego*, vol. 3, no. 65, February 2007, 3–33.

Andelman, Bob. *Will Eisner: A Spirited Life*. Raleigh, NC: TwoMorrows Publishing, 2015.

Arndt, Richard J. "The First Amazon." *Alter Ego*, vol. 3, no. 157, March 2019, 3–34.

——. "Tales from the Code: The Sequel." *Alter Ego*, vol. 3, no. 113, October 2012, 43–50.

Austen, Jake, and Yuval Taylor. *Darkest Africa: Black Minstrelsy from Slavery to Hip-Hop*. New York: Norton, 2012.

Barker, Martin. "Fredric Wertham: The Sad Case of the Unhappy Humanist." In *Pulp Demons: International Dimensions of the Postwar Anti-Comics Campaign*, edited by John A. Lent, 215–233. Madison, NJ: Fairleigh Dickinson University Press and Associated University Presses, 1999.

——. *A Haunt of Fears: The Strange Case of the British Horror Comics Campaign*. Jackson: University Press of Mississippi, 1984.

Barr, Marleen S. *Lost in Space: Probing Feminist Science Fiction and Beyond*. Chapel Hill: University of North Carolina Press, 1993.

Barrier, Michael. *Funnybooks: The Improbable Glories of the Best American Comic Books*. Berkeley: University of California Press, 2015.

Barson, Michael. *Agonizing Love: The Golden Era of Romance Comics*. New York: Harper Design, 2011.

Beaty, Bart. *Fredric Wertham and the Critique of Mass Culture*. Jackson: University Press of Mississippi, 2005.

Benson, John. *Confessions, Romances, Secrets, and Temptations: Archer St. John and the St. John Romance Comics*. Seattle: Fantagraphics, 2007.

Benton, Mike. *The Comic Book in America: An Illustrated History*. Dallas: Taylor Publishing, 1989.

Berenstein, Rhona J. "White Heroines and Hearts of Darkness: Race, Gender, and Disguise in 1930s Jungle Films." *Film History* 6, no. 3 (1994): 314–339.

Berlatsky, Noah. *Wonder Woman: Bondage and Feminism in the Marston/Peter Comics, 1941–1948*. New Brunswick, NJ: Rutgers University Press, 2017.

Blickenstaff, Clark. "Women and Science Careers: Leaky Pipeline or Gender Filter?" *Gender and Education* 17, no. 4 (2005): 369–386.

Blythe, Hal, and Charlie Sweet. "Superhero: The Six Step Progression." In *The Hero in Transition*, edited by Ray B. Browne and Marshall W. Fishwick, 180–187. Bowling Green, OH: Popular Press, 1983.

Bogle, Donald. *Toms, Coons, Mulattoes, Mammies, and Bucks: An Interpretive History of Blacks in American Film*. New York: Bloomsbury, 2001.

Booker, Keith M., ed. *Comics through Time: A History of Icons, Idols, and Ideals*. Santa Barbara, CA: ABC-Clio, 2014.

Boskovich, Desirina. *Lost Transmissions: The Secret History of Science Fiction and Fantasy*. New York: Abrams, 2019.

Bould, Marc, and Sherry Vint. *The Routledge Concise History of Science Fiction*. New York: Routledge, 2011.

Buchanan, Kimberly Moore. *Apache Women Warriors*. Southwestern Studies 79. El Paso: Texas Western Press, 1986.

Burton, Richard. "Interview: Chris Claremont." *Comic Reader*, no. 164, January 1979.

Butler, Judith. "Performative Acts and Gender Constitution: An Essay in Phenomenology and Feminist Theory." *Theatre Journal* 40, no. 4 (1988): 519–531.

Cameron, Kenneth M. *Africa on Film: Beyond Black and White*. New York: Continuum, 1994.

Carlson-Ghost, Mark. "Coming up Aces!" *Alter Ego*, vol. 3, no. 144, January 2017, 3–34.

Carter, Sarah, ed. *Montana Women Homesteaders: A Field of One's Own*. Helena, MT: Farcountry Press, 2009.

Cassell, Dewey. *Marie Severin: The Mirthful Mistress of Comics*. Raleigh, NC: TwoMorrows Publishing, 2012.

"CBA Roundtable: The Great Women Cartoonists' Slumber Party of 1999." *Comic Book Artist*, no. 10, October 2000, 20–41.

Chaykin, Howard. *The Art of Ramona Fradon*. Mt. Laurel, NJ: Dynamite Entertainment, 2013.

Chute, Hillary. *Graphic Women: Life Narrative and Contemporary Comics*. New York: Columbia University Press, 2010.

——. *Why Comics? From Underground to Everywhere*. New York: Harper, 2017.

Cocca, Carolyn. *Superwomen: Gender, Power, Representation*. New York: Bloomsbury, 2016.

Cole, William, and Florett Robinson, eds. *Women Are Wonderful*. Boston: Houghton Mifflin, 1956.

Conrad, Joseph. *Heart of Darkness*. Cambridge: Cambridge University Press, 2018.

Coogan, Peter. "Comics Predecessors." In *The Superhero Reader*, edited by Charles Hatfield, Jeet Heer, and Kent Worcester, 7–15. Jackson: University Press of Mississippi, 2013.

——. "The Hero Defines the Genre, the Genre Defines the Hero." In *What Is a Superhero?*, edited by Robin S. Rosenberg and Peter Coogan, 3–10. New York: Oxford University Press, 2013.

Coontz, Stephanie. "The Way We Weren't." *National Forum* 75, no. 3 (1995): 11–15.

Couch, N. C. Christopher. *Jerry Robinson: Ambassador of Comics*. New York: Abrams ComicArts, 2010.

Cowsill, Alan, and Daniel Wallace. *DC Comics Year by Year: A Visual Chronicle*. London: DK Publishing, 2010.

Creed, Barbara. *The Monstrous-Feminine: Film, Feminism, and Psychoanalysis*. New York: Routledge, 1993.

Crist, Judith. "Horror in the Nursery." *Collier's Magazine*, March 27, 1948, 22–23, 95–97.

Daniels, Les. *Marvel: Five Fabulous Decades of the World's Greatest Comics*. New York: Harry N. Abrams, 1991.

——. *Wonder Woman: The Complete History*. San Francisco: Chronicle Books, 2003.

Davin, Eric Leif. *Partners in Wonder: Women and the Birth of Science Fiction, 1926–1965*. Lanham, MD: Lexington Books, 2005.

Davis, Blair. "*All-Negro Comics* and the Birth of Lion Man, the First African American Superhero." *Inks: The Journal of the Comics Studies Society* 3, no. 3 (Winter 2019): 273–297.

——. *Movie Comics: Page to Screen / Screen to Page*. New Brunswick, NJ: Rutgers University Press, 2017.

Depree, Peter. "Night of the Paper Noir." In *Will Eisner: Conversations*, edited by M. Thomas Inge, 131–175. Jackson: University Press of Mississippi, 2011.

Devlin, William J. "No Country for Old Men: The Decline of Ethics and the West(ern)." In *The Philosophy of the Western*, edited by Jennifer L. McMahon and B. Steve Csaki, 221–240. Lexington: University of Kentucky Press, 2010.

Dingle, Adrian. *Nelvana of the Northern Lights*. Edited by Hope Nicholson. Winnipeg, MB: Bedside Press, 2017.

Donawerth, Jane L., and Carol A. Kolmerten. *Utopian and Science Fiction by Women: Worlds of Difference*. Syracuse, NY: Syracuse University Press, 1994.

Dvorsky, George, and James Hughes. *Postgenderism: Beyond the Gender Binary*. Hartford, CT: Institute for Ethics and Emerging Technologies, 2008.

Eisenstein, Hester. "Hegemonic Feminism, Neoliberalism, and Womenomics: 'Empowerment' Instead of Liberation?" *New Formations*, no. 91 (2017): 35–49.

Eisner, Will. *Will Eisner: Conversations*. Edited by M. Thomas Inge. Jackson: University Press of Mississippi, 2011.

Elmy, Jack. "In Search of Lloyd Jacquet." *Alter Ego*, vol. 3, no. 22, March 2003, 24–29.

Evanier, Mark. "An Introduction." In *Jack Kirby's Dingbat Love*, edited by John Morrow, 5–7. Raleigh, NC: TwoMorrows Publishing, 2019.

Fanon, Frantz. *Black Skin, White Masks*. London: Pluto Press, 2008.

Farrimond, Katherine. *The Contemporary Femme Fatale: Gender, Genre and American Cinema*. New York: Routledge, 2017.

Filipovic, Jill. "Trump's Stone-Age Views on 'Women's Work.'" CNN, May 19,

2020. https://www.cnn.com/2020/05/19/opinions/trump-pompeo-remarks-misogyny-filipovic/index.html.

Fink, Deborah. *Agrarian Women: Wives and Mothers in Rural Nebraska, 1880–1940.* Chapel Hill: University of North Carolina Press, 1992.

Foucault, Michel. *Security, Territory, Population.* Basingstoke, UK: Palgrave Macmillan, 2007.

Friedan, Betty. *The Feminine Mystique.* New York: Norton, 1963.

Gabilliet, Jean-Paul. *Of Comics and Men: A Cultural History of American Comic Books.* Translated by Bart Beaty and Nick Nguyen. Jackson: University Press of Mississippi, 2010.

Gagné, Michel. "Simon and Kirby's Romance Comics: A Historical View." In Joe Simon and Jack Kirby, *Young Romance: The Best of Simon & Kirby's Romance Comics*, 198–201. Seattle: Fantagraphics Books, 2012.

Galvan, Margaret, and Leah Misemer. "Introduction: The Counterpublics of Underground Comics." *Inks: The Journal of the Comics Studies Society* 3, no. 1 (Spring 2019): 1–5.

Garceau-Hagen, Dee, ed. *Portraits of Women in the American West.* New York: Routledge, 2005.

Gilbert, James B. *A Cycle of Outrage: America's Reaction to the Juvenile Delinquent in the 1950s.* Oxford: Oxford University Press, 1988.

Goffman, Erving. *Stigma: Notes on the Management of Spoiled Identity.* New York: Touchstone, 1963.

González, Jesús Ángel. "New Frontiers for Post-Western Cinema: *Frozen River, Sin Nombre, Winter's Bone.*" *Western American Literature* 50, no. 1 (2015): 51–76.

Goldstein, Nancy. *Jackie Ormes: The First African American Woman Cartoonist.* Ann Arbor: University of Michigan Press, 2008.

——. "The Trouble with Romance in Jackie Ormes's Comics." In *Black Comics: Politics of Race and Representation*, edited by Sheena C. Howard and Ronald L. Jackson, 23–44. New York: Bloomsbury, 2013.

Goodrum, Michael, Tara Scott, and Phillip Smith. *Gender and the Superhero Narrative.* Jackson: University Press of Mississippi, 2018.

Gordon, Ian. *Comic Strips and Consumer Culture, 1890–1945.* Washington, D.C.: Smithsonian Institution Scholarly Press, 1998.

Gordon, Sarah Barringer. "Law and the Contact of Cultures." In *A Companion to the American West*, edited by William Deverell, 130–142. Malden, MA: Blackwell Publishing, 2004.

Goulart, Ron. *Good Girl Art.* New Castle, PA: Hermes, 2007.

——. *Great American Comic Books.* Lincolnwood, IL: Publications International, 2001.

Grant, Barry Keith. *The Dread of Difference: Gender and the Horror Film*, 2nd ed. Austin: University of Texas Press, 2015.

——. *Shadows of Doubt: Negotiations of Masculinity in American Genre Films.* Detroit, MI: Wayne State University Press, 2010.

Grewell, Greg. "Colonizing the Universe: Science Fictions Then, Now, and in the (Imagined) Future." *Rocky Mountain Review of Language and Literature* 55, no. 2 (2001): 25–47.

Grossman, Julie. *Rethinking the Femme Fatale in Film Noir: Ready for Her Close-Up*. New York: Palgrave Macmillan, 2009.

Guinn, Jeff. *Go Down Together: The True Untold Story of Bonnie and Clyde*. New York: Simon and Schuster, 2012.

Hadju, David. *The Ten-Cent Plague: The Great Comic-Book Scare and How It Changed America*. New York: Picador, 2008.

Hanley, Tim. "Introduction." In Adolphe Barreaux, *Sally the Sleuth*. Winnipeg: Bedside Press, 2018.

——. *Wonder Woman Unbound*. Chicago: Chicago Review Press, 2014.

Hanson, Helen, and Catherine O'Rawe, eds. *The Femme Fatale: Images, Histories, Contexts*. New York: Palgrave, 2010.

Harpold, Terry. "European Science Fiction in the Nineteenth Century." In *The Cambridge History of Science Fiction*, edited by Gerry Canavan and Eric Carl Link, 50–68. Cambridge: Cambridge University Press, 2018.

Harvey, Robert C. *The Art of the Comic Book: An Aesthetic History*. Jackson: University Press of Mississippi, 1996.

——. *The Art of the Funnies: An Aesthetic History*. Jackson: University Press of Mississippi, 1994.

Hatfield, Charles, Jeet Heer, and Kent Worcester, eds. *The Superhero Reader*. Jackson: University Press of Mississippi, 2013.

Hetherington, Naomi. "Creator and Created in Mary Shelley's Frankenstein." *Keats-Shelley Review* 11, no. 1 (1997): 1–39.

Hills, Matt. *The Pleasures of Horror*. London: Continuum, 2005.

hooks, bell. *Feminism Is for Everybody: Passionate Politics*. New York: Routledge, 2015.

——. *Talking Back: Thinking Feminist, Thinking Black*. Cambridge, MA: South End Press, 1989.

Honey, Maureen. *Creating Rosie the Riveter: Class, Gender, and Propaganda During World War II*. Amherst: University of Massachusetts Press, 1984.

Horn, Maurice, ed. *Comics of the American West*. New York: Winchester Press, 1977.

——. *Women in the Comics*. Vol. 1. Philadelphia: Chelsea House Publishers, 2001.

——. *The World Encyclopedia of Comics*. New York: Avon, 1976.

Howard, Sheena C. *Encyclopedia of Black Comics*. Golden: Fulcrum, 2017.

Howe, Sean. *Marvel Comics: The Untold Story*. New York: Harper, 2012.

Howell, Richard. "Introduction." In Joe Simon and Jack Kirby, *Real Love—The Best of the Simon and Kirby Romance Comics, 1940s–1950s*. Forestville, CA: Eclipse Books, 2008.

Hufsmith, George W. *The Wyoming Lynching of Cattle Kate, 1889*. Glendo, WY: High Plains Press, 1993.

Hyman, David. *Revision and the Superhero Genre*. Cham, Switzerland: Palgrave Pivot, 2017.

Inge, M. Thomas. *Comics as Culture*. Jackson: University Press of Mississippi, 1990.

"Interview: Al Feldstein." In *The Comics Journal Library*, vol. 10, *The EC Artists Part 2*, 58–73. Seattle: Fantagraphics Books, 2016.

"Interview: Johnny Craig." In *The Comics Journal Library*, vol. 8, *The EC Artists Part 1*, 99–111. Seattle: Fantagraphics Books, 2013.

"Interview: Marie Severin." In *The Comics Journal Library*, vol. 10, *The EC Artists Part 2*, 84–95. Seattle: Fantagraphics Books, 2016.

"Interview: Mike Gold." *Comics Interview*, no. 68, 1989.

"Interview: William M. Gaines." In *The Comics Journal Library*, vol. 8, *The EC Artists Part 1*, 63–72. Seattle: Fantagraphics Books, 2013.

Jackson, Rosemary. *Fantasy: The Literature of Subversion*. New York: Routledge, 1981.

Jackson, Tim. *Pioneering Cartoonists of Color*. Jackson: University Press of Mississippi, 2016.

Jameson, Elizabeth. "Bringing It All Back Home: Rethinking the History of Women and the Nineteenth-Century West." In *A Companion to the American West*, edited by William Deverell, 179–199. Malden, MA: Blackwell Publishing, 2004.

Jay, Alex. "Comics: Marcia Snyder, Artist." *Tenth Letter of the Alphabet* (blog), January 18, 2018. http://alphabettenthletter.blogspot.com/2018/01/comics-marcia-snyder-artist.html.

Jones, Gerard. *Men of Tomorrow: Geeks, Gangsters, and the Birth of the Comic Book*. New York: Basic Books, 2004.

Kanigel, Rachele. *The Diversity Style Guide*. Hoboken, NJ: John Wiley & Sons, 2019.

Karasik, Paul, ed. *Turn Loose Our Death Rays and Kill Them All!: The Complete Works of Fletcher Hanks*. Seattle: Fantagraphics Books, 2016.

Kearney, Mary Celeste. "Recycling Judy and Corliss: Transmedia Exploitation and the First Teen-Girl Production Trend." *Feminist Media Studies* 4, no. 3 (2004): 265–295.

Kennedy, Martha H. *Drawn to Purpose: American Women Illustrators and Cartoonists*. Jackson: University Press of Mississippi, 2018.

Kirkpatrick, Ellen, and Suzanne Scott. "Representation and Diversity in Comics Studies." *Cinema Journal* 55, no. 1 (2015): 120–124.

Knopf, Christina M. "'Hey Soldier!—Your Slip Is Showing!': Militarism vs. Femininity in World War II Comic Pages and Books." In *The Ten Cent War: Comic Books, Propaganda, and World War II*, edited by Trischa Goodnow and James M. Kimble, 26–45. Jackson: University Press of Mississippi, 2016.

Knowles, Chris. *Our Gods Wear Spandex: The Secret History of Superhero Comics*. San Francisco: Wieser Books, 2007.

Labarre, Nicholas. *Understanding Genres in Comics*. Cham, Switzerland: Palgrave Pivot, 2020.

Lamont, Victoria. *Westerns: A Women's History*. Lincoln: University of Nebraska Press, 2016.

Lemmo, Demmo. *Tarzan, Jungle King of Popular Culture*. Jefferson, NC: McFarland, 2017.

Lepore, Jill. *The Secret History of Wonder Woman*. New York: Knopf Doubleday, 2014.

Lewis, Paul. *Comic Effects: Interdisciplinary Approaches to Humor in Literature*. Albany: SUNY Press, 1989.

Linde, Maurice. "Truth Is Held in Disrepute: O. Henry and the Dismantling of Paradigms." *Miscelanea: A Journal of English and American Studies*, no. 38 (2008): 11–27.

"Lisa Yaszek Interview." *Geek's Guide to the Galaxy* (podcast), February 2, 2019. https://geeksguideshow.com/2019/01/24/ggg346-lisa-yaszek/.

Lopes, Paul. "Culture and Stigma: Popular Culture and the Case of Comic Books." *Sociological Forum* 21, no. 3 (2006): 387–414.

Lupack, Barbara, ed. *Early Race Filmmaking in America*. New York: Routledge, 2016.

Lustig, John. "The Terrible, Tragic (>Sob!<) Death of Romance Comics." *Back Issue*, no. 13, December 2005, 16–23.

Mabbott, Alastair. "Graphic Mogul: Stan Lee." In *Stan Lee: Conversations*, edited by Jeff McLaughlin, 121–125. Jackson: University Press of Mississippi, 2007.

Mackay, Christopher S. *The Hammer of Witches: A Complete Translation of the Malleus Maleficarum*. Cambridge: Cambridge University Press, 2009.

Maglio, Mitch. *Fiction House: From Pulps to Panels, from Jungles to Space*. San Diego, CA: IDW Publishing, 2017.

Marston, William Moulton. "Why 100,000 Americans Read Comics." *The American Scholar* 13, no. 1 (Winter 1943): 35–44.

Marvel Masterworks: Atlas Era Jungle Adventure. Vol. 2. New York: Marvel Comics, 2011.

Matheson, Sue. *Women in the Western*. Edinburgh, UK: Edinburgh University Press, 2020.

McBratney, John. *Imperial Subjects, Imperial Space: Rudyard Kipling's Fiction of the Native-Born*. Columbus: Ohio State University Press, 2002.

McClancy, Kathleen. "Editor's Introduction: Comics and History." *Feminist Media Histories* 4, no. 3 (Summer 2018): 1–11.

McGillis, Roderick. *He Was Some Kind of a Man: Masculinities in the B-Western*. Waterloo, ON: Wilfrid Laurier University Press, 2011.

McWilliams, John P. *Against the Wind: Courageous Apache Women*. Staten Island, NY: Page Publishing, 2015.

Merino, Ana. "Women in Comics: A Space for Recognizing Other Voices." Translated by Derek Peterey. *Comics Journal*, no. 237, September 2001.

Meyerowitz, Joanne. "Beyond the Feminine Mystique: A Reassessment of Postwar Mass Culture, 1946–1958." *Journal of American History* 79, no. 4 (1993): 1455–1482.

Miles, Johnny E. *Superheroes and Their Ancient Jewish Parallels: A Comparative Study*. Jefferson, NC: McFarland, 2018.

Mills, Tarpé. *Miss Fury: Sensational Sundays 1941–1944*. Edited by Trina Robbins. San Diego: IDW Publishing, 2013.

Mitchell, Kurt, and Roy Thomas. *American Comic Book Chronicles: 1940–1944*. Raleigh, NC: TwoMorrows Publishing, 2019.

Moore, Dorothy, and Paul Witty. "Interest in Reading the Comics among Negro Children." *Journal of Educational Psychology* 5, no. 36 (December 1941): 303–308.

Mulvey, Laura. *Visual and Other Pleasures*. New York: Palgrave, 1989.

Murray, Chris. "*Pop*aganda: Superhero Comics and Propaganda in World War II." In *Comics & Culture: Analytical and Theoretical Approaches to Comics*, edited by Anne Magnussen and Hans-Christian Christiansen, 141–155. Copenhagen: Museum Tusculanum Press, 2000.

Murray, Will. "Introduction." In *Golden Age Marvel Comics Omnibus*, 8–23. New York: Marvel, 2009.

——. "The Roots of Superman." *Comic Book Marketplace*, no. 63, October 1998.

Nicholson, Hope. *The Spectacular Sisterhood of Superwomen: Awesome Female Characters from Comic Book History*. Philadelphia: Quirk Books, 2017.

Nolan, Michelle. "Introduction." In Joe Simon and Jack Kirby, *Young Romance: The Best of Simon and Kirby's Romance Comics*, 6–9. Seattle: Fantagraphics Books, 2012.

——. *Love on the Racks: A History of American Romance Comics*. Jefferson, NC: McFarland, 2015.

Nyberg, Amy Kiste. *Seal of Approval: The History of the Comics Code*. Jackson: University Press of Mississippi, 1998.

Patrick, Kevin. *The Phantom Unmasked: America's First Superhero*. Iowa City: University of Iowa Press, 2017.

Peek, Wendy Chapman. "The Romance of Competence: Rethinking Masculinity in the Western." *Journal of Popular Film and Television* 30, no. 4 (2003): 206–219.

Peppard, Anna F. "'This Female Fights Back!' A Feminist History of Marvel Comics." In *Make Ours Marvel: Media Convergence and a Comics Universe*, edited by Matt Yockey, 105–137. Austin: University of Texas Press, 2017.

Phillips, Robert W. *Roy Rogers: A Biography, Radio History, Television Career Chronicle, Discography, Filmography, Comicography, Merchandising and Advertising History, Collectibles Description, Bibliography, and Index*. Jefferson, NC: McFarland, 1995.

Pinedo, Isabel Cristina. *Recreational Terror: Women and the Pleasures of Horror Film Spectatorship*. Albany: SUNY Press, 1997.

Pizzino, Christopher. "Comics History and the Question of Delinquency: The Case of *Criminal*." In *Comics Memory: Archives and Styles*, edited by Maaheen Ahmed and Benoît Crucifix, 165–185. London: Springer International Publishing, 2018.

Poovey, Mary. "My Hideous Progeny: Mary Shelley and the Feminization of Romanticism." *Publications of the Modern Language Association of America* 95, no. 3 (1980): 332–347.

"Power Lunch—1974." *Alter Ego*, vol. 3, no. 13, March 2002, 4–11.

Pruitt, Dwain Carlton. "It Rhymes with Lust? Matt Baker and the Ironic Politics of Race, Sex and Gender in the Golden Age." *Journal of Graphic Novels and Comics* 7, no. 2 (2016): 197–209.

Quattro, Ken. "Eisner-Blum Addendum." *Alter Ego*, vol. 3, no. 127, August 2014, 27.

——. "The Gospel According to Archer St. John." *Alter Ego*, vol. 3, no. 77, May 2008, 3–58.

Quinlan, Adrian. "A Real Life Comic-Book Superhero." *Newsweek*, July 30, 2010. https://www.newsweek.com/real-life-comic-book-superhero-74267.

Radway, Janice A. *Reading the Romance: Women, Patriarchy, and Popular Literature*. Chapel Hill: University of North Carolina Press, 1984.

Rapp, David N. "Dell Comics." In *Icons of the American Comic Book*, edited by Randy Duncan and Matthew J. Smith, 193–205. Santa Barbara, CA: Greenwood, 2013.

Rifas, Leonard. "Race and Comix." In *Multicultural Comics: From Zap to Blue Beetle*, edited by Frederick Luis Aldama, 27–38. Austin: University of Texas Press, 2010.

Riley, Shannon E. "Women in Comics Roundtable with Barbara Randall Kesel, Gail Simone, and Jill Thompson." *Back Issue*, no. 54, February 2012, 36–51.

Robbins, Trina. "Albino Jo, the Man with the Tigre Eyes." In Tarpé Mills, *Miss Fury: Sensational Sundays, 1944–1949*, edited by Trina Robbins, 215. San Diego, CA: IDW Publishing, 2011.

——. *Babes in Arms: Women in Comics during the Second World War*. New Castle, PA: Hermes Press, 2017.

——. *A Century of Women Cartoonists*. Northhampton, MA: Kitchen Sink Press, 1993.

——. *From Girls to Grrrlz: A History of Women's Comics From Teens to Zines*. San Francisco: Chronicle Books, 1999.

——. *Gladys Parker: A Life in Comics, a Passion for Fashion*. New Castle, PA: Hermes Press, 2019.

——. *The Great Women Super Heroes*. Northampton, MA: Kitchen Sink Press, 1996.

——. "Miss Fury and the Very Personal Universe of Tarpé Mills." In Tarpé

Mills, *Miss Fury: Sensational Sundays, 1944–1949*, edited by Trina Robbins, 7–18. San Diego, CA: IDW Publishing, 2011.

——. *Pretty in Ink: North American Women Cartoonists, 1896–2013*. Seattle: Fantagraphics Books, 2013.

Roth, Mitchel P. *Crime and Punishment: A History of the Criminal Justice System*. Boston: Cengage, 2010.

Rowett, John L., ed. *Genre Theory and Historical Change: Theoretical Essays of Ralph Cohen*. Charlottesville: University of Virginia Press, 2017.

Russ, Joanna. *The Image of Women in Science Fiction*. Andover, MA: Warner Modular Publications, 1973.

Salisbury, Mark. *Writers on Comics Scriptwriting*. London: Titan Books, 1999.

Sargent, Pamela. *Women of Wonder: Science Fiction Stories Written by Women about Women*. New York: Vintage Books, 1974.

Sarseke, Gulnar. "Under-Representation of Women in Science: From Educational, Feminist and Scientific Views." *NASPA Journal about Women in Higher Education* 11, no. 1 (2018): 89–101.

Schenkar, Joan. "Patricia Highsmith and the Golden Age of American Comics." *Alter Ego*, vol. 3, no. 90, December 2009, 35–40.

——. *The Talented Miss Highsmith: The Secret Life and Serious Art of Patricia Highsmith*. New York: St. Martin's Press, 2009.

Schrum, Kelly. *Some Wore Bobby Sox: The Emergence of Teenage Girls' Culture, 1920–1945*. New York: Palgrave Macmillan, 2004.

Schumacher, Michael. *Will Eisner: A Dreamer's Life In Comics*. New York: Bloomsbury, 2010.

Schumer, Arlen. "Superhero Comics of the Twenty-First Century: Origins." In *The Education of a Comics Artist: Visual Narrative in Cartoons, Graphic Novels, and Beyond*, edited by Michael Dooley and Steven Heller. New York: Allworth Press, 2005.

Scott, Naomi, ed. *Heart Throbs: The Best of DC Romance Comics*. New York: Fireside, 1979.

Seifart, Mark. "Meeting Golden Age Art Goddess, Lily Renée." Bleeding Cool. November 9, 2011. https://www.bleedingcool.com/2011/11/09/meeting-golden-age-art-goddess-lily-renee/.

Sheppard, Alice. *Cartooning for Suffrage*. Albuquerque: University of New Mexico Press, 1994.

Simon, Joe. *My Life in Comics*. London: Titan Books, 2011.

Simone, Gail. *You'll All Be Sorry!* Thousand Oaks, CA: About Comics, 2008.

Singer, Marc. *Breaking the Frames: Populism and Prestige in Comics Studies*. Austin: University of Texas Press, 2018.

Smith, Clive. "The Great Canadian Comic Books." *Alter Ego*, vol. 3, no. 71, August 2007, 3–44.

Sostaric, Mia. "The American Wartime Propaganda during World II: How Comic Books Sold the War." *Australasian Journal of American Studies* 38, no. 1 (2019): 17–43.

Spiegelman, Art, and Chip Kidd. *Jack Cole and Plastic Man*. San Francisco: Chronicle Books, 2001.

"Spotlight on Marie Severin." In Colleen Coover, Trina Robbins, and G. Willow Wilson, *Girl Comics*. New York: Marvel, 2010.

Stanfield, Peter. *Horse Opera: The Strange Case of the 1930s Singing Cowboy*. Urbana: University of Illinois Press, 2002.

Stewart, Maria Miller. "Religion and the Pure Principles of Morality, the Sure Foundation on Which We Must Build." In *Words of Fire: An Anthology of African-American Feminist Thought*, edited by Beverly Guy-Sheftall, 27–42. New York: The New Press, 1995.

Thomas, Roy. "A Moon . . . A Bat . . . A Hawk: A Candid Conversation with Sheldon Moldoff." *Alter Ego*, vol. 3, no. 4, Spring 2000, 4–14.

Thrasher, Fredric M. "The Comics and Delinquency: Cause or Scapegoat." *The Journal of Educational Sociology* 23, no. 4 (December 1949): 195–205.

Tilley, Carol L. "A Regressive Formula of Perversity: Wertham and the Women of Comics." *Journal of Lesbian Studies* 22, no. 4 (2018): 354–372.

——. "Seducing the Innocent: Fredric Wertham and the Falsifications That Helped Condemn Comics." *Information & Culture* 47, no. 4 (2012): 383–413.

Turner, William B. *A Genealogy of Queer Theory*. Philadelphia: Temple University Press, 2000.

Van Pelt, Lori. "Cattle Kate, Homesteader or Cattle Thief?" In *Wild Women of the Old West*, edited by Glenda Riley and Richard W. Etulain, 154–176. Golden, CO: Fulcrum Publishing, 2003.

Vollum, Scott, and Cary D. Atkinson. "The Portrayal of Crime and Justice in the Comic Book Superhero Mythos." *Journal of Criminal Justice and Popular Culture* 10, no. 2 (2003): 96–108.

Walton, Michael. *The Horror Comic Never Dies: A Grisly History*. Jefferson, NC: McFarland, 2019.

Wandtke, Terrence. *The Comics Scare Returns: The Contemporary Resurgence of Horror Comics*. Rochester, NY: RIT Press, 2018.

——. *The Dark Night Returns: The Contemporary Resurgence of Crime Comics*. Rochester, NY: RIT Press, 2015.

Wanzo, Rebecca. *The Content of Our Caricature: African American Comic Art and Political Belonging*. New York: New York University Press, 2020.

Waugh, Coulton. *The Comics*. Jackson: University Press of Mississippi, 1991.

Weiner, Stephen. "The Development of the American Graphic Novel." In *The Cambridge Companion to the Graphic Novel*, edited by Stephen E. Tabachnick, 41–57. Cambridge: Cambridge University Press, 2017.

Wertham, Fredric. *Seduction of the Innocent*. New York: Rinehart & Company, 1954.

Wertham, Fredric, and Frank Santana. *The Circle of Guilt*. New York: Rinehart & Company, 1956.

Weston, Gavin. "Superheroes and Comic-Book Vigilantes versus Real-life Vigilantes: An Anthropological Answer to the Kick-Ass Paradox." *Journal of Graphic Novels and Comics*, no. 2 (2013): 223–234.

Whaley, Deborah Elizabeth. *Black Women in Sequence: Re-inking Comics, Graphic Novels, and Anime*. Seattle: University of Washington Press.

Wheeler-Nicholson, Nicky. *DC Comics before Superman: Major Malcolm Wheeler-Nicholson's Pulp Comics*. Neshannock, PA: Hermes Press, 2018.

Whitted, Qiana. *EC Comics: Race, Shock, and Social Protest*. New Brunswick, NJ: Rutgers University Press, 2019.

Williams, Maren. "She Changed Comics: Pre-Code and Golden Age." Comic Book Legal Defense Fund, March 4, 2016. http://cbldf.org/2016/03/she-changed-comics-pre-code-golden-age/.

Wilson, David Laurence. "A Timely Pair." *Jack Kirby Collector*, no. 69, Fall 2016, 32–35.

Wise, Andrew. *Places of Their Own: African American Suburbanization in the Twentieth Century*. Chicago: University of Chicago Press, 2009.

Woo, Benjamin. "An Age-Old Problem: Problematics of Comic Book Historiography." *International Journal of Comic Art* 10, no. 1 (2008): 268–279.

Wylie, Leslie. *Colonial Tropes and Postcolonial Tricks: Rewriting the Tropics in the Novela de la Selva*. Liverpool, UK: Liverpool University Press, 2009.

Yekani, Elahe Haschemi. *The Privilege of Crisis: Narratives of Masculinities in Colonial and Postcolonial Literature, Photography and Film*. Frankfurt, Germany: Campus Verlag, 2011.

Zorbaugh, Harvey. "The Comics—There They Stand!" *Journal of Educational Sociology* 18, no. 4 (December 1944): 196–203.

Comics Cited

Action Comics, no. 29, Detective Comics, October 1940.

Adventures into the Unknown, no. 6, American Comics Group, August–September 1949.

Adventures into the Unknown, no. 9, American Comics Group, February–March 1950.

All-American Comics, no. 20, All-American Comics Inc., November 1940.

All-American Comics, no. 21, All-American Comics Inc., December 1940.

All-American Comics, no. 22, All-American Comics Inc., January 1941.

Amazing Man Comics, no. 6, Centaur Publications, October 1939.

Amazing Man Comics, no. 7, Centaur Publications, November 1939.

Amazing Man Comics, no. 8, Centaur Publications, December 1939.

Amazing Mystery Funnies 2, no. 2, Centaur Publications, February 1949.

Batman, no. 1, Detective Comics Inc., Spring 1940.

Blue Bolt, no. 2, Novelty Press, July 1940.

Blue Bolt, no. 4, Novelty Press, September 1940.

Blue Ribbon Comics, no. 20, M. L. J. Magazines, January 1942.

Bomber Comics, no. 1, Elliot Publishing Co., March 1944.

Boy Comics, no. 9, Comic House Inc., April 1943.

Captain Aero Comics 3, no. 11, Et-Es-Go Magazines Inc., January 1944.

Captain America Comics, no. 66, Timely Comics, April 1948.

Cave Girl, no. 11, Magazine Enterprises, 1953.

Champion Comics, no. 4, Harvey Comics, February 1940.

Cow Puncher Comics, no. 1, Avon Comics, January 1947.

Cow Puncher Comics, no. 2, Avon Comics, February 1947.

Cow Puncher Comics, no. 3, Avon Comics, 1947.

Cow Puncher Comics, no. 4, Avon Comics, May 1948.

Crack Western, no. 63, Quality Comics, November 1949.

Crack Western, no. 64, Quality Comics, January 1950.

Crime Does Not Pay, no. 22, Comic House Inc., July 1942.

Crime Does Not Pay, no. 39, Comic House Inc., May 1945.

Crime SuspenStories, no. 1, EC Comics, October–November 1950.

Crimes by Women, no. 1, Fox Feature Syndicate, June 1948.

Crimes by Women, no. 2, Fox Feature Syndicate, August 1948.

Dale Evans Comics, no. 4, National Comics Publications Inc., March–April 1949.

Dale Evans Comics, no. 18, National Comics Publications Inc., July–August 1951.

Dale Evans Comics, no. 19, National Comics Publications Inc., September–October 1951.

Dale Evans Comics, no. 23, National Comics Publications Inc., May–June 1952.

Daring Mystery Comics, no. 3, Timely Comics, April 1940.

Daring Mystery Comics, no. 4, Timely Comics, May 1940.

Daring Mystery Comics, no. 5, Timely Comics, June 1940.

Daring Mystery Comics, no. 7, Timely Comics, April 1941.

Dell Four Color, no. 438, Dell, 1952.

Famous Funnies, no. 82, Famous Funnies Inc., May 1941.

Fantastic Comics, no. 18, Fox Publications, May 1941.

Feature Comics, no. 42, Quality Comics, March 1941.

Fight Comics, no. 34, Fiction House, October 1944.

Fight Comics, no. 36, Fiction House, February 1945.

Fight Comics, no. 38, Fiction House, April 1945.

Firehair Comics, no. 1, Fiction House, Winter 1948.

Firehair Comics, no. 7, Fiction House, Spring 1951.

Ghost Comics, no. 11, Fiction House, 1954.

Heart Throbs, no. 25, Quality Comics, December 1953.

Indian Chief, no. 3, Dell, July 1951.

Indians, no. 1, Fiction House, 1950.
Indians, no. 2, Fiction House, 1950.
It Rhymes with Lust, St. John Publications, 1950.
Jumbo Comics, no. 2, Fiction House, October 1938.
Jungle Comics, no. 1, Fiction House, June 1940.
Jungle Comics, no. 2, Fiction House, February 1940.
Jungle Comics, no. 3, Fiction House, March 1940.
Jungle Comics, no. 27, Fiction House, March 1942.
Jungle Comics, no. 56, Fiction House, November 1944.
Jungle Tales, no. 4, Timely Comics, March 1955.
Just Married, no. 5, Charlton, October 1958.
Justice Traps the Guilty, no. 4, Prize Comics, May–June 1948.
Love Scandals, no. 5, Quality Comics, October 1950.
Miss America Magazine, vol. 4, no. 6, Timely Comics, October 1946.
Miss America Magazine, vol. 5, no. 3, Timely Comics, January 1947.
Monster, no. 1, Fiction House, 1953.
Moon Girl and the Prince, no. 1, EC Comics, 1947.
More Fun Comics, no. 7, More Fun Magazines Inc., January 1936.
My Love, no. 4, Timely Comics, April 1950.
National Comics, no. 1, Quality Comics, July 1940.
National Comics, no. 8, Quality Comics, February, 1941.
Negro Romance, no. 1, Fawcett Comics, June 1950.
Negro Romance, no. 2, Fawcett Comics, August 1950.
New Fun, no. 1, National Allied Publications, February 1935.
Patsy Walker, no. 103, Marvel Comics, October 1962.
Planet Comics, no. 3, Fiction House, March 1940.
Planet Comics, no. 4, April 1940.
Pocket Comics, no. 3, Harvey Comics, November 1941.
Prize Comics, no. 1, Feature Publications, March 1940.
Prize Comics, no. 2, Feature Publications, April 1940.
Rangers Comics, no. 20, Fiction House, December 1944.
Rangers Comics, no. 23, Fiction House, March 1945.
Rangers Comics, no. 24, Fiction House, April 1945.
Rangers Comics, no. 27, Fiction House, July 1945.
Romantic Marriage, no. 13, Ziff-Davis Publishing Co., May 1952.
Slave Girl Comics, no. 2, Avon, 1949.
Star Ranger, no. 2, Centaur Publishing, April 1937.
Star Studded Comics, no. 1, Cambridge House, May 1946.
Tales from the Crypt, no. 32, EC Comics, October–November 1952.

Teen Confessions, no. 52, Charlton, November 1968.
The Chief, no. 2, Dell, April 1951.
The Haunt of Fear, no. 14, EC Comics, July–August, 1952.
The Vault of Horror, no. 31, EC Comics, June–July 1953.
This Magazine Is Haunted, no. 18, Charlton, July 1954.
Tim Holt, no. 25, Magazine Enterprises, August–September 1951.
Torchy, no. 1, Quality Comics, November 1949.
Torchy, no. 2, Quality Comics, December 1949.
True Crime Comics, no. 2, Magazine Village Inc., May 1947.
Western Adventures, no. 1, Ace Magazines, October 1948.
Western Adventures, no. 2, Ace Magazines, December 1948.
Western Adventures, no. 5, Ace Magazines, June 1949.
Western Crime Busters, no. 3, Trojan Magazines, February 1951.
Western True Crime, no. 15, Fox Feature Syndicate, August 1948.
Women Outlaws, no. 1, Fox Feature Syndicate, July 1948.
Wonder Woman, no. 12, All American Publications, March 1945.
Wonderworld Comics, no. 3, Fox Feature Syndicate, July 1939.
Young Love, no. 1, Prize Comics Group, February 1949.
Young Romance, no. 1, Feature Publications Inc., September–October 1947.
Young Romance, no. 2, Feature Publications Inc., November–December 1947.
Young Romance, no. 11, Feature Publications Inc., May–June 1949.
Young Romance, no. 197, DC Comics, January–February 1974.

INDEX

www.ingramcontent.com/pod-product-compliance
Lightning Source LLC
LaVergne TN
LVHW011230200826
845811LV00015B/185
* 9 7 8 1 4 7 7 3 2 4 1 2 7 *